S0-BJI-189

The New Americans
Recent Immigration and American Society

Edited by
Steven J. Gold and Rubén G. Rumbaut

A Series from LFB Scholarly

Chain Migration Explained
The Power of the Immigration Multiplier

Bin Yu

Dear Prof. White,
Thank you very much for your guidance. I would not have written this book without your teaching encouragement and advices. support, Thanks!

Your student

LFB Scholarly Publishing LLC
New York 2008

Copyright © 2008 by LFB Scholarly Publishing LLC

All rights reserved.

Library of Congress Cataloging-in-Publication Data

Yu, Bin, 1962-
  Chain migration explained : the power of the immigration multiplier /
Bin Yu.
     p. cm. -- (The new Americans)
  Includes bibliographical references and index.
  ISBN 978-1-59332-235-9 (alk. paper)
  1. United States--Emigration and immigration--Mathematical models.
2. Emigration and immigration--Mathematical models. I. Title.
  JV6465.Y8 2008
  304.8'730015118--dc22

2007038020

ISBN 978-1-59332-235-9

Printed on acid-free 250-year-life paper.

Manufactured in the United States of America.

To my wife, Weijie,

who is the source of my support, energy and happiness,

and to my sons, Jovian and Zane,

who are the light of my life.

Table of Contents

List of Figures

List of Tables

Preface

This research began in 2002, when I noticed, and was amazed and puzzled, that the Immigration Multiplier is one of the least researched topics in the field of migration, despite the fact that immigration has been one of the hot topics in the field of sociology and demography (let alone in policy making). Studies on chain migration have focused more on the socio-economic factors. Few have assessed the effectiveness of the multiplier effect that is implied by the chain migration theory, although there have been several academic debates on the "explosiveness" of migration in the U.S. since the 1980s. The reason no one has found a better way to calculate it, as some scholars suggested, is that the method for calculating the Immigration Multipliers is very complicated. I was very curious. I wanted that challenge. Little did I know that I had taken on a huge task and that I would spend the next few years working on it.

Before I developed the method, I spent much time reviewing the literature on chain migration and the Immigration Multiplier. Although most studies rarely dealt directly with the Immigration Multiplier, they helped me formulate the overall scheme of my research. Thanks to the availability of immigration data from 1972 through 2000 published by ICPSR at the University of Michigan (from then INS—Immigration and Naturalization Services, currently USCIS—United States Citizenship and Immigration Services), I was able to develop and test the method by combining the immigration data with the U.S. Census data from IPUM at Minnesota (1980, 1990, and 2000).

The results were very exciting, because they provided a new way to examine the chain migration process, which is crucial for us to understand the multiplier effect. The successful development of this method is the direct result of the encouragement and support of Dr. Michael White, Dr. Frances Goldscheider, Dr. David Lindstrom, Dr. Gregory Elliot, and Dr. Roger Avery from Brown University. During

xv

the past few years, I have revised the method a few times, and performed the calculations. Dr. White's comments on the Immigration Multipliers and on nativity, Dr. Goldscheider's advice on immigrant fertility, and Dr. Avery's suggestions on methodology were quite helpful during my research.

This book summarizes my research and presents this method. I hope it will shed light to other scholars of chain migration studies.

I would like to acknowledge my debt to Leslie Oh and Jovian Yu, who have taken significant time to read and edit this book. Leslie, who spent several weeks reading my book several times, has offered me much advice, and I am grateful for her help. I would also like to thank my family. They have always encouraged me to complete this book and have been tremendously patient during the last few years. Without the support and encouragement of Weijie, my wife, it would have been entirely impossible for me to accomplish this. I want to thank Weijie for her love, patience, comprehension, and encouragement over the many years we have been together. Without her and my sons' enormous love, optimism, persistence, and support I would not have come even close to what I have achieved today.

Bin Yu
Rhode Island College
Providence, RI

June 24, 2007

CHAPTER 1

Introduction

The growth of ethnic populations in the United States has been the focus of much academic research on various aspects of population studies (economic, sociological, political, and interdisciplinary). Some of these studies have focused on the growth of the immigrant population in the context of immigration theories and some on the immigrant reproduction in the destination countries. This book studies and demystifies the chain migration process and presents the Immigration Multiplier as an indicator that explains the chain migration process that has driven the overall growth of the immigrant population and ethnic groups within the United States.

THE GROWTH OF IMMIGRANT POPULATION IN THE U.S.

The history of population growth in the United States shows that natural increase was once the major source, particularly during the mid 20th Century. However, immigration has now become a significant contributing factor. From 1965 through 2006, the foreign-born population in the United States has significantly increased. Table 1-1 shows the historical trend of immigrants admitted to the U.S. by immigrant-sending regions from 1820 through 2006, and Table 1-2 displays the distribution of immigrants to the U.S. by immigrant-sending region during the same period.

Data suggests that Western immigrants (from Europe, North America, and Oceania) were the main sources of U.S. immigrant populations until the first half of the century. However, during the last five decades, the proportion of Western immigrants began steadily to decrease.

Table 1-1 Immigrants to the U.S. by Region: 1820~2006

Period	Europe	Latin Am	Asia	N. America	Africa	Oceania	Total
1820-29	99,272	7,358	34	2,297	15	19,526	128,502
1830-39	422,771	20,030	55	11,875	50	83,600	538,381
1840-49	1,369,259	16,231	121	34,285	61	7,380	1,427,337
1850-59	2,619,680	19,974	36,080	64,171	84	74,565	2,814,554
1860-69	1,877,726	12,314	54,408	117,978	407	18,428	2,081,261
1870-79	2,251,878	20,700	134,128	324,310	371	10,750	2,742,137
1880-89	4,638,677	31,961	71,151	492,865	763	13,151	5,248,568
1890-99	3,576,411	34,252	61,285	3,098	432	18,816	3,694,294
1900-09	7,572,569	154,742	299,836	123,067	6,326	45,848	8,202,388
1910-19	4,985,411	361,824	269,736	708,715	8,867	12,827	6,347,380
1920-29	2,560,340	641,992	126,740	949,286	6,362	10,790	4,295,510
1930-39	444,399	67,616	19,231	162,703	2,120	3,306	699,375
1940-49	472,524	167,524	34,532	160,911	6,720	14,397	856,608
1950-59	1,404,973	568,441	135,844	353,169	13,016	23,825	2,499,268
1960-69	1,133,443	1,241,044	358,605	433,128	23,780	23,749	3,213,749
1970-79	825,590	1,725,088	1,406,544	179,267	71,408	40,306	4,248,203
1980-89	668,866	2,539,016	2,391,356	156,313	141,990	346,838	6,244,379
1990-99	1,348,612	4,942,955	2,859,899	194,788	346,416	82,728	9,775,398
2000-06	1,073,726	2,865,971	2,265,696	171,151	446,792	185,986	7,009,322
Total	39,346,127	15,439,033	10,525,281	4,643,377	1,075,980	1,036,816	72,066,614

Table 1-2 Distribution of Immigrants to the U.S. by Region: 1820~2006

Period	Europe	Latin America	Asia	North America	Africa	Oceania	Total
1820-29	77.25%	5.73%	0.03%	1.79%	0.01%	15.20%	100.00%
1830-39	78.53%	3.72%	0.01%	2.21%	0.01%	15.53%	100.00%
1840-49	95.93%	1.14%	0.01%	2.40%	0.00%	0.52%	100.00%
1850-59	93.08%	0.71%	1.28%	2.28%	0.00%	2.65%	100.00%
1860-69	90.22%	0.59%	2.61%	5.67%	0.02%	0.89%	100.00%
1870-79	82.12%	0.75%	4.89%	11.83%	0.01%	0.39%	100.00%
1880-89	88.38%	0.61%	1.36%	9.39%	0.01%	0.25%	100.00%
1890-99	96.81%	0.93%	1.66%	0.08%	0.01%	0.51%	100.00%
1900-09	92.32%	1.89%	3.66%	1.50%	0.08%	0.56%	100.00%
1910-19	78.54%	5.70%	4.25%	11.17%	0.14%	0.20%	100.00%
1920-29	59.61%	14.95%	2.95%	22.10%	0.15%	0.25%	100.00%
1930-39	63.54%	9.67%	2.75%	23.26%	0.30%	0.47%	100.00%
1940-49	55.16%	19.56%	4.03%	18.78%	0.78%	1.68%	100.00%
1950-59	56.22%	22.74%	5.44%	14.13%	0.52%	0.95%	100.00%
1960-69	35.27%	38.62%	11.16%	13.48%	0.74%	0.74%	100.00%
1970-79	19.43%	40.61%	33.11%	4.22%	1.68%	0.95%	100.00%
1980-89	10.71%	40.66%	38.30%	2.50%	2.27%	5.55%	100.00%
1990-99	13.80%	50.57%	29.26%	1.99%	3.54%	0.85%	100.00%
2000-06	15.32%	40.89%	32.32%	2.44%	6.37%	2.65%	100.00%
Notes	*Calculated from Statistical Abstract of the United States: 2006*						

By 2000-06, only about 20% of the legal immigrants to the United States came from Western countries (Europe, Canada, and Oceania). At the same time, the proportion of Asian immigrants significantly increased—from 0.03% in the 1820s, to 6% in the 1950s, to 32% by 2000-06. The total number of Asian immigrants admitted to the U.S. from 1990 through 2006 was 5 million, about one third of all admitted immigrants combined (16.8 million). During the same period, the largest number of immigrants, almost 8 million, were from Latin America. These comprised almost half of all immigrants admitted during the same period. Between 2000 and 2006, the percentage of Latin American immigrants admitted to the U.S. was about 40%. The total number of African immigrants has also grown, especially since the 1950s. However, compared to the growth of immigrants from Asia and Latin America, the growth of African immigrants has not been significant. During 2000-06, the percentage of African immigrants admitted to the U.S. was about 6.4%.

The Growth of Second-Generation Immigrants in the U.S.

The accelerated growth of immigration in the United States has triggered the growth of a new population—the immigrant second-generation. In their analysis on "Foreign-Stock Population," Fix and Passel (1994) studied the growth pattern of second-generation immigrants (defined as the children of foreign-born parents), and demonstrated that this generation outpaced the first-generation immigrant population. Other scholars have confirmed these findings (Portes and Rumbaut, 2001; Farley and Alba, 2002).

According to the 2000 Census, 11.1% of the U.S. population was foreign-born. The combined number of first- and second-generation immigrants and their children reached a total of 55 million, or about one out of five Americans (Portes and Rumbaut 2001).

According to projections by the Urban Institute, authors Edmonston and Passel (1994a) assume a 5% annual growth rate through the 1990s, and a 3.6% growth rate between 2000 and 2010. At these rates, for example, the U.S. population of Asian-Americans should increase from 2.9% in 1990 to 5.7% in 2010 (17.1 million), and to 9.7% in 2040 (34.5 million) (Exter 1992).

Some estimates suggest that Latin American immigrants account for nearly half of all immigrants to the U.S. today (legal and undocumented combined). Based on its estimates of the relative high birth rate of Latin American immigrants, the U.S. Census Bureau has predicted that foreign-born population (first-generation) and U.S.-born (second-generation) Latinos will make up more than 40% of the U.S. population growth in the next decade, compared to less than 25% for non-Hispanic whites (Suro 1999).

Kahn (1988, 1994) concluded that most European immigrants have an average of 2.2 to 2.5 children, while those from Asia and Latin America have an average of 1.8 to 4.0 children (Kahn 1988, 1994). He suggests that further studies are needed to understand the variability in fertility levels among immigrant groups, especially those from less-developed regions.

Bean and Stevens (2003) noted that immigration has become the major component of population changes in the U.S. because almost 20% of all U.S. births in the 1990s have been attributed to foreign-born mothers. Consequently, almost 60% of the annual population growth in the U.S. can be directly attributed to immigration and indirectly attributed to childbearing immigrants (Bean, Swicegood and Berg 2000; Bean and Stevens 2003).

Much research has demonstrated that immigration has changed the composition of the U.S. population. It further suggests that new waves of immigration will continue this change in the future.

It suggests that the migration process will change the population composition of the destination country not only instantly (upon the completion of the migration), but also cumulatively (upon producing future generations of the immigrants). For example, with more than 30% of Asians and Hispanics marrying outside of their communities, the current boundaries of race and ethnic populations are certain to change dramatically in the coming years (Smith and Edmonston 1997).

A better understanding of the current immigration process and the reproductive patterns of immigrants will help us understand the future ethnic composition of the U.S. population.

THE IMPORTANCE OF CHAIN MIGRATION

Migration is more complex than a simple mechanical process of moving people, as assumed by crude "push-pull" or other economic models. Numerous contemporary studies in Europe, Africa, Asia, Latin America, and the United States have concluded that sociological factors, such as social networks (especially family units), have played significant roles in the international migration process.

Immigration studies around the world have noted that family migration (defined as family reunification related migration) has become the dominant form of migration in many countries. For example, Guiraudon and Joppke (2001) note that although the level of immigration in most OECD [1] countries (especially the European countries) has been relatively flat or has dropped to the level of 10 years earlier (measured as the ratio of the total number of immigrants over the total population); family migration has been the predominant mode within existing legal immigration; and all of these family migrations are the direct result of the settled labor migrants in the European countries who were granted rights to sponsor their family members.

Some U.S. scholars have suggested that the dominance of family migration is the leading cause of the "explosiveness" of the migration waves in the last 30 years. Some suggest that the dramatic growth of immigration is the direct result of chain migration, which is characterized by a series of "chains" of sponsorship by a number of family members and relatives.

In 1978, the Congress and President Carter approved the creation of the Select Commission on Immigration and Refugee Policy (SCIRP) to study the immigration issue in the U.S. In its March 1981 report, SCIRP argued that the current immigration law permitted "runaway demand" or an explosive chain migration multiplier:

> To illustrate the potential impact, assume one foreign-born married couple, both naturalized, each with two siblings who are also married and each new nuclear family having three children. The foreign-born married couple may petition for the admission of their siblings. Each has a spouse and three

---

[1] Organization for Economic Cooperation and Development, with membership countries: Australia, Austria, Belgium, Canada, Czech Republic, Denmark, Finland, France, Germany, Greece, Hungary, Iceland, Ireland, Italy, Japan, Luxembourg, Mexico, Netherlands, New Zealand, Norway, Poland, Portugal, Slovakia, South Korea, Spain, Sweden, Switzerland, Turkey, UK, U.S.

children who come with their parents. Each spouse is a potential source for more immigration, and so it goes. It is possible that no less than 84 persons will become eligible for visas in a relatively short period. (SCIRP 1981 :334-335)

One of the conclusions of the SCIRP report concerns the effects of chain migration, caused by siblings of U.S. citizens:

The inclusion of a preference for brothers and sisters of adult U.S. citizens creates a runaway demand for visas .... The reason is simple. Once any person enters the country under any preference and becomes naturalized, the demand for the admission of brothers and sisters increases geometrically. (SCIRP 1981:334-335)

SCIRP had considered altering the preference system to reduce the *chaining* that accounts for this phenomenon, but it did not succeed. Several congressional attempts in this direction also failed, largely because of effective pressures from the affected ethnic groups and constituencies (Zolberg 1999).

With the new waves of immigration affecting every part of American society over the past forty years—demographically, economically, politically, and culturally—there has been a surge of studies in the field of immigration studies, especially on immigration to the United States. This book reviews recent studies on chain migration within the economic, sociological, and non-socioeconomic frameworks, and develops a method to measure the chain migration process and its impact, if there is any.

Chain Migration and the Immigration Multiplier

Many studies on chain migration [2] demonstrate that immigration patterns can be explained in terms of Principal Immigrants and family

---

[2] Please see research by Price 1963a; McDonald and McDonald 1964, 1974; Banerjee 1983a, 1983b; Menon 1988; Boyd 1989; Fuller, Kamnuansilpa and Lightfoot 1990; Mahmood 1991; Singhanetra-Renard 1992; Lindquist 1993; Böcker 1994; Kahn 1994; Hugo 1981, 1995; Azam 1998; Gunatilleke 1991, 1998; Shah and Menon 1999; Helmenstein and Yegorov 2000.

immigrants. Efforts have been made to measure the scope and magnitude of chain migration. The Immigration Multiplier, as an indicator for measuring chain migration, has proved to be effective for measuring the chain effect of migration (Jasso and Rosenzweig 1986, 1989, 1990; Reimers 1985, 1992; Arnold *et al.* 1989; Gunatilleke 1998).

According to Jasso and Rosenzweig (1986), the Immigration Multiplier is defined as "the number of future immigrants who come to the United States as a result of the admission of one current immigrant (Jasso and Rosenzweig 1986:291)," who "is not him or herself sponsored for a family reunification visa by a previous immigrant" (Jasso and Rosenzweig 1989:858).[3]

Among studies, there are two different methods for calculating the Immigration Multipliers.

In their studies, Reimers (1985, 1992), Arnold *et al.* (1989), and Gunatilleke (1998) try to estimate the Immigration Multipliers via case studies and/or surveys. Their estimates range from as low as 0.5 to as high as 18. Two main factors cause these variations: the researchers studied two different regions, and they used different definitions of Immigration Multipliers. The research of Reimers (1985, 1992) and Arnold *et al.* (1989) focused on U.S. immigrants, whereas Gunatilleke (1998) focused on South Asia. The definition of Immigration Multiplier used by Reimers (1985, 1992) and Arnold *et al.* (1989) included family members (relatives) only, while Gunatilleke's (1998) Immigration Multiplier included friends in addition to family members.

To date, the research of Jasso and Rosenzweig (1986, 1989) is considered the only theoretical calculation of the Immigration Multipliers. They conclude that the Immigration Multiplier is in the range of 1.16 to 1.40. The method they used for calculating the Immigration Multiplier was widely analyzed and attracted some critics.

---

[3] Some demographers and sociologists define the term "Immigration Multiplier" quite differently and use it for a totally different purpose. For example, Bongaarts and Bulatao (1999) defines the 'Immigration Multiplier" as the ratio of Ps/Pn, where Ps is the total of standard population, which is the sum of native population and immigrants; Pn is the total of natural population, which is the total of native population without including immigrants.

After studying their calculation, certain scholars voiced concern about several key issues such as the method, sample size, research criteria, *etc.* (Passel and Woodrow 1987; Arnold *et al.* 1989; Teitelbaum 1989).

Having reviewed all of the studies on the Immigration Multiplier, Goering (1989) concluded:

> There are substantial methodological and analytic difficulties associated with reliably measuring the size and characteristics of immigrant multiplication. ...... That is, there are no technically simple means to calculate the size and growth of the expansion of immigrant chain. (Goering 1989, p. 809)

However, despite some concern about their calculations, many scholars seemed to accept the Immigration Multiplier as 1.16 to 1.40. For example, some scholars (Goering 1989; Massey *et al.* 1994) concluded that the concern about the chain migration process was overstated because the results of Jasso and Rosenzweig's Immigration Multiplier were lower than expected. This may have discouraged further research on the Immigration Multiplier in the 1990s and later. Yet, concern about the research on chain migration and the Immigration Multiplier still remain.

Massey and associates (Massey *et al.* 1994) suggested that the Immigration Multiplier might be low (based on Jasso and Rosenzweig's research) because of the limitations of their sample. They suggest that the potential for future immigration through such multiplier effects is still real because of the long backlog of immigrants from many countries, especially Mexico, who are waiting to be granted legal entry visas. They continue to suggest that:

> [t]he evidence accumulated so far is thus strong and consistent in confirming the powerful role of migrant networks in structuring individual and household migration decisions, and in promoting and directing aggregate flows of immigrants. .... In particular, more and better research on non-Mexican samples is clearly needed to confirm the generality of findings. (Massey *et al.* 1994)

Edmonston (1996) also concludes that "There is currently inadequate information on the rates at which immigrants sponsor new immigrants and thus on the size of the Immigration Multiplier" (Edmonston 1996: 52). Furthermore, there is a need to develop a useful method to measure the chain migration process and the immigration multiplication effects.

THE IMMIGRATION MULTIPLIER BREAKTHROUGH

With the magnitude of immigration growth in the United States since the 1970s, there are more questions about the possible effects of chain migration. However, since 1989—knowing the known and complicated nature of the Immigration Multiplier—few scholars have successfully tried to reevaluate it or to find a better calculation method.

Since the 1990s, scholars have continued their research in chain migration and have demonstrated its existence in many cases, such as in the family immigrants in Europe (Kofman, 2004), Muslim immigrants in Britain (Baxter, 2006), immigrants from selected countries in New Zealand (Johnston *et al.* 2006), Asian (Luk and Phan, 2006), Syrian (Gualtieri, 2004), Mexican immigrants in the U.S. (Yeh, 2004), and refugee settlement in the U.S. (Brown *et al.* 2007). These studies, among many others, reiterated the existence and importance of chain migration. However, none of them provided an actual assessment of its impact. The problem is that there is no simple way to measure the chain migration process.

In this book, I will discuss a method I developed for calculating the Immigration Multipliers and for measuring the chain migration process. My method focuses on the chain migration from a completely different perspective using the Complete Chain Migration Model, and it is based on the definition of the Immigration Multiplier originally studied by Jasso and Rosenzweig (1989). It further breaks down the complicated chain migration processes into two phases: the immigration unification phase and the immigration reproduction phase. Therefore, my Immigration Multiplier, which I will call Yu's Immigration Multiplier, measures the multiplier effect of immigrant fertility as well as that of immigrant sponsorship.

Within the immigration unification phase, my method further studies various sponsorship types and their corresponding multiplier effects. The study of various unification phases during the migration chains is unprecedented, because my method studies the sponsorship of spouses, children, parents, and siblings separately so that the multiplier effects can be measured at each level.

Another key advancement of Yu's Immigration Multiplier is that it includes a family reproduction component that measures the impact of immigrant children. Since second-generation immigrants (immigrant children) are the direct product of the first-generation immigrants, Yu's Immigration Multiplier can measure and compare differential immigrant fertility patterns or the reproduction multiplier effect among immigrants from different regions/countries of origin during the migration chain process.

As the final product, Yu's Complete Chain Migration Model not only answers many of the questions about chain migration theories, but for the first time also provides the accurate calculation of Immigration Multipliers for evaluating the multiplier effect of chain migration.

This book will present Yu's Complete Chain Migration Model and explain in detail the method for calculating the Immigration Multiplier, as well as the multiplier effect in the chain migration process. The focus of this book will be on Yu's Complete Chain Migration Model and the Immigration Multiplier for demystifying the complicated nature of the Immigration Multiplier. Further, this book will use Yu's Immigration Multiplier to illustrate that the chain immigration process has been the basis for the significant growth of some ethnic populations in the United States during the past several decades.

CHAPTER 2
Research Background

CHAIN MIGRATION AND U.S. IMMIGRATION LAWS

Brief History of U.S. Immigration Laws

The U.S. immigration system is highly regulated by immigration laws designed to balance economic and humanitarian needs. The U.S. immigration laws have many different preference categories, most of them having numerical ceilings. Ethnicity is now no longer a component of current U.S. immigration laws.

The major changes of U.S. immigration laws started with the Immigration and Nationality Act of 1952. It continued the national origins quota system, and the annual ceiling remained. The most significant piece of this legislature was that it abolished immigration and naturalization exclusions against Asians, and it instituted the preference system to allow admission of foreigners with education or skills, as well as relatives—this was the base of the current preference system. Immigration from Latin America and the Caribbean remained exempt from numerical limits. Since 1952, there have been three major phases of change in U.S. immigration law since 1965. Each of these allowed an increase in the immigration limits. The first phase is the Immigration and Nationality Act Amendments of 1965, which were in effect from 1965 to 1977. The second phase began with the Immigration and Nationality Act Amendments of 1978 and the Refugee Act of 1980 that were in effect from 1978 to 1991. During the final phase, the Immigration Act of 1990, which went in effect since 1992, and the Illegal Immigration Reform and Immigrant Responsibility Act of 1996, which, both which have formed the legal basis for most of the immigration policies today.

As we recall, the significant immigration growth (Tables 1-1 and 1-2) took off during the 1950s and 1960s, which is the direct result of the Immigration and Naturalization Act of 1952 and the 1965 Amendments. The 1952 Act still limits the number of immigrants admitted annually based upon a quota by country, but it also sets half of all admission slots for immigrants with high educational credentials. The Immigration and Nationality Act Amendments of 1965 repealed the system of quotas based on national origins and established an eligibility system based on "family reunification" and employment skills. The changes in these laws made the selection of immigrants fairer.

The Immigration and Nationality Act Amendments of 1978 combined separate ceilings for Eastern and Western Hemisphere immigrants into one worldwide limit. The Refugee Act of 1980 has contributed to a substantial relative growth in legal immigration (Zolberg 1999, 2001), and it allows the President, in consultation with Congress, to set the numerical limit of refugees admitted. The Immigration Reform and Control Act of 1986 allows the government to impose fines on employers who hire undocumented workers,[4] while granting amnesty to those who have lived in the country illegally since 1982.

The Immigration Act of 1990 tripled the numerical limits for employment-based immigration and increased the limits on family-based immigration. Many of the current immigration policies are from this Act. The Illegal Immigration Reform and Immigrant Responsibility Act of 1996, among many other things, restricted the eligibility of legal immigrants from receiving many federal benefits (such as food stamps and welfare payments) and expedited the deportation of undocumented immigrants and immigrants who were convicted of crimes.

The Patriot Act of 2001, passed right after the September 11, 2001 terrorist attacks, added the enhanced enforcement of border patrol and immigration inspection, along with many other processes (such as the expansion of terrorism-related procedures, the proposed

---

[4] To some critics, the effort has largely failed for lack of enforcement, and illegal immigration has continued (see Zolberg 1999).

implementation of new technology, the implementation of the student visa monitoring program, and the new special immigrant status).

Immigration Growth and Immigration Laws

In studying the immigration flow to the U.S., it is very important to understand the key components of U.S. immigration laws and the immigration processes.

The 1965 law has been cited as one of the most important immigration laws in U. S. history, because of its emphasis on family reunification. Many scholars argue that the growth in immigration during the last few decades is the direct result of the provision of this law for allowing family reunification or chain migration, a term that describes the process of initial migration being followed by additional immigrants from the same family or community (Price 1963a). For example, in fiscal year 1988, about 80% of all immigrant admissions were family-related (Fix, Zimmermann and Passel 2001). Another significant indication of the growth of immigrant population comes from census data. In general, households headed by non-U.S. citizens are significantly more likely to contain children than those headed by U.S. citizens. In addition, 85% of immigrant families with children are "mixed-status" families—that is, families in which at least one parent is a non-U.S. citizen and one child is a U.S. citizen (Fix, Zimmermann and Passel 2001).

Family members of immigrants are admitted to the United States under the preference categories defined by U.S. immigration laws, most which have numerical limits defined by country. One of the most important features of the post-1965 immigration laws is that some immediate family members of U.S. citizens (parents, spouses, and children of U.S. citizens) were placed in the categories that do not have quota limits.

The post-1965 immigration data shows that immigrants admitted through these non-quota categories (as family members of U.S. citizens) are the key components of the dramatic increase of legal immigration during the last four decades. For example, in 1990, the total number of immigrants in non-quota categories was 234,090; this jumped to 347,870 in 2000 (a 50% net increase in 10 years), and it climbed to 406,074 in 2004 (another 17% net increase in four years) (U.S. Statistical Abstract 2006, Table 6, p. 10). At the same time, the baseline limit of 366,000 annual immigrants for the other preferences categories has not changed.

As part of the U.S. immigration laws, the U.S. refugee policies have also played a significant role in shaping the size of the U.S. immigrant population. The Refugee Act of 1980 made refugees a special immigration category for the admission of individual asylum-seekers. Under the law, the U.S. has accepted several major waves of refugees from different countries (including Cuba, Vietnam, Indonesia, and the former Soviet Union). It has been noted that, since the 1970s, Asia and Latin America have replaced Europe as the main source of refugee admission (Hein 1993).

"Amnesty" is one of the key components in the Immigration Reform and Control Act (IRCA), which allows illegal residents who entered the U.S. before 1982 to adjust their status to legal immigrants. As a result, it created a pool of some three million permanent residents and prospective citizens, who would eventually stimulate more immigration by way of family reunification. Therefore, it has been suggested that the IRCA of 1986 has significantly increased the legal immigrant population, yet failed to curb undocumented entry (Zolberg 1999, 2001; Castles 2004). The data shows that there has been a significant increase in immigration since the IRCA of 1986. From 1990 to 1993, about 2.2 million undocumented immigrants were legalized under this category (Zolberg 1999).

The Immigration Act of 1990 also converted a few hundred thousand illegal Salvadorans into legal permanent immigrants. Later, the Illegal Immigration Reform and Immigrant Responsibility Act of 1996 was passed to cut down illegal immigration (Zolberg 1999, 2001).

However, many researchers on immigration policy have suggested (Portes 1997; Zolberg 1999, 2001; Meyers 2002; Castles 2004) that the immigration policies of the U.S., as well as those of many other countries,[5] have achieved almost the opposite of their original intent.

---

[5] Examples of failed immigration policies include those of Australia, whose postwar immigration policy led to the creation of a very racially diverse society, although its original intent was to keep the country primarily white and British; and Germany, whose "guest worker" program between 1955 and 1973 actually increased the permanent settlement of the ethnic minority population (Castles 2004). Similar results in France, Britain, and the Netherlands, where policies designed to reverse labor migration have

They argue that the existing and past U.S. immigration policies have not effectively controlled the immigration flow as originally intended. Instead, they have played important roles in driving the growth of the immigration population, thus shaping the U.S. immigration process and the growth of the U.S. population.

One of the key factors of such policy failures, as some argue (Castles 2004), is that migration is a social process with its own inherent dynamics. Immigration policies, therefore, will always have socioeconomic consequences, because immigrants are the key players in the chain migration process that is part of the overall social process.[6] Therefore, it will be very meaningful to investigate the relationship between the magnitude of immigration waves (as the result of changes in U.S. immigration laws) and the family reunification sponsorship and family reproduction process within the migration chain.

In the case of the United States, any immigrants admitted (regardless of the types of admission, whether as employees or asylum-seekers or refugees) will be immediately eligible to sponsor their relatives through a family reunification process. Therefore, as many sociologists and demographers have suggested, the "family-friendly" post-1965 U.S. immigration laws have had a great impact on the recent immigration wave of the last four decades. Many studies have concluded that the pattern of contemporary immigration to the U.S. is characterized as family-reunification-based immigration (which brings a significant portion of immigrants to the U.S. for family reunification) (Hein 1993; Krafft 1994; Carter and Sutch 1998; Zolberg 1999, 2001, Castles 2004).

At the same time, some researchers have tried to measure the impact of these new immigration laws on the immigration process. Research does show that most of the post-1965 immigration laws have had a positive impact on recent immigration waves. However, although there have been many studies of the chain migration process since 1965, few have been able to develop an effective method for

---

generally ended up promoting further immigration and the emergence of permanent ethnic settlements (Hollifield 1994; Enoch 1994; Kurthen 1995; Body-Gentrot 1995; Portes 1997; Castles 2004).

[6] One perfect example of such dynamics is the family unification process that is mainly driven by the immigrants.

measuring the migration chain. Some scholars (see Jasso and Rosenzweig 1986, 1989; Arnold *et al.* 1989) have proposed to measure the chain migration through the so-called Immigration Multipliers. Their results, however, have received some criticism and challenges, and it has been concluded that this is case needs further study.

TRADITIONAL APPROACH TO STUDYING CHAIN MIGRATION

Chain Migration is a sequence of migration stages, as initially defined by Price (1963a): the initial immigrants arrive at the destination country and then, over time, encourage and help their relatives and friends to join them. This process establishes links between local communities in the countries of origin and specific locations in the destination countries; therefore, it has a considerable influence on the origins of immigrants, as well as on their destinations. It focuses on stages in a sequence of movements through time (Rowland 2003).

Price (1963a, 1963b) pioneered the chain migration research on Mediterranean migrants to Australia. He identified the migration chains as new structures that are crucial not only for the immediate settlement of the initial immigrants but that are also the building blocks for the longer-term development of communities. *Chain Migration* theory has proved to be a very powerful tool in many immigration studies. Both micro-level analysis (Burnley 1988; Ware 1988) and macro-level studies (Lever-Tracy and Holton 2001) on chain migrations have revealed the strong presence of migration chains between particular towns (in Italy, Australia, Ireland) and specific settlement locations (Wegge 1998).

The migration chains connect family members and relatives (and sometimes friends) across distances and over time. The concept of the chain migration helps explain which persons from a given location migrates, where and with whom they settle, and how they meet many of the challenges of that settlement (Friedl 1976). Chain migration is also an issue in policy-making, especially for family reunification and its priorities (Birrell, R. 1994; Freeman and Birrell. 2001).

Chain migration has been identified as the migration pattern in eastern and southern European populations in the past (Wegge 1998), as well as in Asian population (to other regions including the Middle East and America) (Rowland 2003). Alba and Denton (2004) noted that chain migration also plays a part in building ethnic enclaves (such as Little Italy communities) in the United States.

According to the chain migration model, the initial migrants migrate to a destination country on their own, although they have no social ties there. These initial immigrants will migrate either driven by the *socioeconomic factors* (such as wages, employment potentials, *etc.*, as validated by all of the economic and sociological immigration theories), or by *non-socioeconomic factors* (wars, natural disasters, refugee and asylum policies, *etc.*, as validated by all of the non-socioeconomic theories). They are either *voluntary* or *involuntary*[7] migrants, depending on their situations. The key is that these initial migrants migrate on their own, and migration for them usually has a high price, both *economically* (in terms of financial cost) and *non-economically* (in terms of the disruption of their family lives and the resulting total cultural shock). Once they arrive at their destination countries, the potential *cost* of the future migration of their friends and relatives is substantially lower. It is relatively easier for them to arrange for the migrations of their family members and friends. The growth and expansion of *migration chains* will reduce both the *costs* and the *risks* for future migrants, eventually making it virtually risk-free and almost cost free, as they can diversify their household labor and earnings after family and friends have joined them in their new countries. Studies in both *economic* and *sociological* frameworks have validated the complete chain migration process (Massey *et al.* 1994; Massey 1999).

At the same time, the migration chains are also regulated by the emigration policies of the countries of origin and the immigration policies of the countries of destination—that is the *non-socioeconomic* aspect of the immigration process. For example, some European countries do not have family-unification-specific immigration laws similar to those in the U.S.[8] The differences among the immigration

---

[7] Some researchers use the term *forced migration* for *involuntary migration* (example see Castles 2004).

[8] One perfect example is the fact that the U.S. immigration laws will allow the siblings of U.S. citizens to be admitted, while there are no corresponding immigration laws in European countries.

laws contribute to the differences in immigration patterns between U.S. and European countries.

The following analysis focuses on the *economic, sociological,* and *non-socioeconomic* aspects of the *chain migration* process.

Economic Component of Chain Migration

Immigration Studies in Economic Framework

Within the economic framework, there are a few immigration theories: *the Neoclassical Economics Theory, the New Economics of Migration Theory* and *the Segmented Labor Market Theory* (Massey *et al.* 1994; Massey 1999).

The Neoclassical Economics Theory used to dominate the migration analysis. It focuses on the internal labor migration in the context of the process of economic development. At the macro level, it considers migration as the response to supply-demand imbalances and the resulting wage differences between geographic locations. At the micro level, the theory assumes that individuals seek maximum returns for their *cost* and *human capital*. It considers the international migration as a form of *investment* in human capital (Sjaastad 1962; Harris and Todaro 1970; Todaro 1969, 1976; Todaro and Maruszko 1987; Borjas 1989; Massey 1999).

The *New Economics of Migration Theory* expands the *Neoclassical Economics Theory* and redefines the concept of "isolated individuals," who make decisions as in the *Neoclassical Economics Theory,* but who make decisions for larger units of related people. It emphasizes the strong relationship between the labor market factors and the family/household/communities variables in the migration decision-making process, and it suggests that people usually act collectively (as families, households, or entire communities). Driven by the capital market, people decide to migrate to gain access to capital (Stark and Taylor 1989, 1991; Stark 1991; Massey 1999).

Constant and Massey (2002) applied these two theories in the case of return migration of German guest workers and concluded that the "parameters associated with the determinants of return migration in any population of international migration will reflect a blending of parameters associated with two distinct economic rationales (Constant and Massey, 2002: pp. 34)."

Segmented Labor Market Theory suggests that variables of social stratification affect migration, where the labor market is stratified into *primary* (established demand with better-paying jobs) and *secondary* (seasonal demand with lower-paying jobs) sectors. It considers international migration as the result of a labor demand that is inherent in the economic *structure* of developed nations. For example, foreign workers in the developed countries are needed because of the shortages of general labor, the need to fill the low-skill-class jobs, and the labor shortages in the segmented labor market. Therefore, immigration is not caused by *push* factors in the sending countries (low wages or high unemployment), but by *pull* factors in the receiving countries (a chronic and unavoidable need for low-wage workers) (Piore 1979; Massey 1999; Jennissen 2003).

Chain Migration Studies in Economic Framework
According to the *Chain Migration Theory*, the family is the core starting point. Based on the *New Economics Theory*, Borjas and Bronars (1991) suggest that household members collectively make decisions to allocate migrating family workers optimally. The decision to select the first migrant in the migration chain is usually made with great care, with the understanding that future migration costs for subsequent family members will be lower. Therefore, the family will usually decide to optimize the migration chaining process to minimize the costs of other family members migrating.

Using the *New Economics of Labor Migration Theory*, other scholars (David 1974; Stark 1991) propose that risk, in additional to cost, is also part of the decisions a family considers when making the decision to migrate. Families will want not only to minimize the costs (therefore to maximize income), but also to minimize the risks. Therefore, a family that plans a chain migration will diversify its income to manage its risk. Some scholars explored this model in some case studies. (Please see Ravuri (2004) on Bolivar State, Venezuela, and Chen and Song (2006) on China.)

Sociological Component of Chain Migration

Immigration Studies in a Sociological Framework
Some scholars suggest that economic immigration theories alone cannot explain the immigration process as a whole. For example, the major problem with most of the economic immigration theories within the economic framework is that they emphasize *individual* decision-

making and the individual migrant, rather than the household. As a result, they focus on calculating *individual* costs and *individual* benefits, rather than on calculating the costs of and benefits to units larger and more complex than the single person (Goldscheider 1987, pp. 690-691). Therefore, the economic theories do not explain many of the social aspects of the immigration processes. This leads to immigration theories within the sociological and demographic research framework.

With their foci on *social behavior, social relations,* and *social process*es some sociologists and demographers (Goldscheider 1987; Massey 1990; Portes 1995) developed a sociological research framework that is quite different from the economic research framework. They propose that the migration process can be understood only in the context of the social relationships and institutional structures in which the immigrants are embedded (in their countries of origin and their destination communities). Their positions derive from the concept of "social embeddedness" (Brown 2002). As Goldscheider (1987) states, "Individuals are embedded in families and families are embedded in communities, linking individuals to the broader society." Migration, as part of the *social process,* will have its determinants and consequences, especially in the local systems of social institutions and social relations in a *community.* According to Portes (1995), social structure plays a critical role in determining the volume and direction of migration and the adaptation of migrants, and it will affect fundamental social processes, structures, and changes.

The *social behavior, social relations,* and *social process* can then be presented in the *social network* that has proved to be very significant in the migration process (Banerjee 1983b; Massey and Espana 1987; Massey and Parrado 1994; Durand, Parrado and Massey 1996; Roberts, Frank and Lozano-Ascencio 1996; Phillips and Massey 1999; Brown 2002; Abenaty 2003). According to the *Social Network* theory, *Migration* and *social networks* are reciprocally related. The volume and direction of migration are affected by information, ideas, and resources embedded in the *networks* that link family, friends, and neighbors across origin and destination communities. *Migration,* in turn, is directly and indirectly responsible for building and transforming these *social networks.* Within the research of migration in the sociological framework, migration is structured by *social networks,* with a multilevel *social process* in which individuals are embedded in households, households are embedded in communities, and so on.

Within this framework, the relationship between migration and community has been explored, and many longitudinal data and statistical methods have been developed to examine the determinants and consequences of migration.

Chain Migration Studies in Sociological Framework

Scholars (Choldin 1973; Todaro 1980; Massey 1999) have long recognized that the *social networks* play important roles in the chain migration process, because potential migrants will gain access to knowledge, assistance, and other resources that will help them migrate through social networks that have connections to relatives and friends who have migrated before them. Tilly and Brown (1967) refer to these connections as the "auspices" of migration; others (Price 1963a, 1963b; McDonald and McDonald 1964, 1974) have labeled them "migration chains;" Mildred and Wadycki (1973) have called them a "family and friends effect." Taylor (1986, 1987) characterizes them as a form of economic "migration capital." Massey *et al.* (1987, 1994) and Massey (1999) identify migrant networks specifically as a form of *social capital*.

From a sociological perspective, the cost of migration has both economic and sociological aspects. Migration will cause disruption to personal relationships (with family members, relatives, and friends). The greater the distance of the migration, the greater the disruption because of the economic consequences of costly long distance travel. Therefore, the sociological aspect of chain migration is represented by the social network, which is essential to the process of chain migration to the destination country, where family members, relatives, and friends have previously migrated and which will reduce such cost and disruption. Thus, one of the important aspects of chain migration is that once it has begun, the sociological cost associated with disruption of interpersonal relationships will decline (Heer 1996), because of the gain of social capital through social networks (Massey *et al.* 1994; Massey 1999. Therefore, the social network will reduce the costs and risks (in terms of financial and social capital, which are not solely economic), making the migration chain sustainable (Williams and Sofranko 1979; Massey *et al.* 1987; Massey, Goldring and Durand 1994; Massey 1999; Palloni *et al.* 2001; Brown 2002).

Social Network, Family Network and Migration Chain

Researchers in chain migration (Boyd 1989; Grieco 1998; Wilson 1998; Yoo 2000; Winters, De Janvry and Sadoulet 2001; Palloni *et al.* 2001) focus on various aspects of social networks (family and community). Within the studies of chain migration, we need to understand that networks play very different roles in the process.

The family network, as its name suggests, consists of family members (sometimes close friends included), while the community network includes friends and any non-family members that are part of the migrant community. Family networks are usually stronger. Therefore, chain migration that occurs through family networks will be more sustainable. Although community networks are considered weaker than family networks, they can still assist the chain migration process. Using this concept of two different types of networks, Winters, De Janvry, and Sadoulet (2001) confirm that networks are important both in making the decision to migrate and in determining the level of migration and that family networks are more important than community networks in the decision-making and network-building processes. Once the migration chains have been well established in a community, family networks become less important, because both community and family networks function together in assisting migration. As many studies have demonstrated, the core of the chain migration process is the expansion of the migration chain within the family network; thus, the presence and size of the migration networks form an important basis for predicting future immigration flows. Hence, such networks can produce chain migration and thereby stimulate rapid increase in immigrant populations (Bean and Stevens 2003: 34). A similar analysis can be found in Castles and Miller (2003), and case studies can be found in Zhao (2003) on China and in Moch (2003) on Europe. [9]

---

[9] It is important to note here that chain migration is not unique to the U.S.; it is also the dominant migration pattern in Europe. Since 1996, there has been a general decline in legal immigration in most OECD countries. However, among legal immigrants, the predominant mode has been family migration, and European countries have to grant to their settled labor migrants the right to sponsor family members (Guiraudon and Joppke 2001).

As Massey (1990) suggests, immigration has many social foundations, and the formation of immigration networks is the most important, because they build into the migration process a self-perpetuating momentum that leads to its growth over time in spite of economic factors (fluctuating wage differentials, recessions) and political factors (increasingly restrictive immigration policies).

Non-Socioeconomic Component of Chain Migration

Immigration Studies in Non-Socioeconomic Framework

Given the conflict between personal and national interest, some have argued that family reunification is a privilege granted to the individual, based on (1) the right to travel and (2) the right to family life. At the same time, governments of every country have the right, derived from principles of sovereignty and reinforced by international agreements, to decide who should be permitted to enter their territories. Therefore, for policy makers, the implementation of family reunification policies is discretionary (Lehav 1997). Immigration laws vary from country to country; some countries have immigration-friendly laws, while others have very strict regulations on immigration.

Most scholars in migration studies tend to take the role of the state for granted, which they demonstrate in various research papers that attribute migration to a variety of socioeconomic factors (the "push-pull" processes, "social networks," *etc.*). It has been suggested that not enough attention has been paid to the role of the state (especially in war making and state building), which contributes to international migration (Torpey 1998; Zolberg 1989, 1999, 2001); Castles and Miller (2003)).

Within the political framework of immigration studies, researchers argue that the state agency and government immigration policies are very important not only in shaping a country's emigration and immigration flows, but that they also play a significant role in the growth of immigrant populations in many developed countries (Hein 1993; Krafft 1994; Carter and Sutch 1998; Zolberg 1989, 1999, 2001; Castles and Miller (2003); Castles 2004). For example, in his extensive review of the evolution of U.S. immigration legislation and its impact on the volume of legal immigrants to the U.S. since the late nineteenth century, Zolberg (1999) argues that migration theories will not be complete unless the role of the state is considered.

Traditionally, most studies on international immigration focus on the *socioeconomic immigrants* (those who migrate for socioeconomic reasons), although the volume of *non-socioeconomic immigrants* (those who migrate for non-socioeconomic reasons) is often comparable. The study of non-socioeconomic immigrants (such as refugees and other forced migrants) is generally separate from studies of socioeconomic immigrants. One of the main reasons is that in most developed nations these two groups of immigrants are treated quite differently under two different sets of immigration laws.

One perfect illustration of the importance of the role of immigration policies is the naturalization policy by which immigrants acquire citizenship. Many studies (Graham 2002; Meyer 2004; Briggs 2003; Castles 2004) suggest that in some countries, such as Germany[10] or Japan, citizenship is tied to the "blood" of its people and generally excludes outsiders. On the contrary, in settler nations with a colonial history (the Americas, Australia, New Zealand, and South Africa), citizenship is generally associated with the land. Not surprisingly, the countries that favor citizenship by birth are those that also have immigration policies that favor more family reunifications (for example, the United States, Australia, and Canada). In these countries, the majority of migrants are family migrants (Serow *et al.* 1990).

Hence, immigration policies have a significant impact on immigration patterns. Unfortunately, such an important non-socioeconomic factor has not been the focus of many prevailing immigration studies, which—though not exclusively—have focused on the importance of economic and social factors in the immigration process.[11] After reviewing a few immigration policy failures in Western countries, Castles (2004) suggested that "states tend towards

---

[10] Germany passed new immigration laws in 2000 and relaxed some of the requirements for becoming a German citizen (Meyer 2004).

[11] In this book, the focus is mainly on permanent migration. However, several studies have explored the temporary nature of the migration process. (See Massey and Singer 1995; Lindstrom and Saucedo 2002.) Such type of migration is possible because of (1) geographical location advantages for Mexican immigrants; and (2) the technological and social changes for other immigrants (in terms of decreasing transportation costs and the easier flow of information around the globe). Therefore, people have greater opportunities to return their native counties (Hirschman 1999).

compromises and contra dictionary policies," which leads to "the failure of states to effectively manage migration and its effects on society."

Chain Migration Studies in Non-Socioeconomic Framework

Petersen (1964) categorizes migration into two types: voluntary and involuntary (forced or impelled) movement. Most migration decisions can have both voluntary and involuntary elements. For example, a decision of an unemployed person to migrate in search of a job may not entirely be voluntary, as such a move is driven by the "push" factor (*involuntary* factor), although the migrant may want to move to find a better job elsewhere (*voluntary* factor).

In the case of chain migration, the original factors that drive the initial migrants to move could be voluntary, involuntary, or both. Many "push" factors (war, famine, epidemics, and natural disasters) could drive migrants from their home countries involuntarily (Peterson 1964). At the same time, both socioeconomic and political factors (such as unemployment, economic opportunities, ethnic discrimination, and political prosecution) can contribute to the migrants' decision to move, the timing of migration, and the choice of destination (Cernea 2000; Brown 2002). The sociological analysis of refugee migration can also link the migration process to danger, in terms of the magnitude of the threat. The greater the danger, the more likely the migrant will move (Joly 2002).

Within the chain migration process, future migrants will be more likely to migrate voluntarily, because they will migrate through the social network. Studies suggest that the migration patterns of refugees are similar to the patterns followed by labor migrants (Bonacich 1973) and that it is a social process in which human agency and social networks play a major part (Hein 1993; Castles 2004). For example, refugees to the United States have also been participating in the chain migration process by sponsoring their family members under the family reunification oriented immigration laws (Zolberg 1999). Like labor migrants, refugees may create a network of supporting institutions and communities in which they set up a variety of associations for the purpose of building entrepreneurship, providing services, passing on culture and religion, and looking after the younger generation and offering them educational work. Family networks are part of these associations, in the sense that they share and compete for resources and opportunities through ethnic mobilization (Bonacich 1973).[12]

U.S. immigration history has shown that government intervention (via immigration laws on refugees) has been one of the important external factors that has affected the efficiency of chain migration in the United States, where immigration has become an important component of the labor market and overall population growth. Understanding the role of U.S. policy in the immigration process is vital because immigration is the only component of the labor market or population growth over which policymakers have direct control (Cobb-Clark 1998).

Studies on Chain Migration and Family Reproduction

Immigrant Fertility: Background
In his classic research on the chain immigration processes in Australia, Price (1963b) actually tried to include fertility as a factor in the migration process. He examined the immigration cycle by looking at the demographic characteristics of the birthplaces of immigrants and their descendents. Although the categories he used are not precise by today's standards, he pioneered research in the immigration process by factoring fertility into his study of the immigration process. As Lindstrom and Saucedo (2002) note,

> An examination of migration and fertility together provides valuable insights into each of the two demographic phenomena. Many of the social and economic processes that are thought to affect fertility.... have also been identified as outcomes of labor migration. (Lindstrom and Saucedo 2002: 1342-1343)

---

[12] However, some researchers argue that chain migration is rarely possible for refugees, because of the legislation and policies governing their admission and because they may not necessarily constitute a social group in the destination country (See Joly 2002.). However, I will argue that this is not quite valid, because there is no difference in the family reunification process (for sponsoring additional family members) between refugees and labor immigrants, although there are significant differences in the process of admitting the Principal Immigrants (refugees vs. labor immigrants).

The dynamics of immigrant settlement will start migration chains that encourage further migration. Massey and Espinosa's study (1997), for example, documents the initiation of Mexico-U.S. migration and the settlement of Mexican immigrants in terms of their fertility. They found that the migration of wives and children and the birth of children in the United States "strongly raises the odds of taking additional U.S. trips, documented or undocumented, and strongly lowers the odds of the immigrants returning to Mexico, especially among those with documents (Massey and Espinosa 1997: 988)."

Recent studies (Kahn 1988; Ford 1990; Blau 1992; Stephen and Bean 1992; Lindstrom 1996; Swicegood *et al.* 1988; Bean, Swicegood and Berg 2000; Lindstrom and Saucedo 2002) have demonstrated that the fertility behavior of immigrant women in U.S. is affected by several factors (such as the career opportunities from the destination countries, the characteristics of the home countries, the selectivity of immigrant streams, and the disruptions associated with migration). While almost all developed nations have seen below-replacement fertility rates over the last twenty years, the United States' fertility rates have remained stable or have even slightly increased. This has coincided with a shift in the national origins of immigrants from the low-fertility countries (Europe) to those countries (Latin America and Asia) with higher childbearing rates. Therefore, it suggests that fertility level of recent immigrant groups has implications for the growth and composition of the United States population (Ahlburg 1993; Bean, Swicegood and Berg 2000; Toulemon, 2004).

Factors Affecting Immigrant Fertility

Studies have shown that there are many factors affecting immigrant fertility. Some studies (Becker 1981; Rosenzweig and Schultz 1985; Esterlin 1987; Hotz, Klerman and Willis 1997) suggest that immigrant fertility can be modeled as a function of cost (*e.g.*, the cost of living and raising children) and income (wages earned by the couple). Some studies on immigrant fertility focus more on analyzing sociological and demographic aspects of immigrant behaviors with the *assimilation model* and/or the *disruption model* (Andorka 1978; Schoorl 1990; Gorwaney *et al.* 1990; Ford 1990; Jasso and Rosenzweig 1990; Blau 1992; Kahn 1994; Mayer and Riphahn 2000). The *assimilation model* suggests that immigrants who migrate from a high-fertility home country (usually a developing country) to a low-fertility destination country (usually a developed country) will initially retain their traditional high-fertility patterns, and then adjust to the lower-fertility norm in the destination country. For example, Abbasi-Shavazi and McDonald (2000) suggest, in the case of Australia, that most immigrants eventually reach the same completed fertility level as the Australian population. Gorwaney *et al.* (1990) also conclude that for those immigrants from developing countries, immigrant fertility patterns fit the assimilation model very well.

However, Gorwaney *et al.* (1990) also suggest that fertility patterns for immigrants from developed countries show signs of the disruption effect. The disruption model suggests that migration will have an initial negative impact on immigrant fertility levels, because migration itself is a disrupting event for immigrants. Therefore, the fertility levels of immigrants will initially drop after migration and will rise again, when their socioeconomic conditions improve (Massey and Mullan 1984; Carlson 1985; Jasso and Rosenzweig 1990; Lindstrom and Saucedo 2002).

Based on these models of the economic (cost/income) and sociological (assimilation and disruption) aspects of immigrant fertility adjustment issues, many studies have further researched the selectivity of immigrants and the relationship between their fertility and their selectivity. For example, it has been suggested that immigrants who have more children in the U.S. are less likely to return to their home countries (Blau 1992; Jasso and Rosenzweig 1990).

Immigrant Fertility Differentials
The key to understanding fertility differentials among different immigrant groups is to understand the different compositions of these groups based on the demographic and socioeconomic characteristics associated with fertility. Research has shown that differences among immigrant groups in age, marriage patterns, and socioeconomic status can influence their aggregate fertility levels (Uhlenberg 1973; Ware 1975; Yusuf and Rockett 1981; Bean, Swicegood and Linsley 1981; Espenshade and Ye 1994; Yusuf and Siedlecky 1996; Abbasi-Shavazi and McDonald 2000).

Studies on immigrant fertility differentials reveal the differences among immigrant-sending countries in terms of their norms, values, and attitudes regarding childbearing, as well as their degree of assimilation in their new countries (Kahn 1988). Many studies on immigrant fertility differentials at the rural-urban level have confirmed that there is a fertility assimilation process for rural-urban migration within many nations.[13]

In the studies on immigrant fertility differentials among different immigrant groups, we have similar conclusions. For example, in the case of Israel, immigrants from different countries have all exhibited "the convergence of fertility *within* their ethnic groups and the great convergence of fertility *between* ethnic groups" (Friedlander and Goldscheider 1978: 313). In the case of Australia, Abbasi-Shavazi and McDonald (2000) noticed that immigrants from many countries seem to have adapted to Australian fertility patterns, while Italian and Greek Australians show evidence of maintaining the fertility patterns of their home countries.

Research examining the relationship between immigration and fertility in the U.S. typically involves comparisons of the fertility rates of women from relatively high-fertility sending countries and U.S.-born non-Hispanic whites, or, as an intermediate group, native-born women of similar race/ethnicity (*e.g.* Gorwaney *et al.* 1990; Stephen and Bean 1992; Kahn 1994; Singley and Landale 1998). For example, Althaus (1990) demonstrated that the fertility rates of Asian immigrants follow the assimilation pattern and approach the U.S. fertility norm, while studies on Mexican immigrants have shown otherwise (Bean and Swicegood 1985; Bean, Swicegood and Berg 2000). It has been noted that the gap between the fertility rates of Mexican Americans and those of non-Hispanic whites increased between the 1970s and 1980s, and it continued to do so in the 1990s. Although such fertility differentials are very likely caused by net immigration of young adults of childbearing age, the data from the generational fertility patterns of Mexican immigrants still suggests that the degree of fertility pattern assimilation by Mexican immigrants is somehow "partial" or limited, because the Mexican "immigrants continue to exhibit substantially

---

[13] For example: Thailand (Goldstein and Goldstein 1981), Malaysia (Bach 1981), Ecuador (Rundquist and Brown 1989), Papua New Guinea (Umezaki and Ohtsuka 1998), Peru (White, Moreno and Guo 1995), China (Goldstein, White and Goldstein 1997), Canada (Ram and George 1990; Ng and Nault 1997), Korea (Lee and Pol 1993), Mexico (Lee and Pol 1993), Cameroon (Lee and Pol 1993), Vietnam (White, Djamba and Anh. 2001), Guatemala (Lindstrom 2003), and the Philippines (Jensen and Ahlburg 2004).

higher fertility levels than do the non-Hispanic white population (Bean, Swicegood and Berg 2000: 416)."

QUANTITATIVE RESEARCH ON CHAIN MIGRATION

With more data available for analysis, it has been suggested that the growth of the immigrant population in the United States since the 1970s is the result of the migration chain that is encouraged by the current family-reunification-oriented immigration laws and the multiplier effect of "chain migration," which allows waves of immigrants to bring their relatives into the country. While researchers in various fields are studying better ways to estimate the socioeconomic impact of the recent migration waves, some policy makers are concerned about the potential "Immigration Multiplier effect" of chain migration. There have been many studies on the impact of the post-1965 U.S. immigration policies on the significant growth of the immigration population (especially Latin American and Asian immigrants). Some researchers of chain migration focused on the scope and magnitude of the Immigration Multiplier effect of chain migration, because there is a strong need for measuring the migration chain.

Quantitative studies of chain migration traditionally has focused on the study of "migration stock," which is defined as the total foreign-born population in the destination country. Therefore, the *migrant chain* is the link between migrants and potential migrants. According to the social network theory, the larger the "migration stock," the stronger the migration chain will be. This is referred to as the "family and friends" effect, or Immigration Multiplication Effect.[14] Most of the existing evidence for the presence of chain migration comes not only from studies using migration figures aggregated at the regional or national levels (Wegge 1998; Shah and Menon 1999), but also from those from community levels (Massey 1986, 1987; Taylor 1987).

---

[14] Some authors interpret the multiplier effect as a measurement of how attractive the destination country is. The more migrants from one's own country, the more desirable it is to live in the destination region (Dunlevy and Gemery 1978; Wegge 1998).

As an extension to the study of "immigrant stock," some scholars have proposed a concept to measure the multiplier effect of chain migration. This new concept is to measure the ratio of "immigration stock" against the first immigrants (or the Principal Immigrants). This is useful because immigration scholars can use the measurement to understand the scope of chain migration better. Since this concept is neutral with regard to gender and economic and political status, it will be a very good indicator for scholars to compare immigrants from different countries or regions of origin. Jasso and Rosenzweig (1986) were the first to develop this indicator.

Quantitative Research on Immigration Multiplier

Using data from the 1971 cohorts of immigrants to the U.S., Jasso and Rosenzweig estimate the chain migration multiplier effect for individual immigrants as a function of their social characteristics, their status under U.S. immigration law, and their home country conditions. Their calculations conclude that the Immigration Multiplier is from 1.2 to 1.4 for each immigrant, which means that for each new independent immigrant admitted (not as a relative of an existing immigrant), 1.2 to 1.4 additional immigrants will be admitted to the United States within 10 years. Since this Immigration Multiplier is very low (compared to theoretical estimates), they challenged the notion that the migration "chaining" is infinite. However, their research immediately introduced some heated debate.

In 1988, the General Accounting Office of the United States (GAO) studied the effect of the Immigration Multiplier effect and concluded that the propensity to sponsor new immigrants is substantially higher for immigrants than for native U.S. citizens. It also suggested that new immigrants tend to petition to sponsor their family members as soon as they are legally able to do so.

According to Liu, Ong and Rosenstein (1991), Medina and Natividad estimated the Immigration Multiplier effect by a survey they conducted in 1985. Based on their interviews with people prior to their departure from the Philippines, they found that the eldest child of a family (whether a boy or girl) was generally the first to start the migration chain for the family; then that child could later sponsor the rest of the family members to migrate. They projected subsequent immigration in the sample by listing all of the family members that could possibly be sponsored and concluded with the Immigration Multiplier effect (Liu, Ong, and Rosenstein 1991).

In 1989, Arnold and associates conducted a similar study on estimating the Immigration Multiplier. They interviewed Korean and Philippine immigrants before their departure to the United States and studied their eligible relatives to learn whether they also intended to migrate. Based on their calculations, the Immigration Multiplier for Philippine immigrants is about 1, while the Immigration Multiplier for Korean immigrants is about 0.5. The conclusion they drew about the Immigration Multiplier is similar to that of Jasso and Rosenzweig, and the value of their Immigration Multiplier is comparable to Jasso and Rosenzweig's estimate.

Reimers (1985, 1992) has done a case study on the Immigration Multiplier effect. The most significant factor in this study is that the siblings and spouses of the original principal immigrants contributed the most additional immigrants (12), compared to the parents (3).

To seriously discuss this Immigration Multiplier issue, a series of papers on "chain migration" was published in the winter edition of the *International Migration Review* (*IMR*) in 1989 (23:4), where many scholars discussed "The 'Explosiveness' of Chain Migration: Research and Policy Issues." Jasso and Rosenzweig (1989) re-affirmed their 1986 research and also confirmed that immigrants from Asian nations do exhibit behavior that maximizes their use of the system of migrant admissions.

In 2000, as an attempt to quantitatively measure chain migration, Helmenstein and Yegorov (2000) developed a stochastic two-country model of the Immigration Multiplier—one with one sending country and one receiving country—and they derived a non-linear differential equation as the solution. They introduced the wage as the key variable in adjusting the dynamics of the migration process, and they focused on the interplay of factors that determine the transitional dynamics of migration flows in the presence of social relationships between migrants. Theirs was, however, a basic "push-pull" economic model that did not provide the actual solution to estimating the Immigration Multiplier.

At the same time, there have been other studies on chain migration, and some scholars have demonstrated that the process exists in many places—Europe (Kofman, 2004), Britain (Baxter, 2006), New Zealand (Johnston *et al.* 2006), and the U.S. (Gualtieri, 2004; Yeh, 2004; Luk and Phan, 2006; Brown *et al.* 2007). However, none of them provides an actual assessment of the impact of chain migration in terms of Immigration Multiplier.

Meanwhile, several studies on the Immigration Multiplier effect in other parts of the world support the role played by the migration chain. Most of these include the studies of family members, friends, and community members. They suggest that the migration experience may provide initial contacts and information or that the migrant may actually sponsor the move by subsequent kin, friends, or community members.[15] Among these studies, there has been no standard method to measure the migration chain; many of them focused only on calculating the distribution of immigrants who provided help to others during their immigration process, instead of focusing on measuring the actual migration chain or calculating the Immigration Multipliers. One of the typical statistics these research papers provided is the total number of people who reportedly have sponsored their family members and helped their friends[16] or the total distribution of immigrant spouses from different countries (Khoo 2001).

In 2005 (Yu 2005, 2006), I proposed a new method for calculating the Immigration Multiplier, which is based on the original definition of the Immigration Multiplier proposed by Jasso and Rosenzweig (1989). The calculation method I developed, however, is significantly different. It breaks down the complicated chain migration processes into the immigration unification phase and the immigration reproduction phase, using the expanded definition of the Immigration Multiplier to include the immigrant fertility component. Therefore, the Immigration Multiplier I developed measures the chain migration's multiplier effect that is the result of both family reunification and immigrant fertility.

---

[15] Please see Gilani *et al.* 1981; Banerjee 1983a, 1983b; Menon 1988; Boyd 1989; Fuller, Kamnuansilpa and Lightfoot 1990; Mahmood 1991; Singhanetra-Renard 1992; Lindquist 1993; Kahn 1994; Böcker 1994; Hugo 1981, 1995; Azam 1998; Gunatilleke 1991, 1998; Shah and Menon 1999.

[16] Please see Gilani *et al.* 1981; Banerjee 1983a, 1983b; Menon 1988; Boyd 1989; Fuller, Kamnuansilpa and Lightfoot 1990; Mahmood 1991; Singhanetra-Renard 1992; Lindquist 1993; Böcker 1994; Kahn 1994; Hugo 1981, 1995; Azam 1998; Gunatilleke 1991, 1998; Shah and Menon 1999.

Table 2-1 Summary of Studies on Estimating the Immigration Multiplier

Researcher(s)	Year	Method	Multiplier	Chain	Population Studied
SCIRP	1981	Theoretical Estimate	48	Relatives	Immigrants to U.S.
Reimers	1985, 1992	Case Study	18	Relatives	Immigrants to U.S.
Jasso and Rosenzweig	1986, 1989	Longitudinal Cohort	1.2~1.3	Relatives	Immigrants to U.S.
Arnold et al.	1989	Survey	1.0~1.8	Relatives	Philipino Immigrants to U.S.
Arnold et al.	1989	Survey	0.5~0.7	Relatives	Korean Immigrants to U.S.
Gunatilleke	1998	Survey	8.5	Relatives & Friends	South Asia
Gunatilleke	1998	Survey	3.3	Relatives & Friends	South Asia
Eldredge	2001	Case Study	6	Relatives & Children	Immigrants to U.S.
Eldredge	2001	Case Study	5	Relatives	Immigrants to U.S.
Yu	2005, 2006	Synthetic Cohort	5.3	Relative	Immigrants to U.S.
Source:		*SCIRP 1981; Reimers 1985, 1992; Jasso and Rosenzweig 1986, 1989; Arnold et al. 1989; Gunatilleke 1998; Elderdge 2001; Yu 2005, 2006.*			

Table 2-1 is the summary of all Immigration Multiplier *values* calculated by various key researchers, along with the famous "theoretical estimate" from SCIRP (1981).

Research Opportunities on Chain Migration and Immigration Multiplier

As we can see, most research on chain migration has been primarily descriptive, and many studies of chain migration have primarily focused on theoretical models, with a technical analysis of the correlations of several socioeconomic variables to validate or invalidate the impact of these variables to the model. More studies are needed on the dynamics of the social exchange that is within the chain migration (Lever-Tracy and Holton 2001). At the same time, there has been little quantitative research on chain migration and the Immigration Multiplier. (See Jasso and Rosenzweig 1986, 1989, 1990; Arnold *et al.* 1989.) Due to the complex nature of the calculation, immigration studies in this field have not yet yielded acceptable calculation models or values of the Immigration Multiplier. Many scholars have voiced their doubts about the results of the Immigration Multipliers (published by Jasso and Rosenzweig and others) and challenged the data and the methods. Massey *et al.* (1994) suggest, when discussing the Immigration Multiplier, that "results thus far come from a relatively small number of community case studies and a small number of quantitative analyses from a limited range of countries and datasets." Therefore, Massey challenged scholars that "more and better research on non-Mexican samples is clearly needed to confirm the generality of findings."

Since chain migration is a socioeconomic immigration process that is directly affected by state control (in terms of immigration laws), the actual Immigration Multiplier should not only reflect the current immigration process, but also measure the impact of state immigration policies, as Zolberg (1999) suggests.

As many studies and current immigration data suggest, there will be a long-term impact on U.S. population growth and composition because of the family reunification provisions of U.S. immigration law. It is clear that immigrants will play a large role in determining who will immigrate to the United States, as they are more likely to have immediate relatives residing abroad than native-born U.S. citizens do. Therefore, as Edmonston (1996) concludes,

> It is thus important to measure the number of immigrants admitted by each immigrant (a phenomenon that it referred to as the Immigration Multiplier in the demographic literature). Whereas the potential multiplication of immigration visa entitlements can be substantial because of family reunification provisions, the actual number depends on the propensity of immigrants to naturalize and to sponsor new immigrants. There is currently inadequate information on the rates at which immigrants sponsor new immigrants and thus on the size of the Immigration Multiplier (Edmonston 1996: 52).

My new method of calculating the Immigration Multiplier (originally proposed in 2005 and 2006) is the direct answer to these calls. Having reviewed the existing studies, we can see that my decision to include various components (the role of the state, immigration policies, immigrant fertility, methodology, and other factors) and my economic, sociological, and non-socioeconomic research framework are very solid. This book will explain my method in detail so that sociologists can use this technique to calculate the Immigration Multipliers to measure the chain migration process.

Immigration Components for Chain Migration

It is very important to take several components (economic, sociological, and non-socioeconomic) into consideration for identifying and differentiating between Principal Immigrants and family immigrants and to add the fertility factor to the final calculation of the Immigration Multiplier, which can be summarized as the following:

1. **Economic component**: Most economic theories on migration target the migration of wage earners and the migration of salaried professionals and entrepreneurs, and their family members (sometimes). However, with a significant portion of immigrants in many countries[17] who are sponsored by the government, it is obvious that economic factors alone are not sufficient to explain the international migration to the United States; immigrants with other motivations—either voluntary or involuntary—should be added to the immigrant pool as part of the study.

2. **Sociological component**: The number of studies on immigrants from other regions and/or countries to the U.S. is pale in comparison to the enormous volume of research done on immigration from Mexico to the United States. As we know, immigrant families and the role of families in the migration process could be very different across different regions and/or countries, and there is a need to understand, in general, the mechanism of the immigration process across different regions. Although the study of social networks, especially the role of family networks, has been one of the prominent areas of immigration studies, few have integrated the role of immigrant fertility, which is the one of the primary demographic functions within immigrant families, into studies of family networks in the migration process.

3. **Non-socioeconomic component (government immigration policy)**: Most immigration theories examine immigrant movements that are relatively voluntary, compared to the forced migration of refugees

---

[17] This usually includes most developed countries, such as the United States and European nations that have received many refugees.

and others who flee social or political conflict and human or natural disasters. These involuntary migrations should be the subject of academic research, because they also contribute to the growth of the U.S. foreign-born population, as well as to the significant growth of the second-generation of immigrants in the U.S. Among all non-socioeconomic factors, the role of the state and its immigration policies are extremely important, because most international immigration processes (whether documented or undocumented) operate within the environment these policies control. Immigration policies have played a role in shaping the immigration histories of each respective country. We have to study and understand the relationship between the immigration process and the immigration policies.

4. **Fertility component**: Although immigrant fertility has been one of the major topics in immigration research, most studies have focused on comparing the rate of immigrant fertility to the fertility rate in the destination country. Some studies have tempted to compare fertility rates across different regions and/or countries, but many scholars have focused on fertility as the adjustment process (both as the assimilation model and the disruption model). It will be a new approach if we treat immigrant fertility as the last phase of the chain immigration process, because this will provide us with a better picture of how immigrants migrate to and settle in the destination county.

5. **Methodology**: The Immigration Multiplier was a newly proposed statistical method in late 1980s. However, the method, along with the data issue, has received some criticism, and it needs improvement. Due to its complex technical features, few have ventured to revisit this method. However, as many scholars suggest (Goering 1989; Massey *et al.* 1994; Edmonston 1996), the importance of research on such a measure is still valid despite the complexity of the method. As Edmonston (1996) concludes, "[t]here is currently inadequate information on the rates at which immigrants sponsor new immigrants and thus on the size of the Immigration Multiplier" (Edmonston 1996: 52). There is a need to develop a useful method to measure the migration process and the immigration multiplication effects.

Table 2-2 Components of the Complete Chain Migration Model

			Economic Component		Sociological & Demographic Component				Non Socioeconomic Component	
			Demand Pull	Supply Push	Demand Pull	Push & Pull	Supply Push		Demand Pull	Supply Push
			A	**B**	**C**	**D**	**E**	**F**	**G**	**H**
1st Generation	Principal Immigrants	Principal Immigrants	Possible reasons for migration and the actual migration channels			Possible reasons for migration and the actual migration channels (especially in the case of marrying citizens of the host country)			Possible reasons for migration and the actual migration channels	
1st Generation	Family Members	Spouses, Children, Parents, and Siblings	Possible reasons for the migration			Possible reasons for migration and the actual migration channels			Possible reasons for the migration	
2nd Generation	Descendents of immigrants	Children born in the host country	Economic factors may disrupt the reproduction process in the short term. In the long, the reproduction process will resume.		Cultural differences may remain among immigrants from different countries of origin, also the fertility patterns and reproductive behaviors. The more young people who immigrate, the more immigrant children will be born in the host country.				Policies on citizenship (both host country and the country of origin) would affect the reproduction process to a certain extent.	
		Notes	• A = Labor Recruitment (e.g. guest workers, etc.) • B = Adverse economic situation (such as unemployment or low wages) • C = Information on economic differences (employment opportunities, etc.) from previously migrated family members & friends • D = Family reunification • E = Pressure from previously migrated family members • F = Pressure from previously migrated friends • G = Immigration Policy to encourage migration (such as immigration lottery from selected countries) • H = Flee war or prosecution or natural disaster, etc. (such as refugees or asylum-seekers)								

Table 2-2 lists all of the major components of chain migration that we have discussed so far, with breakdown of push and pull factors from economic, social, demographic, and non-socioeconomic aspects.   I have also listed the immigrants (first-generation) and their descendents (second-generation), along with their roles in this process.

Immigration Multiplier: Yu's Method

Since the initial research by Jasso and Rosenzweig on the Immigration Multiplier in 1989, we did not have a quantitative model to explain the "explosion" of the international immigration phenomenon, until the new method that I now propose (2005, 2006). In this book, I will (1) further refine the method and concept developed by previous scholars in chain migration and the Immigration Multiplier, (2) use the new concept to explain the chain migration process, and (3) provide a detailed analysis of my method for calculating the Immigration Multiplier and using it to measure the magnitude of chain migration process.

It is important to understand that there are two key elements in this book. First is the logic and rationale of my new method to calculate the Immigration Multiplier, which is, although statistical in nature, very straightforward and easy to comprehend. Second is the new definition of the Immigration Multiplier concept, that I call Yu's Immigration Multiplier, which includes the reproduction factor of immigrants.

This new method of studying the chain migration process is unique because no study on chain immigration so far has actually combined the immigrants' reproduction process with the immigrants' family reunification process as an integrated process. By better understanding the reproduction behavior of immigrants and including that as a component of the chain migration process, we can better understand the overall chain migration process.

CHAPTER 3

Research Framework

The research framework presented in this chapter will begin with the concept of the chain migration process and its components, which, as previous research has demonstrated, are driven by many socioeconomic and non-socioeconomic factors. The building blocks of my research framework on the chain migration model has three parts: (1) the individual migrants, who are defined as Principal Immigrants, (2) the immigrant family, which is the family network during the chain migration process, and (3) the immigrant children, the final product of the successful migration to foreign countries.

CHAIN MIGRATION COMPONENTS

Since Price (1963a, 1963b) proposed the concept of *chain migration*, many scholars have used the term to describe only the explosiveness of chain immigration, while others have used the term *social network* to describe similar immigration processes, without using the term *chain*. The term *chain migration* has also been loosely defined as either the migration chain that operates within a social network (including family, friends, community, *etc.*) (Reimers 1982, 1992; Gunatilleke 1998; Shah and Menon 1999) or as the migration chain that operates only within family members (Jasso and Rosenzweig 1986, 1989; Arnold *et al.* 1989).

In this book, I will define the *Complete Chain Migration Model* to describe the overall chain migration process. The Model deals with two different types of migration: the *family migration*, defined as people who migrate via the sponsorship of members within the family networks, and the *non-family migration*, which refers to the migration process initiated by non-family members. The Complete Chain

Migration Model defines that *chain migration always begins with non-family migration and is then joined by family migration.* The process of non-family migration begins with the original Principal Immigrants, who are sponsored by non-family members in the destination country. Once the Principal Immigrants are ready to move, they will initiate the family migration by sponsoring their family members, therefore, starting the migration chain as part of the *family reunification process.* All future family immigrants sponsored by this Principal Immigrant could also initiate new migration chains by sponsoring other family members, as the family reunification process continues. Once immigrants have arrived at the destination country, they will settle down and begin the *immigrant reproduction process,* producing second-generation immigrants. Since the immigrant children born in the destination country will become the citizens of that country,[18] they will become the final nodes of the migration chain, marking the end of the complete chain migration process. Therefore, most of the Model explains the *chain migration* within the context of *family chain migration,* which is a chain that begins with an individual and perpetuates within the family network when that individual immigrant sponsors family members.

Three Phases of the Complete Chain Migration Model

The Complete Chain Migration Model consists of the following three phases:

Initiation Phase
The *initiation phase* of the Model is the migration of the *Principal Immigrants,* who are sponsored by non-family entities. These non-family entities include employers who sponsor immigrants as professional immigrants (or through investment as investment immigrants), the government that sponsors immigrants as refugees, asylum-seekers, or diversity immigrants, and U.S.-born citizens who sponsor immigrants as foreign-born spouses. Theoretically,

---

[18] This is the case in the United States. Some other countries (such as Germany and Japan) have special rules dealing with acquired citizenship, and people born in these countries do not automatically acquire citizenship (Briggs 2003; Meyer 2004).

undocumented immigrants could also be considered initial immigrants, because they might obtain legal immigration status and someday sponsor family members.

Unification Phase

The unification phase of the Model is the *cumulative* migration of family members. During this phase, all prospective migrants immigrate via the sponsorship of previously migrated family members. Migration chains are usually established through the sponsorship of family members who were sponsored by other family members, and so on. It is important to understand that the original Principal Immigrants usually sponsor only their immediate family members, and they usually do not and cannot sponsor other relatives (such as nieces and nephews, for example) of their family members. These relatives are, in fact, sponsored by the sponsored family members of the Principal Immigrants, who can later sponsor their own immediate family members, and the chain migration process, therefore, can progress to bringing more *derived* family members into a country. However, the Model states that the Principal Immigrants are truly *responsible for* all of the derived family members. This is the phase where the Immigration Unification Multiplier is defined. Yu's Immigration Unification Multiplier measures the multiplier effect of the chain migration during this immigration unification process.

Reproduction Phase

The reproduction phase of chain migration is the settlement stage of the immigrant family, during which the immigrant second-generation[19] will be born in the destination country. This important component of the

---

[19] It is very important for this model to label all children who are born in the destination country (in the United States in this case), as the U.S.-born *second-generation immigrant population is* parallel to the *first-generation* immigrants, who were born in foreign countries. There have been some discussions about how to identify young children who "fall between" these generations, because they migrated when they were young, and grew up as if they had been born in the destination country, although they are still considered *first-generation*. (This is not the main topic of this research. Please see Portes and Rumbaut (2003) for more discussion on this subject.)

Model is the phase where immigrant fertility plays a significant role in affecting the size of the second-generation immigrant population. As immigrants arrive from different countries, their respective fertility patterns will become one of the factors that determine the multiplier effect that Yu's Immigration Reproduction Multiplier measures.

Major Factors in the Complete Chain Migration Model

In the Complete Chain Migration Model, we notice that the following factors can affect the strength and length of the migration chain:

The Total Number of Principal Immigrants
It is clear that in the Complete Chain Migration Model, the total number of Principal Immigrants will determine the total number of migration chains to be initiated, hence, the total potential number of future family immigrants to be sponsored during the complete chain migration process. Therefore, the greater the number of Principal Immigrants, the greater the number of migration chains will be generated during the process and the greater the potential number of future family immigrants will be.

The Size and Structure of Immigrant Family
According the Complete Chain Migration Model, each future family immigrant could be sponsored either directly by a Principal Immigrant, or indirectly by previous family immigrants (non-Principal Immigrants). Every such sponsorship is a *chain migration event* that will bring an additional family member into the country. Since each newly sponsored family immigrant could later also initiate his or her own migration chain (for a spouse, children, parents, siblings, and in-laws), the new migration chain, combined with the existing migration chains derived from the same Principal Immigrant, could become a large *family migration network* or the *Complete Migration Chain*. It is clear that the potential total number of family members to be sponsored is directly linked to the family sizes of these immigrants, which is determined by the culture of their countries of origin. Therefore, the larger the immigrant family is (determined by the culture in their own countries), the larger the total number of family immigrants and the stronger and longer the migration chain will be.

Immigrant Fertility Patterns

All immigrants (both principal and family immigrants) will eventually settle down in the destination country. As we know, immigrants with a higher fertility rate will produce more children (fertility factor). In addition, a larger immigrant population could produce more immigrant children than a smaller population with even a lower fertility rate. This suggests that both the total number of all immigrants (determined by the previous two factors) and their *fertility patterns* (determined by the culture in their countries of origin) will decide the total number of second-generation immigrants in the destination country. Therefore, the greater the total number of immigrants and the higher the immigrant fertility rate, the greater the immigrant second-generation population will be.

Other Factors

The actual realization of the chain effects could differ greatly among various immigrant groups, because of the socioeconomic and non-socioeconomic factors involved. The following lists other possible determinants:

- The *attractiveness* of the destination country

The more attractive the destination country is relative to the country of origin, the more family members will want to be part of the chain. According to existing research on international migration, developed countries are highly attractive to immigrants from under-developed or developing countries.

- The *openness* of the immigration policy of the destination country

The more open the immigration policy of the destination country is, the greater the potential for more multiple chains in the immigration process. Most European countries are among the least open in terms of immigration policies.[20]

---

[20] The citizenship policies of many countries place a great emphasis on the "blood" or ethnic heritage of the person to be naturalized, whereas most countries with colonial histories (United States, Canada, Mexico, *etc.*) will emphasize the person's birthplace (the "soil"), instead of "blood" (Briggs 2003; Meyer 2004).

Table 3-1 Analysis of the Complete Chain Migration Model

Immigrant Population	Structure of Migration Chains	Roles in Chain Migration	Migration Chain Analysis
1st Generation	Principal Immigrants	• Initiating Migration Chains	• Migration chain would not exist if Principal Immigrants migrate alone with no future sponsorship of family members or future descendents.
	Spouses, Children, Parents, and Siblings (Sponsored by Principal Immigrants)	• Expanding the Migration Chains by sponsoring their family members	• The family sizes of the Principal Immigrants and of their spouses will decide the potentials of the migration chain.
	Spouses, Children, Parents and Siblings of Family Relatives (Sponsored by Family Members -- other than the original Principal Immigrants)		• Migration chain would grow with more sponsorship of the family members: the more immigrants in this population pool, the stronger the multiplier effects.
2nd Generation	Descendents of immigrants: Final Product of Chain Migration	• Anchoring the immigrant families in the host country • Acting as the end of the Migration Chains • Becoming the new **Principal Immigrants**	• The more immigrant children born in the host country, the more mixed-family will appear in the host country. Welfare policies, for example, might affect the fertility rate of some economically disadvantaged immigrants. • With immigrant children, immigrant families are less likely to go back their home countries. • Although these immigrants are the end of the existing migration chains, they can also initiate new migration chains through the sponsorship of foreign spouses.

- The *culture* factor of the immigrant home country

Assimilation is one of the most discussed topics in international migration research. During the assimilation process, the greatest challenge for immigrants is usually the process of cultural adaptation and adjustment.

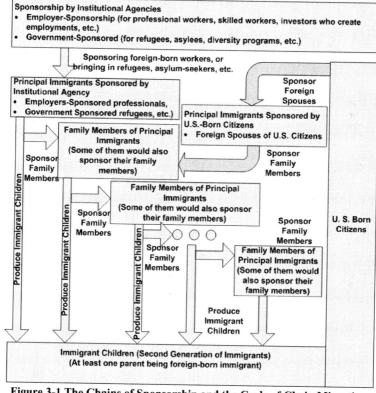

Figure 3-1 The Chains of Sponsorship and the Cycle of Chain Migration

Table 3-1 summarizes the chain migration model with more analysis of each components within the Model. It is worth noting that only a few countries in the world (among the countries that receive a high volume of immigrants) have immigration policies that favor family reunification. Among these, the United States is the one that allows the sponsorship of non-exempt family members of U.S. citizens (such as siblings or adult children of U.S. citizens). Therefore, this research will focus only on the international immigration process to the United States, using the Complete Chain Migration Model with the immigration components discussed earlier.

Figures 3-1 summarizes the flow of sponsorship within the chain migration and the relationship between the immigrants and the U.S.-born population. It illustrates the potential "unlimited" cycles of sponsorship, along with the reproduction phase for every immigrant that is sponsored. As discussed earlier, we focus only on first-generation immigrants (the foreign-born population) and second-generation immigrants (U.S.-born population).

In the following sections, we will study the Complete Chain Migration Model in more detail.

Major Components of Chain Migration

Principal Immigrants: the Initiators of Immigration Chains
Principal Immigrants are immigrants who are sponsored by anyone other than family members. In the case of U.S. immigration, the Principal Immigrant will usually belong to one of the following groups:[21]

- Professional immigrants sponsored by their employers
- Refugees
- Asylum-Seekers
- Immigration lottery winners
- Entrepreneurial Immigrants (investors with $1 million or more to create employment for at least 10 U.S. residents)
- Spouse immigrated via the sponsorship of a U.S.-born citizen (*N.B.*: Spouses sponsored by naturalized U.S. citizens are not considered Principal Immigrants, because they are family members of original immigrants whose applications for naturalization have been granted after U.S. residency and whose naturalization requirements have been fulfilled.)

---

[21] Please note that undocumented immigrants, who come to the United States, cannot sponsor their family members. An illegal immigrant can have children in the U.S., who can sponsor their parent(s) once they reach the age of 18. Therefore, the above categories do not include undocumented immigrants.

- Other immigrants, including the following:
  - o Immigrants from the Diversity Programs, as defined in three laws intended to diversify immigration (P.L. 99-603, P.L. 100-658, and P.L. 101-649)
  - o Amerasians, as defined in law P.L. 100-202

By definition, Principal Immigrants will have the following characteristics:

- Principal immigrants may or may not be motivated to move. Therefore, their migration could be either voluntary or involuntary, determined by economic, sociological, political, and/or other factors (natural disasters, *etc.*).
- Principal immigrants are usually the first in their families to move, and they must either be sponsored by non-family entities (such as employers, government agencies, or policies, *etc.*), or they must marry natives of the destination country to be sponsored.

The Principal Immigrants are responsible for the following chain migration events:

- Principal immigrants sponsor their family members (spouses, children, parents, siblings, and other family members). The sponsorship could either be *direct* or *indirect*. It is important to note that the sponsorship of each new family member, in fact, creates a new chain within the chain migration process begun by the Principal Immigrant. Therefore, the more family members a Principal Immigrant sponsors, the longer the migration chain will be.
  - a. *Direct Sponsorship*: Family members defined above are directly sponsored by the Principal Immigrant.
  - b. *Indirect Sponsorship*: Family members defined above are sponsored by family members who were previously sponsored (directly or indirectly) by the Principal Immigrant.
- The Principal Immigrant produces offspring in the destination country. The birth of second-generation immigrants is the last phase of the immigration process. These children will anchor their immigrant parents in the destination country, reducing their potential to leave the country.

● *Spouses of U.S. Citizens*

There are only two types of U.S. citizens: native born and naturalized. U.S.-born citizens, whose family members most likely reside in the U.S., may sponsor foreign spouses, which is a process of sponsoring new Principal Immigrants (who are *foreign spouses of U.S.-born citizens*). Since these foreign-born spouses usually come to the United States alone for the marriage, they can initiate their own migration chains by later sponsoring their own family members (children, siblings, and parents). Therefore, it is quite logical to treat all foreign spouses of U.S.-born citizens as the "seeds" of migration chains or as Principal Immigrants.

Naturalized U.S. citizens, on the other hand, are immigrants who came to the U.S. earlier. They are part of the first-generation immigrants whose family members are all foreign-born. Therefore, sponsoring foreign spouses is part of the total immigration process for them. Hence, we should treat them as dependents of other immigrants in the Complete Chain Migration Model.

● *Chain Migration and Principal Immigrants*

Since chain migration begins with the Principal Immigrants, it is very important to understand the process that generates their movement. The Principal Immigrants can take the following actions after they enter the U.S.: 1) They can sponsor new family members, which is part of the *Immigration Unification Process;* and 2) they can have children in the United States, which is part of the *Immigration Reproduction Process.* Both actions will contribute to the population growth of the Principal Immigrant's ethnic group in the United States.

Immigration Unification Component

To study the immigration unification component, we must understand all of the non-Principal Immigrants first. They are usually in one of the following categories:

- Spouses of naturalized U.S. citizens
- Unmarried, minor children of naturalized Principal Immigrants
- Parents of naturalized Principal Immigrants
- Adult children (unmarried and married) of naturalized Principal Immigrants
- Brothers and sisters of naturalized Principal Immigrants

- Spouses of Principal Immigrants with permanent resident status
- Unmarried children (minor and adult) of Principal Immigrants with permanent resident status
- Other relatives

All immigrants with legal status will be eligible to sponsor their relatives, who will sponsor others, who will then begin new migration chains. Therefore, these new migration chains are extensions of the original migration chains created by the original Principal Immigrants. The difference between the original migration chain and the new migration chains is that the original migration chains, created by the original Principal Immigrants, mark the very beginning of the migration chain process, while all new migration chains are built *within* the existing migration chains and all sponsored family members are related and sponsored by previously migrated family immigrants. Therefore, the more immigrants who are sponsored within the same family chain, the more immigrants there are who are likely to create new family migration chains that will lengthen and strengthen the chain migration process.

To further study the immigrant unification component of the chain migration process, we will further break down the immigration unification process by the type of family immigrants sponsored by the Principal Immigrants. In the United States, the breakdown of these groups is based on the immigrant visa categories:

Phase 1 Sponsorship: Principal immigrants can sponsor their spouses and children under the *accompanying family members* category. This type of sponsorship would allow Principal Immigrants to migrate with their family members (spouses and minor children only). This type of migration is usually defined as *family unit migration.*[22]

Phase 2 Sponsorship: All immigrants with legal status can sponsor their spouses and children under the normal *family reunification* category. This type of sponsorship would allow family members

---

[22] *Family unit migration* refers to a type of migration in which the original Principal Immigrants migrate to the destination country together with their family members (who are admitted as *accompanying dependents*) (Hondagneu-Sotelo 1994).

(spouses and minor children only) to join the Principal Immigrants in the U.S. after they have settled down. This type of migration is also called a *family stage migration.*[23]

Phase 3 Sponsorship: All U.S. citizens[24] can sponsor their family members (spouses, children, and parents) under the *exempt* category. This type of sponsorship would allow U.S. citizens to bring their family members (spouses, minor children, and parents) to the U.S. with *no numerical limit.*

Phase 4 Sponsorship: All U.S. citizens can sponsor their siblings and adult children under the *non-exempt* category. This type of sponsorship does have a numeric limit.

Family Reproduction Component

In this section, the focus will be on the reproduction component of chain migration, which will eventually explain the fertility patterns among immigrants from different regions after they settle in the destination country. As discussed earlier, immigrant fertility is another important multiplier during the chain immigration process. For example, the fact that both the Latin American and the Asian populations have increased dramatically in the U.S. might be related to following facts:

- Both Latin American and Asian immigrants may have a family reunification component as a very significant part of their immigration process, [25] and hence, of the family reunification process.
- Both Latin American and Asian immigrants may have contributed a significant volume of second-generation immigrants born in the United States via their family

---

[23] *Family stage migration* refers to a type of migration in which the original Principal Immigrants settle in the destination country first and sponsor their family members later (Hondagneu-Sotelo 1994).

[24] Although the U.S. immigration laws do not differentiate the types of U.S. citizens, the most likely type of U.S. citizens to use the Phase 3 and 4 Sponsorship are those who are naturalized U.S. citizens. The only exception is the foreign spouses of U.S.-born citizens.

[25] There have been many studies (Price 1963a, 1963b; McDonald and McDonald 1964; Jasso and Rosenzweig 1986, 1989) on this subject.

reproduction mechanism. [26] This immigrant reproduction process is the newly defined component of the Complete Chain Migration Model, which is one of the focus points of this research.

Table 3-2 Complete Chain Migration Model Explained

Phases	Immigration Visa Preferences	Category
Initial Phase		
	Principal Immigrants	
Phase 0	Employment-related	Professional, skilled workers, etc.
	Government-sponsored	Refugees, asylum-seekers, immigrants of diversity programs, etc.
	Foreign spouses of U.S.-born citizens	Foreign nationals marrying U.S.-born citizens
Unification Phases		
	Immigrant (Permanent Resident): Eligible for sponsoring:	
Phase 1	N/A (Same visa categories)	Accompanying spouses and unmarried sons and daughters of immigrants
Phase 2	2nd Preference	Spouses and unmarried sons and daughters of immigrants
	U.S. Citizens (*usually naturalized immigrant -- after 5 years of immigration*): **Eligible for sponsoring:**	
Phase 3	1st Preference	Unmarried adult children of U.S. citizens and their children
	Exempt (Unlimited)	Immediate relatives of U.S. citizens: spouses, minor children, parents of U.S. citizens at least 21 years of age
Phase 4	3rd Preference	Married children of U.S. citizens and their spouses and children
	4th Preference	Brothers and sisters of adult U.S. citizens and their spouses and children
Reproduction Phase		
	All immigrants (*regardless of immigrant status*): **Eligible for producing**	
Reproduction Phase	N/A	All children born in the United States are U.S. citizens.

---

[26] Research on this subject includes Singley and Landale (1998), Kahn (1994), Jonsson and Rendall (2004), and many others.

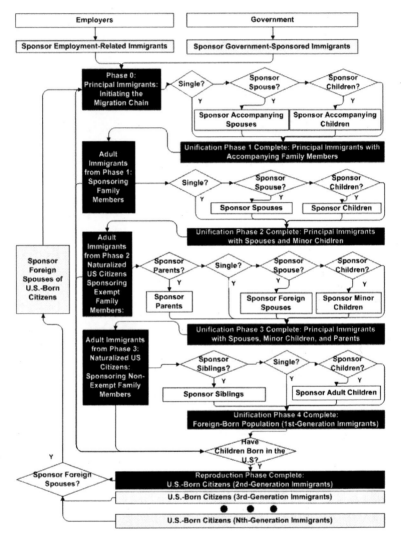

Figure 3-2 Complete Chain Migration Model with Multiple Phases

As proposed earlier, the Complete Chain Migration Model will not be complete without further study of the fertility factor of a particular immigration group. There are different patterns among immigrants from different regions and different countries.

Since the reproduction process involves two people, we have two different scenarios:

- Scenario 1: An immigrant child's parents are both immigrants. That is, both immigrant parents are responsible for bearing the immigrant child in the U.S.
- Scenario 2: An immigrant child's parents are one immigrant and one U.S.-born. In this case, the immigrant parent and U.S.-born spouse will be jointly responsible for his or her children.

Since the cultural backgrounds of immigrants might affect their fertility patterns in the destination country, the study of the immigration reproduction process will help us to understand the immigrant fertility differential.

THE COMPLETE CHAIN MIGRATION MODEL

A good understanding of the Complete Chain Migration Model is essential for us to develop a method to evaluate and measure the variations of both the immigration unification process and the immigration reproduction patterns among different immigrant populations. The development of a measurable method will further our understanding of this process, as well as the impact it has on immigration policies.

Both Table 3-2 and Figure 3-2 summarize the multiple phases within the chain migration under the concept of the Complete Chain Migration Model. The Complete Chain Migration Model breaks down the chain migration process into an initial phase (Principal Immigrants), four unification phases (for sponsoring family members), and one reproduction phase (for family reproduction). It shows the relationship between immigrants and the U.S.-born population. Table 3-2 also shows the matching visa categories under the U.S. immigration laws for some of the unification phases.

As discussed earlier, we will focus only on first-generation immigrants (foreign-born population) and second-generation immigrants (U.S.-born population). In the next chapter, we will develop a method based on this Complete Chain Migration Model.

CHAPTER 4

The Method

The new statistical method developed in this chapter is to measure the chain migration process in terms of multiplier effects, using Yu's *Immigration Multiplier*.[27] Please keep in mind that Yu's *Immigration Multiplier* is significantly different from those used by any previous research; it has been completely redefined and given a new scope and meaning.

As the new indicator measuring the chain migration process, the *Immigration Multiplier* is the product of two components: the *Immigration Unification Multiplier* and the *Immigration Reproduction Multiplier*.

The *Immigration Unification Multiplier* is the total number of first-generation immigrants each Principal Immigrant generates. To calculate this value divide the total number of all first-generation immigrants by the total number of Principal Immigrants[28] The value is, therefore, the multiplier factor that measures the family reunification process in migration chains.

---

[27] In mathematics, the smaller of the two factors, regardless of the order, is usually defined as the **multiplier**. In physics, the **multiplier** is a multiplication of the number of electrons emerging from an electrode as compared with the number incident upon it. In economics, the **multiplier** is the amount by which a change in investment will be multiplied in achieving its final effect on incomes or expenditures.

[28] Since no reliable data is available on undocumented immigrants and since not all undocumented immigrants can obtain legal immigration status to sponsor their family members at any time after they arrive, the methods of calculation discussed here do not include undocumented immigrants.

Since Principal Immigrants are part of the first-generation immigrants, the value of the Immigration Unification Multiplier (*IUM*) will have to be 1 or greater. The extreme case of the *IUM* being 1 would mean that the Principal Immigrants migrate to the destination country all by themselves without sponsorship of family members. In reality, however, immigrants will most likely sponsor some of their family members. Therefore, with the assumption that the additional family members will join the Principal Immigrants, we should always see a value greater than 1 for the *IUM*. Since the family reunification process is heavily influenced by the immigrants' cultural backgrounds (such as family size, family values, etc.), it is easy to suggest that the larger the immigrant family is and the stronger its family values are, the higher the *IUM* value it will have, and the stronger its effect will be in the Immigration Unification Multiplier .

The *Immigration Reproduction Multiplier* is the combined total of the first- and the second-generation immigrants that each first-generation immigrant generates. To obtain its value, divide the combined total of the first- and second-generation immigrants by the total number of all first-generation immigrants. This is the multiplier for measuring the family reproduction component of the chain migration process.

Since all first-generation immigrants are responsible for all of their immigrant children (*i.e.* the second-generation immigrants), the Immigration Reproduction Multiplier (*IRM*) will also have to be 1 or greater. If, in an extreme case, the *IRM* is equal to 1, the Principal Immigrants (and their sponsored family members, if *IUM* is greater than 1) will not produce any children in the destination country after their migration. In reality, immigrants do usually have children in the destination country. Therefore, we can use this new tool to measure the fertility component of the chain immigration process, because producing children in the destination country is the final phase of the migration chain. Usually, the higher the immigrant fertility rate and the higher the *IRM* value, the stronger the immigration reproduction multiplier effect will be. As some research suggests, when children are born in the destination country, immigrants tend to stay there permanently (Krafft 1994; Carter and Sutch 1998). Therefore, this fertility component in chain migration process is very important.

The *Immigration Multiplier* is the product of the *Immigration Unification Multiplier* and the *Immigration Reproduction Multiplier*. Its value, in fact, is the combined total of the first- and the second-generation immigrants that each Principal Immigrant generates. Since Principal Immigrants are part of the first-generation immigrants, therefore, the value of the Immigration Multiplier should be at least 1. If the Immigration Multiplier is 1, it means simply that the Principal Immigrant did not sponsor any family members or produce any immigrant children. In this case, there would be no Immigration Multiplier effect. This scenario exists only in theory. The higher the value of the Immigration Multiplier, the stronger the multiplier effect will be, which reflects both the unification multiplier factor as well as the reproduction multiplier effect.

Using this new definition of the Immigration Multiplier, including the *IUM* and the *IRM*, we could understand the internal migration process much more clearly. Figure 4-1 summarizes the definitions of all Immigration Multipliers.

From these definitions, we see that the denominators of both the *IUM* and the *IRM* are part of the numerators. Therefore, we can also derive the *Net IUM* and the *net IRM* from the *IUM* and the *IRM* to exclude the denominators from the numerators. Now, we will have the following:

The *Net IUM*:

- The *denominator* of the *Net IUM* is the same as the denominator of *IUM*, which is the total number of principal Immigrants.
- The *numerator* of the *Net IUM* is the total number of derived family dependents, whom the Principal Immigrants sponsor. It differs from the numerator of *IUM* in that the Principal Immigrants are not part of the numerator in *Net IUM*.
- The value of *Net IUM* can be explained as the total number of family immigrants for whom each Principal Immigrant eventually will be responsible.

The *net IRM*:

- The *denominator* of the *net IRM* is the same as the denominator of *IRM*, which is the total number of first-generation immigrants.
- The *numerator* of the *net IRM* is the total number of second-generation immigrants, and that is different from the numerator of *IRM*, which also includes the total number of first-generation immigrants.

Defining Immigration Multipliers (Formulas)

$$IUM = \frac{\text{Total Number of First Generation Immigrants}}{\text{Total Number of Principal Immigrants}}$$

$$IRM = \frac{\text{Combined Total of First and Second Generation Immigrants}}{\text{Total Number of First Generation Immigrants}}$$

$$IM = IUM * IRM = \frac{\text{Combined Total of First and Second Generation Immigrants}}{\text{Total Number of Principal Immigrants}}$$

$$NetIUM = IUM - 1 = \frac{\text{Total Number of Derived Immigrants (Family Dependents)}}{\text{Total Number of Principal Immigrants}}$$

$$NetIRM = IRM - 1 = \frac{\text{Total Number of Second Generation Immigrants}}{\text{Total Number of First Generation Immigrants}}$$

$$NetIM = IM - 1 = \frac{\text{Combined Total of Drived and Second Generation Immigrants}}{\text{Total Number of Principal Immigrants}}$$

==

===

where:

IUM ≥ 1 and net IUM >=0

When: *IUM*=1 (or *net IUM* =0)

If and only if the total number of family immigrants is 0, *i.e.* no new immigrants admitted to the United States through family unification sponsorship.

When: *IUM*>1 (or *net IUM* >0)

This is the real-life case. Here, the total number of family immigrants is always greater than 0. The larger the value of *IUM* (or *net IUM*), the more new immigrants will be admitted into the United States through family unification sponsorship.

Note:

It is impossible for *IUM* to be smaller than 1 (or for *net IUM* to be smaller than 0). According to the definition of the Immigration Unification Multiplier, the total number of Principal Immigrants is a subset of the total number of first-generation immigrants. Therefore, it is impossible for the total number of first-generation immigrants to be smaller than the total number of Principal Immigrants.

IRM>=1 and net IRM >=0

When: *IRM*=1 (or *net IRM* = 0)

If and only if the total number of immigrant descendents is 0, *i.e.* no children born to immigrant parent(s) in the United States.

When: *IRM*>1 (or *net IRM* >1)

This is the real-life case. Here, the total number of immigrant descendents is always greater than 0. The larger the value of *IRM* (or *net IRM*), the more children will be born to immigrant parent(s) in the destination country.

Note:

It is impossible for *IRM* to be smaller than 1 (or for *net IRM* to be smaller than 0). According to the definition of the Immigration Reproduction Multiplier, the total number of first-generation immigrants is a subset of the combined total of the first-generation immigrants and the second-generation. Therefore, it is impossible for the combined total of the first-generation immigrants and the second-generation to be smaller than the total number of first-generation immigrants.

Figure 4-1 Immigration Multipliers Defined

- The value of *net IRM* is the total number of native-born children for whom each foreign-born immigrant will eventually be responsible.

These new indicators (*IM, IUM, IRM*) are valuable tools for measuring the Immigration Multiplier effects as part of our study on immigration.

THE CONCEPT OF COHORT ANALYSIS

We all know the difference between the TFR (Total Fertility Rate) and the CFR (Complete Fertility Rate). The TFR is a period indicator obtained by summing the age-specific birth rates for a specific year. The CFR, however, is a cohort indicator computed by summing a set of age-specific birth rates for a given cohort. Here, the data collected over a number of years for a given cohort represents a *real cohort*, while the data collected for the population in a given year will represent only a *synthetic cohort*. While cohort data would be ideal, the most practical way of understanding most demographic situations would be to use the period data for generating the numbers we need. The cohort analysis model illustrated here provides an explanation for the process flow of immigrant admission into the U.S. and the timeline of when these immigrants can sponsor their family members.

In the research framework of migration studies, the time variable is an essential component. In the case of international migration to the U.S., immigrants initially can sponsor their spouses and unmarried children under the second preference category. After five years, they can apply for U.S. citizenship and then sponsor their parents, siblings, and adult children under other visa categories.[29]

In the Complete Chain Migration Model discussed earlier and from the proposed formulas for calculating Immigration Multipliers in Figure 4-1, we can see that the ideal calculations would be to use longitudinal data. This would mean that all calculations of all *IUMs*, *IRMs*, and *IMs* need a complete immigrant cohort from the Principal

---

[29] Jasso and Rosenzweig suggest that "most of the multiplier effects occur within the first 10 years after a person immigrates to the United States" (Jasso and Rosenzweig 1986, p296).

Immigrants to all directly or indirectly sponsored family immigrants, and their U.S.-born children. Such ideal cohort data sets obviously do not exist. However, since it is best to use the most available data sets to build synthetic cohorts, it is more practical to calculate the Complete Chain Migration Models using the synthetic cohorts. (Figures 4-2 and 4-3 show the differences.) Therefore, the method proposed in this chapter will use the synthetic cohort for measuring the sponsorship patterns. The concept is parallel to using the TFR concept in fertility analysis.

Longitudinal (Cohort) Analysis vs. Cross-Sectional Analysis

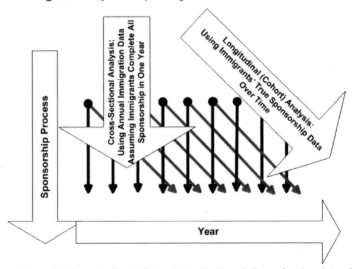

Figure 4-2 Longitudinal (Cohort) Analysis and Cross-Sectional Analysis

CALCULATING IMMIGRATION UNIFICATION MULTIPLIER

Immigration Unification Multiplier: Measuring Family Reunification Process

As discussed earlier, the *IUM* measures the total number of first-generation immigrants each Principal Immigrant generates during the family reunification process. If we examine the first-generation immigrants as a whole, we notice the following:

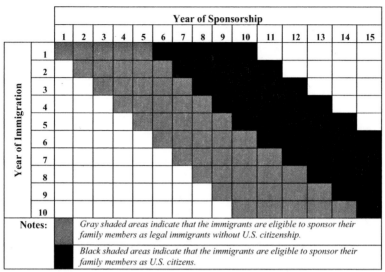

Figure 4-3 Longitudinal vs. Synthetic Cohort Sponsorship

$$I = P + D$$

where P is the total number of Principal Immigrants, and D is the total number of derived family immigrants. Hence, I is the total number of first-generation immigrants.

We have also defined the *IUM* as the ratio of all first-generation immigrants to all Principal Immigrants. Thus, we have the following expression for calculating the *IUM*:

$$IUM = \frac{P + D}{P} = \frac{I}{P}$$

where

P is the total number of Principal Immigrants to the U.S.;

D is the total number of derived family immigrants to the U.S.;

I is the total number who immigrated into the U.S. This is the total number of Principal Immigrants P and the Derived Family Immigrants D.

According to this definition, the *IUM* is the total number of all immigrants (principal and derived family immigrants combined) that each Principal Immigrant contributes. It can also be interpreted as the sum of all immigrants admitted to the U.S. (including the original

Principal Immigrant) after original Principal Immigrant has been admitted.

If we calculate the annual *IUM*, we have the following:

$$IUM = \sum_{j=1\sim\infty}(IUM_j) = \frac{\sum\limits_{j=1\sim\infty}(P_j + D_j)}{\sum\limits_{j=1\sim\infty}P_j} = \frac{\sum\limits_{j=1\sim\infty}I_j}{\sum\limits_{j=1\sim\infty}P_j}$$

where IUM is the Immigration Unification Multiplier over time.

We can also re-write the formula as an *n*-year measure:

$$IUM_{i,i+n} = \frac{\sum\limits_{j=i,i+n}I_j}{\sum\limits_{j=i,i+n}P_j}$$

where

    $IUM_{i,i+n}$ is the Immigration Unification Multiplier from year i to i+n;

    $\sum\limits_{j=i,i+n}D_j$ *is the total number of family members sponsored (directly or*

        indirectly) and admitted to the U.S. between years i and i+n;

    $\sum\limits_{j=i,i+n}P_j$ *is the total number of Principal Immigrants admitted to the U.S.*

        between years i and i+n.

Here, we assume that all family members admitted to the U.S. during this period (years *i* to *i+n*) are sponsored by the total number of Principal Immigrants during the same period, because this is a method using a synthetic cohort.

The relationship between the *Net IUM* and the *IUM* is the following:

$$IUM = \frac{I}{P} = \frac{P+D}{P} = 1 + \frac{D}{P} = 1 + NetIUM$$

Obviously, the difference between the *Net IUM* and *IUM* is the inclusion of the *original Principal Immigrant*. The *Net IUM* focuses on the *additional* derived family immigrants that each original Principal Immigrant will bring to the United States, while the *IUM* assesses the total number of *all* immigrants to the U.S., including the original Principal Immigrant. Therefore, we should also know that the *Net IUM* is equivalent to *the total number of additional immigrants for whom the original Principal Immigrant is responsible* (via either direct or indirect sponsorship).

In order to calculate the *IUM* and the *Net IUM*, we need to set up a model to differentiate more between these family immigrants. As we discussed earlier, the Complete Chain Migration Model has several phases based on the timing (immediate vs. delayed sponsorship[30]) and the types of sponsorship (whether sponsoring *immediate* family members—spouses, children, or non-exempt family members of U.S. citizens like siblings, *etc.*).

Calculating Principal Immigrants

Since the Immigration Multipliers measure chain migration, it is natural that the Principal Immigrants are the foundation of this measure. As discussed earlier, the Principal Immigrants consist of three major types of non-family-member-sponsored immigrants: Employment Related Immigrants (ERI Principals), Government Sponsored Immigrants (GSI Principals), and Foreign Spouses of U.S. Born Citizens (FSUSB Principals). The following sections will discuss the method that I developed for calculating the numbers of these Principal Immigrants.

Assuming that we have E_0 as ERI Principals, G_0 as GSI Principals, and S_0 as FSUSB Principals, then we have:

$$Z_0 = E_0 + G_0$$

Here *0* denotes the *Phase 0* immigrants (Principal Immigrants) and Z_0 is the total number of Principal Immigrants sponsored by non-family entities (either employers or government agencies):

$$P = Z_0 + S_0$$
$$= E_0 + G_0 + S_0$$

where

0 is the Phase 0 immigrants (Principal Immigrants);
E_0 is the total number of ERI Principals;
G_0 is the total number of GSI Principals;

---

[30] The case of immediate sponsorship is *family unit migration* when Principal Immigrants bring accompanying dependents with them. The case of delayed sponsorship is *family stage migration* when Principal Immigrants will immigrate first, and sponsor their spouses and children after they are settled in the destination country. Please see Chapter 3.

Z_0 is the total number of ERI Principals and GSI Principals;
S_0 is the total number of FSUSB Principals;
P is the total number of Principal Immigrants sponsored by non-family members.

Calculating Sponsored Family Immigrants

As discussed earlier, chain migration is a process in which the original Principal Immigrants sponsor the immigration of members of their families. Since many original Principal Immigrants cannot sponsor all of their family members at the same time, they must sponsor them in stages, or during several *Unification Phases* (as part of the family reunification process) and one *Reproduction Phase* (as part of the immigration reproduction process) to reflect the Complete Chain Migration Model.

In the following sections, we will develop the methods of calculation for all four unification phases as phase-specific Immigration Unification Multipliers:

- Chain Migration Unification Phase 1: for sponsoring *Accompanying Family Members* (or *AFM Immigrants*), which include:
    - Spouses (or *AFM Spouses*)
    - Minor children (or *AFM Children*)
- Chain Migration Unification Phase 2: for sponsoring *Later-Sponsored Family Members* (or *LFM Immigrants*), which include:
    - Spouses (or, *LFM Spouses*)
    - Minor children (or, *LFM Children*)
- Chain Migration Unification Phase 3: for sponsoring exempt family members of U.S. citizens, which include:
    - Parents of U.S. Citizens (or PUSC Immigrants)
    - Foreign Spouses of Naturalized U.S. Citizens (or FSUSN Immigrants)[31]
    - Minor Children of U.S. citizens and/or their spouses (or MC Immigrants)

---

[31] It is important to note here that this category includes only the foreign spouses of naturalized U.S. citizens, because the foreign-born spouses of U.S.-born citizens are categorized as Principal Immigrants.

- Chain Migration Unification Phase 4: for sponsoring non-exempt family members of U.S. citizens, which include:
    - Married Adult Children of U.S. Citizens (or MAC Immigrants)
    - Unmarried Adult Children (or UAC Immigrants)
    - Siblings of U.S. Citizens (SIB Immigrants)

In the following chapters, I will sometimes refer to the Chain Migration Unification Phases simply as Phase 1 through Phase 4.

Immigration Unification Phase 1: AFM Immigrants

The total number of Phase 1 AFM Immigrants sponsored by the Principal Immigrants is defined as D_1. Since D_1 can also be broken down into the categories of accompanying spouses (S_1) and accompanying children (C_1), we then have the following:

$D_1 = S_1 + C_1$

We also have:

$S_1 = SE_1 + SG_1$

where

SE_1 *is the total number of AFM Spouses of ERI Principals E_0 (Phase 1);*
SG_1 *is the total number of AFM Spouses of GSI Principals G_0 (Phase 1);*

$C_1 = CE_1 + CG_1$

where

CE_1 *is the total number of Phase 1 AFM Children of ERI Principals E_0;*
CG_1 *is the total number of Phase 1 AFM Children of GSI Principals G_0.*

Immigration Unification Phase 2: LFM Immigrants

The total number of *Phase 2* LFM (later-sponsored family members or family members) is defined as D_2. Please note that the main reason this population (D_2) differs from D_1 is that D_1 joins the Principal Immigrant as AFM Immigrants because D1 immigrates to the U.S. *at the same time* as the Principal Immigrants, while D_2 immigrants must wait and join the Principal Immigrants *later* (usually referred as the *Family Stage Migration* process).

If we break down *Phase 2* LFM dependents into categories of LFM Spouses and LFM Children, we then have the following:

$D_2 = S_2 + C_2$

where

S_2 *is the total number of LFM Spouses of Z_0.*

C_2 *is the total number of LFM Children of* Z_0

Immigration Unification Phase 3: Exempt Family Members of U.S. Citizens

Phase 3 immigrants are exempt family members of U.S. citizens (either U.S.-born or naturalized), who are defined as D_3.

If we break down the dependents into detailed categories (such as spouses, minor children, and parents), we then have the following:

$D_3 = S_3 + C_3 + P_3$

where

> S_3 *is the total number of foreign spouses of naturalized U.S. citizens (from the immigrant pool of* $Z_0, D_1,$ *and* D_2*);*
>
> C_3 *is the total number of MC children whose parents are either naturalized U.S. citizens or U.S.-born citizens;*
>
> P_3 *is the total number of PUSC parents of U.S. citizens.*

Immigration Unification Phase 4: Non-Exempt Family Members of U.S. Citizens

Phase 4 immigrants are defined as the non-exempt family members of U.S. citizens, which is labeled as D_4. D_4 should have the following categories:

- *UAC* Immigrants (unmarried adult children of U.S. citizens and their families)
- *MAC* Immigrants (married adult children of U.S. citizens and their families)
- *SIB* Immigrants (siblings and their families).

These family members of U.S. citizens could be sponsored by any U.S. citizens (whether naturalized or U.S.-born).[32]

The total number of D_4 immigrants could be calculated as follows:

$D_4 = C_4 + M_4 + B_4$

where

> C_4 *is the total number of UAC Immigrants and their families;*
>
> M_4 *is the total number of MAC Immigrants and their families;*
>
> B_4 *is the total number of SIB Immigrants and their families.*

---

[32] U.S.-born citizens, though, are less likely to have foreign-born extended family members.

Immigration Unification Multiplier: Standardized Formula for All Unification Phases

We can now generalize all *IUM* formulas as the following:

$$NetIUM = \frac{\sum_{i=1\,to\,4}(S_i + C_i + M_i + B_i + P_i)}{E_0 + G_0 + S_0}$$

$$= \frac{\sum_{i=1\,to\,4}(S_i + C_i + M_i + B_i + P_i)}{Z_0 + S_0}$$

$$= \frac{\sum_{i=1\,to\,4}(S_i + C_i + M_i + B_i + P_i)}{P}$$

$$IUM = NetIUM + 1 = \frac{Z_0 + S_0 + \sum_{i=1\,to\,4}(S_i + C_i + M_i + B_i + P_i)}{Z_0 + S_0}$$

$$= \frac{P + \sum_{i=1\,to\,4}(S_i + C_i + M_i + B_i + P_i)}{P}$$

It is worth noting that we must introduce the time variable as part of the calculation of *IUM*s, because this study will use cross-sectional data to simulate the longitudinal phenomenon (chain migration process). Assuming that we are in a perfect world where we have complete immigration data on all the variables presented above, then the *IUM* will be the true *IUM*.

In reality, we have only the following data: (We will discuss more date in next chapter.)

- USCIS Immigration Data: Immigrants Admitted to the U.S.: 1972-2000
- U.S. Census Data: 1970-2000

From these two major data source, I have the following:

$$NetIUM \approx \frac{\sum_{\substack{i=1\,to\,4 \\ j=1972\,to\,2000}}(Sij + Cij + Mij + Bij + Pij)}{\sum_{j=1972\,to\,2000}(Z_{0j} + S_{0j})}$$

$$= \frac{\displaystyle\sum_{i=1\,to\,4}^{j=1972\ to\ 2000} (Sij + Cij + Mij + Bij + Pij)}{\displaystyle\sum_{j=1972\ to\ 2000} P_j}$$

$$IUM = \frac{\displaystyle\sum_{j=1972\,to\,2000}(Z_{0j} + S_{0j}) + \sum_{i=1to4}^{j=1972\,to\,2000}(Sij + Cij + Mij + Bij + Pij)}{\displaystyle\sum_{j=1972\,to\,2000}(Z_{0j} + S_{0j})}$$

$$= \frac{\displaystyle\sum_{j=1972\,to\,2000} P_j + \sum_{i=1to4}^{j=1972\,to\,2000}(Sij + Cij + Mij + Bij + Pij)}{\displaystyle\sum_{j=1972\,to\,2000} P_j}$$

CALCULATING IMMIGRATION REPRODUCTION MULTIPLIER

In this section, I will examine the fertility behavior of first-generation immigrants. In order to measure the Immigration Reproduction Process, we must first measure the total number of children born to immigrants, *i.e.*, the total number of second-generation immigrants. We will identify the second-generation immigrants by the birthplaces of their parents. The concept of second-generation immigrants is same as the concept of the population of U.S.-born children who have at least one foreign-born parent. This would lead to the study of the fertility patterns of immigrants. It is important to note that the majority of demographic studies have been on female fertility behavior; few have studied male fertility patterns. Since the majority of Principal Immigrants are male (as data in this research shows), this study must measure the fertility patterns of male immigrants, as well as the immigratio reproduction process. In studying the fertility of both genders, I will take a different approach to calculating the Total Fertility Rates (TFRs) for first-generation immigrants. Unlike the traditional method, which considers children in connection only to their mothers, I will split the "credit" for each U.S.-born child between the mother and the father. Therefore, we have the following:

- If both parents of the U.S.-born child are foreign-born immigrants, both the receive half credit for each child.
- If only one parent of the U.S.-born child is a foreign-born immigrant and the other is U.S.-born, the foreign-born parent (either mother or father) will get half credit for the child in the calculation. The other half credit will be assigned to the U.S.-born parent and will *not* be included in the calculation.
- In the case of a single-parent family, if the single parent is foreign-born, he or she will receive half credit for each of his or her children. We will discard the other half credit because of the unknown status of the other parent.

Of course, this research excludes all U.S.-born children whose parents are both U.S.-born parents, regardless of their ethnicity.[33]

First-Generation Immigrants

First-generation immigrants are foreign-born immigrants who are responsible for the birth of second-generation immigrants in the United States. Therefore, in order for us to develop a method to measure the *IRM*, we should first understand the first-generation immigrants. From the USCIS data (Immigrants Admitted to the United States: 1972-2000), we have:

$$I = I_f + I_m$$

where:

I is the total number of newly admitted immigrants (first-generation);
f indicates that the gender of the first-generation immigrant is female;
m indicates that the gender of the first-generation immigrant is male;
I_f is the total number of newly admitted female immigrants;
I_m is the total number of newly admitted male immigrants.

We can also rewrite the expression, as follows, to take into consideration the year the immigrant was admitted:

---

[33] It is important to note that these children are the descendents of second-generation immigrants and are beyond the scope of this research. As discussed earlier, this research will study only the first-generation immigrants and their children (i.e. second-generation immigrants). This research does not include future generations of immigrants.

$$I_i = I_{f,i} + I_{m,i}$$

where:

> *i is the year when the immigrants are admitted to the U.S.;*
> $I_{f,i}$ *is the total number of newly admitted female immigrants in year i;*
> $I_{m,i}$ *is the total number of newly admitted male immigrants in year i.*

Since we have two sources of data (the USCIS and the U.S. Census), I will use F to represent all foreign-born immigrants identified in the census data (U.S. Census 1980, 1990 and 2000). Therefore, we have:

$$F = F_f + F_m$$

where

> *F is the total number of foreign-born immigrants in the U.S.;*
> F_f *is the total number of foreign-born female immigrants in the U.S.;*
> F_m *is the total number of foreign-born male immigrants in the U.S.*

The following will make this census-year-specific:

$$F_i = F_{f,i} + F_{m,i}$$

where

> *i is the census year from which the data is calculated;*
> F_i *is the total number of foreign-born immigrants in the U.S. in census year i (1980, 1990 or 2000);*
> $F_{f,i}$ *is the total number of foreign-born female immigrants in the U.S. in census year i (1980, 1990 or 2000);*
> $F_{m,i}$ *is the total number of foreign-born male immigrants in the U.S. in census year i (1980, 1990 or 2000).*

If we take into consideration the age of the immigrants, we have:

$$F_{i,a} = F_{f,i,a} + F_{m,i,a}$$

where

> *i is the census year from which the data is calculated;*
> *a is the age range (15-49 for female immigrant, and 15-59 for male immigrants);*
> $F_{f,i,a}$ *is the total number of foreign-born female immigrants of age a in the U.S. in census year i (1980, 1990 or 2000);*
> $F_{m,i,a}$ *is the total number of foreign-born male immigrants of age a in the U.S. in census year i (1980, 1990 or 2000)*

Immigrant Second Generation: U.S.-Born Immigrant Children

In the study of second-generation immigrants, demographers have used the information on the birthplace of the parents to classify the native population by parentage: native born of native parentage (*NNP*), native born of foreign parentage (*NFP*), and native born of mixed parentage (*NMP*). The *NNP* population is native by definition because both of their parents are native. At the same time, both the *NFP* population (both parents are foreign-born) and the *NMP* population (one parent is native and the other is foreign-born) make up the immigrant second-generation.

In this research, the total number of second-generation immigrants is derived from the assumption that each parent contributes only half credit for each child they have in order to avoid counting immigrant children twice and to provide fertility information for immigrants of both genders. Therefore, we have the following:

- A *NFP* child (whose parents are both foreign-born) will be counted as 1 child—each parent gets 0.5 child as his/her contribution from his/her country of origin;
- A *NMP* child (who has one foreign-born parent and one U.S.-born parent) will be counted as 0.5 child. The foreign-born parent gets 0.5 child as his/her contribution from his/her country of origin, and the native born parent also gets 0.5 child, but that will be discarded because only foreign-born parents will be studied.

In addition to the standard breakdown of the native population by parentage, I would like to add three new categories:

- Native born of unknown parentage (*NUP*, or unknown place of birth for at least one parent);
- Native born of mixed parentage with one foreign-born parent (*NMP-F*, or one parent who is foreign-born and the other is unknown);
- Native born of mixed parentage with one native born parent (*NMP-N*, or one parent who is native born and the other is unknown).

These new categories are important, because this research specifically studies the immigrant fertility based on the birthplaces of the foreign-born parents of the native-born population.

We have no choice but to discard *NUP* (native born of unknown parentage, or birthplace of both parents unknown). We will also discard *NMP-N*, because we do not study native-born parents, and we do not have information for the other parent. In the case of *NMP-F*, we will discard the unknown parents, but we will use the foreign-born parents, along with the ½ child assigned to each of them, because known foreign-born parents are meaningful to this research.[34] These foreign-born parents (*NMP-F*), along with the foreign-born parents of *NFP* and *NMP*, make up the complete cohort of parents of second-generation immigrants. Table 4-1 details the logic of the inclusions and exclusions in this research.[35]

So, the total number of second-generation immigrants is equal to the total number of U.S.-born children to foreign parent(s). One of the best sources of data to calculate the total number of this population comes from the U.S. Census. I will use the IPUMS data sets to identify these children by verifying that their parents were born outside the U.S.[36]

Assuming that B is the total number of second-generation immigrants (*i.e.* the U.S.-born children, *USB Children,* who have at least one foreign-born parent) from the census data, we know that B could be the children of any immigrants in population groups Z_0, D_1 D_2, S_0, S_3, D_3, or D_4, as discussed in the previous section.

-----

[34] It is also possible to estimate a fertility rate better by adjusting the calculation method. One possible method is to assign the nationality of the parent who is known to the missing parent, i.e. the parent with positive identification would be given full weight under the assumption that the unknown parent is of the same type. However, since the goal of this research is to estimate the minimum multiplier effect and not the immigrant fertility rate, we will not use this method.

[35] It is also worth mentioning that this research, because of its method of calculation, has excluded children who died. No calculations can be done because the census data does not include that information.

[36] IPUMS data was used here. It has special fields that identify father records (POPLOC) and mother records (MOMLOC). Please see Ruggles *et al.*, *Integrated Public Use Microdata Series; Version 3.0.* Minneapolis, MN: Minnesota Population Center (http://www.ipums.org).

Table 4-1 Relationship Between the Native Born Children and the Place of Birth of their Parents

Category	Description	Father	Calculation	Mother	Calculation
NFP	Native Born of Foreign Parentage	Foreign Born	0.5 Child	Foreign Born	0.5 Child
NMP	Native Born of Mixed Parentage (with a foreign mother and a native father)	Foreign Born	0.5 Child	U.S. Born	Exclude
NMP	Native Born of Mixed Parentage (with a foreign father and a native mother)	U.S. Born	Exclude	Foreign Born	0.5 Child
NMP-F	Native Born of Mixed Parentage (with a foreign father and an unknown mother)	Foreign Born	0.5 Child	Unknown	Exclude
NMP-N	Native Born of Mixed Parentage (with a foreign father and an unknown mother)	Unknown	Exclude	Foreign Born	0.5 Child
NNP	Native Born of Native Parentage	U.S. Born	Exclude	U.S. Born	Exclude
NUP	Native Born of Unknown Parentage	Unknown	Exclude	Unknown	Exclude

Assuming that the total number of USB children is B, it follows that half of B is the fathers' responsibility, while the other half is the mothers'. Therefore, we have the following:

$B_{n,n}$ *defined as the total number of children born to parents who are both foreign-born immigrants;*

$B_{n,u}$ *defined as the total number of children born to one U.S. -born parent and one foreign-born parent;*

$B_{u,u}$ *defined as the total number of children born to parents who are both U.S.-born.*

Since we are interested only in the second-generation immigrants who are the children of $B_{n,n}$ and $B_{n,u}$ and because each immigrant parent will contribute only half of each child, we have the following:

$B= \frac{1}{2} * B_{n,u} + B_{n,n}$

Now, I will look at this from a different angle. I want to re-group this Total B into two new groups: B_f —the total number of U.S.-born children of a foreign-born mother, and the other as B_m —the total number of U.S.-born children of a foreign-born father. Then we have:

$B = B_f + B_m$

Or:

$B_{i,a} = B_{f,i,a} + B_{m,i,a}$

where

f indicates that female immigrants are responsible for these children;

m indicates that male immigrants are responsible for these children;

i indicates the census year from which the data is calculated;

a is the age range of the immigrant parents (15-49 for female immigrant, and 15-59 for male immigrants);

$B_{i,a}$ *is the total number of U.S.-born children of at least one foreign-born parent in age group a in census year i;*

$B_{f,i,a}$ *is the total number of U.S.-born children of foreign-born mothers in age group a in census year i;*

$B_{m,i,a}$ *is the total number of U.S.-born children of foreign-born fathers in age group a in census year i.*

Therefore, the total number of children B_f and B_m represents the second-generation immigrants as gender-specific contributions of first-generation immigrants. [37] The following discussions will provide further information on the fertility patterns of first-generation immigrants.

---

[37] Again, I want to stress the importance of the underlying calculation method here, which takes into account that first-generation immigrants contribute second-generation immigrants. I will give credit to both parents for each child they produce. To avoid double counting, I will give only half of the credit to each parent, *i.e.* for each U.S.-born child, half of the credit will go to the mother and half to the father.

Immigrant Fertility Rates

Using the census data, we can calculate the total number of first-generation immigrants as well as second-generation immigrants. Therefore, we have the following Crude Birth Rate for first-generation immigrants (F) with the total number of second-generation immigrants, *i.e.* the U.S.-born children or USB children (B):

$$\frac{B}{F} * 1,000$$

Or, we can calculate the age-specific fertility rate by gender, as follows:

$$R_{f,i,a} = \frac{B_{i,a}}{F_{i,a}} \text{ (female age-specific fertility rate in the census year i)}$$

where:

a is the age range from 15 to 49 for female immigrant parents;

$B_{f,i,a}$ *indicates the total number of U.S.-born children who have foreign-born mothers of age a in census year i;*

$F_{f,i,a}$ *indicates the total number of foreign-born mothers of age a in census year i;*

$R_{f,i,a}$ *is the age-specific fertility rate for foreign-born female immigrants of age a in census year i*[38].

And

$$R_{m,i,a} = \frac{B_{m,i,a}}{F_{m,i,a}} \text{ (male age-specific fertility rate in census year i)}$$

where:

a is the age range from 15 to 59 years for male immigrant parents;

$B_{m,i,a}$ *indicates the total number of U.S.-born children of foreign-born fathers of age a in census year i;*

$F_{m,i,a}$ *indicates the total number of foreign-born fathers of age a in census year i;*

---

[38] Please note that I have decided not to use the per 1,000 rate, because the Immigration Multiplier is calculated per original Principal Immigrant. Therefore, none of the *IRM*-related fertility rate calculations use the per 1,000 rate.

$R_{m,i,a}$ is the age-specific fertility rate for foreign-born male immigrants of age a in census year i.

Therefore, we can calculate the Total Fertility Rates from the census data for both female and male immigrants, as follows:

1)   Total Fertility Rate for Female Immigrants:

$$TFR_{f,i} = \sum_{a=15}^{49} R_{f,i,a} = \sum_{a=15}^{49} \frac{B_{f,i,a}}{F_{f,i,a}} \qquad \text{(single year)}$$

$$TFR_{f,i} = 5 * \sum_{a=15-19}^{45-49} R_{f,i,a} = 5 * \sum_{a=15-19}^{45-49} \frac{B_{f,i,a}}{F_{f,i,a}} \qquad \text{(5-year age group)}$$

2)   Total Fertility Rate for Male Immigrants:

$$TFR_{m,i} = \sum_{a=15}^{59} R_{m,i,a} = \sum_{a=15}^{59} \frac{B_{m,i,a}}{F_{m,i,a}} \qquad \text{(single year)}$$

$$TFR_{m,i} = 5 * \sum_{a=15-19}^{55-59} R_{m,i,a} = 5 * \sum_{a=15-19}^{55-59} \frac{B_{m,i,a}}{F_{m,i,a}} \qquad \text{(5-year age-group)}$$

Hence, the overall TFR from the census data will be:

$$TFR_i = TFR_{f,i} + TFR_{m,i}$$

where:

TFR_i is the TFR calculated from the census year i data;

$TFR_{f,i}$ is the foreign-born female immigrant TFR calculated from the census year i data;

$TFR_{m,i}$ is the foreign-born male immigrant TFR calculated from the census year i data.

Estimating Second Generation Immigrants

Using the census data, we can calculate the age-specific fertility rate by gender. In order to estimate the total number of second-generation immigrants from the annual admission of immigrants using the USCIS data, we assume the following:

1.   If U.S. immigrants recorded in the USCIS data follow the same fertility patterns as the foreign-born immigrants recorded in the U.S. Census, we can then apply the age-specific fertility rates (from the census data) for both genders to the USCIS immigrant cohort.

2.   If the USCIS immigrants follow this fertility pattern for the rest of their lives in the U.S., we can use the age- and gender-specific TFR to estimate the total number of second-generation immigrants for

whom these first-generation immigrants will be responsible in the future.

Therefore, we can estimate the total number of USB children of these newly admitted immigrants in the census year, as follows, assuming that these first-generation immigrants follow the fertility pattern calculated from the census data (assumption 1). C represents the estimated total number of this second-generation population:

$$C_{f,i,a} = R_{f,i,a} * I_{f,i,a} = \frac{B_{f,i,a}}{F_{f,i,a}} * I_{f,i,a}$$

(Estimated U.S.-born children of female immigrants of age a who are admitted in year i)

$$C_{m,i,a} = R_{m,i,a} * I_{m,i,a} = \frac{B_{m,i,a}}{F_{m,i,a}} * I_{m,i,a}$$

(Estimated U.S.-born children of male immigrants of age a who are admitted in year i)

where:

a is the age range from 15-49 for female immigrants and 15-59 for male immigrants;

$R_{f,i,a}$ *is the age-specific fertility rate for female immigrants of age a in census year i;*

$I_{f,i,a}$ *is the total number of female immigrants of age a admitted to the U.S. in year i;*

$B_{f,i,a}$ *is the total number of U.S.-born children of female immigrants of age a in year i;*

$F_{f,i,a}$ *is the total number of female immigrants of age a in year i;*

$R_{m,i,a}$ *is the age-specific fertility rate for male immigrants of age a in census year i;*

$I_{m,i,a}$ *is the total number of male immigrants of age a admitted to the U.S. in year i;*

$B_{m,i,a}$ *is the total number of U.S.-born children of male immigrants of age a in year i;*

$F_{m,i,a}$ *is the total number of male immigrants of age a in year i;*

Since the TFR is the total number of children a woman or man bears in her or his lifetime,[39] we have the following:

1.   The estimated total number of future immigrant children in the U.S.-born to female immigrants of age *a*, using the fertility pattern from year *i*:

$$TFR_{f,i,a} = \sum_{j=a}^{49} R_{f,i,j} = \sum_{j=a}^{49} \frac{B_{f,i,j}}{F_{f,i,j}} \qquad \text{(single year)}$$

$$TFR_{f,i,j} = 5 * \sum_{j=a}^{44-49} R_{f,i,j} = 5 * \sum_{j=a}^{44-49} \frac{B_{f,i,j}}{F_{f,i,j}} \quad \text{(5-year age group)}$$

2.   The estimated total number of future immigrant children in the U.S. in the future born to male immigrants of age *a*, using the fertility pattern from year *i*:

$$TFR_{m,i,a} = \sum_{j=a}^{59} R_{m,i,j} = \sum_{j=a}^{59} \frac{B_{m,i,j}}{F_{m,i,j}} \qquad \text{(single year)}$$

$$TFR_{m,i,a} = 5 * \sum_{j=a}^{54-59} R_{m,i,j} = 5 * \sum_{j=a}^{54-59} \frac{B_{m,i,a}}{F_{m,i,a}} \quad \text{(5-year age group)}$$

Therefore, we can calculate the estimated total number of future immigrant children in the U.S.-born to immigrants of any age *a* (from USCIS data), using fertility patterns from the census data and immigrant data from the USCIS:

1.   The estimated total number of future immigrant children born to female immigrants of age *a*, using the fertility pattern from the census data:

$$C_{f,i,a} = I_{f,i,a} * TFR_{f,i,a} = I_{f,i,a} * \sum_{j=a}^{49} R_{f,i,j} = I_{f,i,a} * \sum_{j=a}^{49} \frac{B_{m,i,j}}{F_{f,i,j}}$$

(single year)

$$C_{f,i,a} = I_{f,i,a} * TFR_{f,i,a} = I_{f,i,a} * 5 * \sum_{j=a}^{44-49} R_{f,i,j} = I_{f,i,a} * 5 * \sum_{j=a}^{44-49} \frac{B_{f,i,j}}{F_{f,i,j}}$$

(5-year age group)

---

[39] In most cases, the TFR is calculated for only the female population (age 15-49). In this research, however, male fertility is considered in the 15-59 age range. The TFR is a measure of fertility for both genders in this research.

where

$C_{f,i,a}$ *is the estimated total number of U.S.-born children of female immigrants of age a using the fertility pattern from year i.*

2.   The estimated total number of future immigrant children born to male immigrants of age *a*, using the fertility pattern from the census data:

$$C_{m,i,a} = I_{m,i,a} * TFR_{m,i,a} = I_{m,i,a} * \sum_{j=a}^{49} R_{m,i,j} = I_{m,i,a} * \sum_{j=a}^{49} \frac{B_{m,i,j}}{F_{m,i,j}}$$

(single year)

$$C_{m,i,a} = I_{m,i,a} * TFR_{m,i,a} = I_{m,i,a} * 5 * \sum_{j=a}^{44-49} R_{m,i,j} = I_{m,i,a} * 5 * \sum_{j=a}^{44-49} \frac{B_{m,i,j}}{F_{m,i,j}}$$

(5-year age group)

where

$C_{m,i,a}$ *is the estimated total number of U.S.-born children of male immigrants of age a under the fertility pattern from year i.*

It is obvious that the younger the first-generation immigrants are, the greater number of second-generation children they will bear. In fact, for any young first-generation immigrants in the age group 0-15, the expected total number of children to be born in the future is equivalent to $TFR_{f,i}$ for females and $TFR_{m,i}$ for males. That is:

$$TFR_{f,j} = TFR_{f,i,j} \qquad \text{where } j = 0 \sim 15$$
$$TFR_{m,j} = TFR_{m,i,j} \qquad \text{where } j = 0 \sim 15$$

Now, we can calculate the estimated total number of future immigrant children to be born to male immigrants of age *a*, using the fertility pattern from the U.S. Census:

$$C_i = \sum_{a=0}^{99} C_{f,i,a} + \sum_{a=0}^{99} C_{m,i,a}$$
$$= \left(I_{f,i,a} * \sum_{a=0}^{99} \frac{B_{f,i,a}}{F_{f,i,a}} + I_{m,i,a} * \sum_{a=0}^{99} \frac{B_{m,i,a}}{F_{m,i,a}} \right)$$

where:

C_i *is the estimated total number of children to be born in the U.S. to all immigrants under the fertility pattern of year i.*

The Immigration Reproduction Multiplier: the Formula

We can define the reproduction process within the migration chain as the *Chain Migration Immigration Reproduction Process.* At the Reproduction Phase, both principal and derived family members are responsible for producing second-generation immigrants. Therefore, we can define the Immigration Reproduction Multiplier (*IRM*) as the following:

$$IRM = \frac{I+C}{I} = \frac{I + \sum_{a=0}^{99} C_{f,a} + \sum_{a=0}^{99} C_{m,a}}{I}$$

$$= \frac{I + \left(I_{f,a} * \sum_{a=0}^{99} \frac{B_{f,a}}{F_{f,a}} + I_{m,i,a} * \sum_{a=0}^{99} \frac{B_{m,a}}{F_{m,a}} \right)}{I}$$

where:

C is the estimated total number of second-generation immigrants, assuming that first-generation immigrants will experience with a fertility pattern of year i;

I is the total number of first-generation immigrants.

Or, we can rewrite this expression using the specific fertility pattern calculated from census year *i* as follows:

$$IRM_i = \frac{I_i + C_i}{I_i} = \frac{I_i + \left(I_{f,i,a} * \sum_{a=0}^{99} \frac{B_{f,i,a}}{F_{f,i,a}} + I_{m,i,a} * \sum_{a=0}^{99} \frac{B_{m,i,a}}{F_{m,i,a}} \right)}{I_i}$$

where:

C_i is the estimated total number of second-generation immigrants, assuming that the first-generation immigrants follow the fertility pattern of year i;

I_i is the total number of first-generation immigrants;

IRM_i is the IRM with fertility pattern of year i.

From this definition of *IRM*, we can see that when *C*=0 (*i.e.*, there are no children born in the U.S. to first-generation immigrants), the *IRM* will be 1. In this special case, there will be no multiplier effect in the reproduction phase during the chain migration. However, in reality,

C is always greater than 0, because immigrants *do* produce offspring. This means that *IRM* is always greater than 1. Therefore, the higher the fertility rate, the larger the *C* value, the higher the *IRM* value, and the stronger the reproduction multiplier effect.

We can also define the *net IRM*, which is used to measure the net ratio of second-generation immigrants to first-generation immigrants:

$$NetIRM = \frac{C}{I} = \frac{\left(I_{f,a} * \sum_{a=0}^{99} \frac{B_{f,a}}{F_{f,a}} + I_{m,i,a} * \sum_{a=0}^{99} \frac{B_{m,a}}{F_{m,a}} \right)}{I}$$

$$NetIRM_i = \frac{C_i}{I_i} = \frac{\left(I_{f,i,a} * \sum_{a=0}^{99} \frac{B_{f,i,a}}{F_{f,i,a}} + I_{m,i,a} * \sum_{a=0}^{99} \frac{B_{m,i,a}}{F_{m,i,a}} \right)}{I_i}$$

We can see that the *net IRM* will be 0 only if *C*=0, *i.e.*, there are no children born in the U.S. to first-generation immigrants, which is impossible. Hence, C is always greater than 0 in reality. Therefore, the *net IRM* is always greater than 0.

CALCULATING IMMIGRATION MULTIPLIER

To construct the overall Immigration Multiplier (*IM*), we need the *IUM* from the immigration unification process, and the *IRM* from the immigration reproduction process. Therefore, we have the following *IM*:

$$IM = IUM * IRM$$
$$= \frac{I}{P} * \frac{I + C}{I} = \frac{I + C}{P} = \frac{P + D + C}{P} = 1 + \frac{D + C}{P} = 1 + NetIM$$

Or, we can rewrite *IM* as:

$$IM = net\ IM + 1.$$

Here, we can define *net IM* as: $NetIM = \frac{D + C}{P}$

where

P is the total number of Principal Immigrants;

    D is the total number of derived family immigrants sponsored (directly or indirectly) by the original Principal Immigrants;

    I is the total number of foreign-born immigrants (i.e. first-generation immigrants), the sum of Principal Immigrants (P), and derived family immigrants (D);

    C is the total number of future children to be born in the U.S. to foreign-born parents. This is also the total number of immigrant second-generation.

If we substitute the formulas for calculating D and C, we have the following:

$$IM = \frac{P + \sum_{i=1to4}(S_i + C_i + M_i + B_i + P_i) + \left(I_{f,a} * \sum_{a=0}^{99}\frac{B_{f,a}}{F_{f,a}} + I_{m,i,a} * \sum_{a=0}^{99}\frac{B_{m,a}}{F_{m,a}}\right)}{P}$$

$$NetIM = \frac{\sum_{i=1to4}(S_i + C_i + M_i + B_i + P_i) + \left(I_{f,a} * \sum_{a=0}^{99}\frac{B_{f,a}}{F_{f,a}} + I_{m,i,a} * \sum_{a=0}^{99}\frac{B_{m,a}}{F_{m,a}}\right)}{P}$$

Weighted Immigration Multiplier

According to the Complete Chain Migration Model, the migration chains start with the Principal Immigrants and then the total multiplier effects are measured by the Immigration Multipliers. This suggests that both the size of the Principal Immigrant population and the size of the Immigration Multipliers can contribute to the growth of the migration chains. Therefore, we need to develop a measure that takes both of these into account so that we can measure the scale of the whole migration chain. This is especially important, when we want to make comparisons under various parameters (such as time, regions, countries, etc.).

    In a case of comparing the multiplier effects of the chain migration among n entities (where n is an integer and entities could be any comparison unit, such as year, immigrants-sending region, or immigrants-sending country), we can define the following by starting a total number of Principal Immigrants of $P_w = 1,000$:

    $P_{w,i} = P_i / P * 1,000$

Where

P_i is the total number of Principal Immigrants for unit i.

P is the grand total all Principal Immigrants combined.

$P_{w,i}$ is the distributed weight within the 1,000 Principal Immigrants for comparison unit i. This could also be interpreted as the total number of Principal Immigrants per 1,000.

Starting with the 1,000 Principal Immigrants P_w, we have:

$$IM_{w,i} = IM_i * P_{w,i}$$

Where:

$P_{w,i}$ is the distributed weight within the 1,000 Principal Immigrants for comparison unit i.

IM_i is the IM value for comparison unit i.

$IM_{w,i}$ is the weighted IM for unit i, which is the total number of immigrants contributed by the weighted Principal Immigrants for comparison unit i.

$$\sum_{i=1 \sim n} IM_{w,i} = IM * 1,000$$

$$\sum_{i=1 \sim n} IM_i = IM$$

$$\sum_{i=1 \sim n} P_{w,i} = P_w = 1,000$$

Therefore, we have the following:

$$NetIUM_{w,i} = P_{w,i} * NetIUM_i$$

- The total number of sponsored family immigrants for unit i is the result of the total number of Principal Immigrants multiplying the net Immigration Unification Multiplier. *Therefore, the impact of the unification phase of the chain migration process is proportional to the size of the Principal Immigrant population and the value of Immigration Unification Multiplier.*

$$NetIRM_{w,i} = (P_{w,i} + NetIUM_{w,i}) * NetIRM_i$$

- The total number of immigrant children (or second-generation immigrants) for unit i is the result of the total number of first-generation immigrants multiplying the net Immigration Reproduction Multiplier. *Therefore, the impact of the reproduction phase of the chain migration is proportional to the size of the population of Principal Immigrants, the size of the sponsored family immigrants, and the value of Immigration Reproduction Multiplier.*

$$WIM_{w,i} = P_{w,i} + NetIUM_{w,i} + NetIRM_{w,i}$$
$$= P_{w,i} + NetIUM_{w,i} + NetIRM_{w,i}$$

$$= P_{w,i} + NetIUM_{w,i} + (P_{w,i} + NetIUM_{w,i}) * NetIRM_i$$
$$= P_{w,i} + NetIUM_{w,i} + P_{w,i} * NetIRM_i + NetIUM_{w,i} * NetIRM_i$$
$$= P_{w,i} + P_{w,i} * NetIUM_i + P_{w,i} * NetIRM_i + P_{w,i} * NetIUM_i * NetIRM_i)$$
$$= P_{w,i} * (1 + NetIUM_i + NetIRM_i + NetIRM_i * NetIUM_i)$$
$$= P_{w,i} * (1 + NetIUM_i) * (1 + NetIRM_i)$$
$$= P_{w,i} * IUM_i * IRM_i$$
$$= P_{w,i} * IM_i$$

- The total number of the combined immigrant population for unit *i* is the total number of Principal Immigrants, the total number of sponsored family immigrants, and the total number of second-generation immigrants, (which is the same as the combined total of first and second-generation immigrants). This total can also be derived by multiplying the total number of Principal Immigrants by the Immigration Multiplier. *Therefore, the total impact of chain migration is proportional to the size of the population of Principal Immigrants and the value of the Immigration Multiplier.*

Estimating IUMs Using Published Data

Using concepts developed here, we can also estimate Immigration Unification Multiplier (*IUM*), using the data from the Statistical Abstract of the United States. As discussed earlier, we know that Principal Immigrants are the source of all future family-based immigrants. In the general immigration categories listed in Table 4-2, we have three groups of immigrants: Family-Based Immigrants (Item 1), Employment-Based Immigrants (Item 2), and Other Immigrants (Item 3). Out of these three groups, we designate Family-Based Immigrants as the "sponsored family immigrants," which includes the "foreign spouses of U.S.-born citizens" but does not include the accompanying family members. Since Employment-Based Immigrants (Item 2) and the Other Immigrants (Item 3) are quite similar to our definition of Principal Immigrants, we will define these two groups as Principal Immigrants, knowing that the foreign-born spouses of U.S.-born Citizens are grouped in the "Family-based Immigrants," category, while all accompanying immigrants are included as principle immigrants.

Table 4-2 Estimating Immigration Unification Multipliers (Annual Data)

Major Categories	1970	1975	1980	1985	1990	1998	2000	2004
Raw Numbers								
Total Immigrants	373,326	386,194	530,639	570,009	1,536,483	660,477	849,807	946,142
1. Family-Based (F)	274,174	283,996	374,599	417,625	448,640	475,750	583,150	620,429
Immediate Relatives	79,213	95945	157,743	204,368	234,090	284,270	347,870	406,074
Family Sponsored	92,432	91,504	216,856	213,257	214,550	191,480	235,280	214,355
Other Family Immigrants	102,529	96,547	NA	NA	NA	NA	NA	NA
2. Employment-Based (E)	34,016	29334	47,511	53,446	58,192	77,517	107,024	155,330
3. Other Immigrants (O)	65,136	72,864	108,529	98,938	1,029,651	107,210	159,633	170,383
Refugees & Asylees	12,332	25,433	88,057	95,040	97,364	54,645	65,941	71,230
Others	52,804	47,431	20,472	3,898	932,287	52,565	93,692	99,153
Estimated IUM = (E+O+F) /(E+O)	3.77	3.78	3.40	3.74	1.41	3.58	3.19	2.90
Estimated Net IUM = F /(E+O)	2.77	2.78	2.40	2.74	0.41	2.58	2.19	1.90
Source:	*Calculations based on Statistical Abstract of the United States: 1986 (Table 128; p. 85); 1995 (Table 6; p. 10), 2000 (Table 6, p. 9), 2006 (Table 6, p. 10)*							

In Table 4-2, we have the estimated Immigration Unification Multiplier:

- *Estimated Immigration Unification Multiplier*, which is defined as the ratio of the total number of immigrants over the combined total number of Employment-Based Immigrants and Other Immigrants, or:

$$Est.IUM = \frac{EmploymentBased(E) + Other(O) + FamilyBased(F)}{EmploymentBased(E) + Other(O)}$$

$$= \frac{All.immigrants\ (E + O + F)}{Employment\ Based\ (E) + Others\ (O)}$$

$$= \frac{E + O + F}{E + O}$$

- *Estimated Net Immigration Unification Multiplier,* defined as the ratio of the total number of Family-Based Immigrants to the combined total number of Employment-Based Immigrants and Other Immigrants, or:

$$EstimatedNetIUM = \frac{FamilyBased(F)}{EmployentBased(E) + Others(O)}$$

$$= \frac{F}{E + O}$$

From this illustration and these two new definitions, we notice the following:

$$Estimated\ IUM = \frac{E + O + F}{E + O} = \frac{F}{E + O} + 1 = Estimated\ Net\ IUM + 1$$

From Table 4-2, we can see that the estimated net *IUM* has been from 2 to 3 since the 1970s. This means that for each immigrant admitted through the Employment-Based or Other categories, 2~3 additional family immigrants will also be admitted to the U.S.

We also notice that changes in immigration laws can affect both the Net IUM and IUM.. As demonstrated in 1990, both the estimated IUM and estimated Net IUM are quite low, because the volume of immigrants in the Other category is exceptionally high. As a result, the denominators of both the estimated IUMs are quite large; therefore reducing the overall values of the estimated and Net IUMs.

SPECIAL NOTES

The focus of this research is on international migrations. Immigrants who come to the United States (for various economic, sociological, political, or other non-socioeconomic reasons) will be identified and categorized as certain types of immigrants (*i.e.* Principal Immigrants or derived family immigrants). However, there are a few exception cases and assumptions.

Adoption

It is clear that the adoption process does not apply to any of the immigration types we have discussed so far. Because of the legal process involved, the adoption process produces minimum probabilities of an additional immigration flow. Therefore, it is reasonable for this study to exclude any adoption related immigrants so that we will be able to focus on the components of international migration.

Emigration

As discussed earlier, migration is a type of life event that is quite different from birth and death in the sense that migration is repeatable, while birth and death are not. Thus, it will be more reasonable to study migration as a two-part process: immigration and emigration. Since the study of immigration is very similar to the study of births, while the study of emigration is similar to the study of deaths, the Immigration Multiplier that measures immigration is very similar to the birth rate that measures births. Therefore, the scope of study on chain migration and Immigration Multiplier would be limited only to immigration. This means that the study of measuring emigration is equivalent to the study the mortality rate, and it is beyond the scope of this research to include emigration.

At the same time, in order for us to study (repeated) migration processes effectively, we will have to separate *temporary migration* from *permanent migration*. In this research, the focus is on international migration, and the population under study is all immigrants who have applied for the admission as *permanent residents* of the United States. In this case, the immigrants involved in this study are all relatively *permanent*, although there is a possibility that some could later emigrate to other countries (including to his/her own country of birth). Kobrin and Speare (1983) reported that substantial ethnic differentials exist among emigrants. They concluded that immigrant groups with a strong network of social and economic ties (as characterized by chain migration processes) do not sponsor emigration.

The issue with emigration could be more than the return of previous immigrants. There is the possibility that the emigration population might consist of not only previous immigrants who came from other countries, but also U.S.-born citizens who have decided to leave the United States permanently for whatever reason. This will obviously complicate the whole process, and it will deserve another separate study. Therefore, emigration is not included as part of this research.

Undocumented Immigrants

Since undocumented immigrants cannot sponsor their family members, they will not affect the family reunification process. However, the undocumented immigrant population will have an impact on the immigrant reproduction process. Some immigrant children are born to these undocumented immigrants, and these children will be included in the U.S. Census data.

As an interesting note, however, we might be able to estimate the number of undocumented immigrants by using the simulation model in the later part of this book.

CHAPTER 5

Data

DATA SOURCE OVERVIEW

Most of the studies on international immigrations to the U.S. have used U.S. Census data, USCIS (United States Citizenship and Immigration Services) data, or other data to perform their analyses. Few have combined two or more data sets to study various aspects of immigrants. In this book, I have developed a method to combine the two most important data sources for immigration studies: IPUMS Census Data (Integrated Public Use Microdata Series) and USCIS data. The USCIS data come from the published datasets on Immigrants Admitted to the United States from 1972-2000, and the IPUMS are 5% samples for census years 1980, 1990 and 2000 (Ruggles *et al.* 2004).

USCIS Data

The USCIS data on *Immigrants Admitted to the United States* (U.S. Department. of Justice, USCIS. 1972-2000) is the main data set used in this research for building the *family reunification* component of the Complete Chain Migration Model, with the main focus on the study of *family reunification process* of the immigrants.

IPUMS Census Data

I used U.S. Census data from 1980, 1990, and 2000 in this research to study the *family reproduction* component of the Complete Chain Migration Model, with the focus on the study of immigrant fertility and family structures of the immigrants. The census also provided data on naturalized citizens, and such information is a perfect supplement to the USCIS data.

The 1980, 1990, and 2000 census data are all from IPUMS. The IPUMS data consists of high-precision samples of the census data, and it assigns uniform codes across all of these, bringing relevant documentation into a coherent form to facilitate the analysis of social and economic change (Ruggles *et al*. 2004). It is also important that the IPUMS records for all three census years (1980, 1990, and 2000) are comparable, because that made it much easier for me to study several key variables across multiple census years.

Other Data

In this research, I have used other data sources as supplemental resources, such as the *Statistical Yearbook of the Citizenship and Immigration Service* and the annual *Statistical Abstract of the United States*. I used these data sources for illustrating the method for calculating the *Estimated İmmigration Unification Multipliers*.

IMPORTANT DATA ELEMENTS

Classes of Admissions

Classes of Admissions (COA) are defined by the USCIS (United States Citizenship and Immigration Services). Throughout this book, we will group all immigrants in the following categories according to their Classes of Admissions upon entering the United States.

Principal Immigrants
Principal immigrants are defined as those who are sponsored by non-family members, such as employers or the government. All Principal Immigrants have the potential to sponsor future family members.

• *ERI Principals*
Employment-Related Principal Immigrants, or ERI Principals are defined as foreign nationals who have been authorized to "live and work permanently in the United States."[40] It is required that the ERI Principals have permanent employment opportunities in the United

---

[40] Please see USCIS Website (http://uscis.gov/graphics/services/residency/ employment.htm) on this subject.

States and that they have sponsorship from employers. Most employment categories require the U.S. employer to complete a labor certification request for the immigrants.

- **GSI Principals**

The category of Government-Sponsored Principal Immigrants, or GSI Principals includes many different types. Most of them are refugees[41] and asylum-seekers.[42] However, it also includes some lesser-known government-sponsored immigration programs like the Diversity Lottery (DV) Program, which makes 55,000 immigrant visas available through a lottery to people who come from countries with low rates of immigration to the United States every year. Of such visas, 5,000 are allocated for use under NACARA, beginning with Diversity Lottery Program in 1999 (DV '99). The State Department (DOS) holds the lottery every year and randomly selects approximately 110,000 applicants from all qualified entries. The DOS selects more applicants than the number of visas it will supply, since many individuals who are chosen will not complete the visa process. Once 55,000 visas are issued or the fiscal year ends, the DV program is closed.

- **FSUSB Principals**

As previously discussed, we will consider all FSUSB Principals (i.e. Foreign Spouses of U.S.-Born Citizens) as *Principal Immigrants* because they all have the potential to sponsor their family members. At the same time, some foreign-born spouses are naturalized U.S. citizens, and they would be considered *derived family immigrants*.

It is very important to note that USCIS data alone could *not* differentiate whether foreign-born spouses are sponsored by U.S.-born citizens or by naturalized citizens. We will need information from the census data to perform calculations to estimate these two groups of immigrants. Hence, as discussed in the previous chapter, we will

---

[41] Defined by the *Immigration and Nationality Act* in Sec. 101(a)(42).

[42] Asylum is a form of protection that allows individuals who are in the United States to remain here, provided that they meet the definition of a refugee. They are not barred from either applying for or being granted asylum, and they eventually adjust their status to lawful permanent resident. (See USCIS Website:

http://uscis.gov/graphics/services/asylum/index.htm.)

calculate the actual number of those foreign-born spouses of U.S.-born citizens using the census data. Meanwhile, all foreign-born spouses of non-U.S. citizen immigrants will be considered *dependents,* who are sponsored by the Principal Immigrants.

- **Calculating Principal Immigrants: FSUSB Principals**

As discussed earlier, Foreign Spouses of U.S.-born Citizens are also considered as Principal Immigrants (hence, *FSUSB Principals*), because they are sponsored by persons outside their families and such sponsorship is not family-unification-based.

In order for us to calculate the total number of U.S.-born citizens who sponsor *foreign-born* spouses, we must use the census data to determine the number of couples made up of one U.S. citizen and one non-U.S. citizen. We will narrow that data down to create a data set for couples, making the following assumptions to estimate the probabilities of foreign-born spouses being sponsored by U.S.-born citizens or by naturalized U.S. citizens:

Table 5-1 U.S. Citizens and Their Foreign Spouses: Sponsorship Patterns

Partner A	Partner B	Conclusion	Assumption
U.S. Born	U.S. Born	Exclude	Not Applicable
Foreign Born Non U.S. Citizen	Foreign Born Non U.S. Citizen	Exclude	No sponsorship
Naturalized U.S. Citizen	Foreign Born Non U.S. Citizen	Include	A sponsors B
Foreign Born Non U.S. Citizen	Naturalized U.S. Citizen	Include	B sponsors A
Naturalized U.S. Citizen	Naturalized U.S. Citizen	Include	Husband sponsors Wife
U.S. Born	Foreign Born Non U.S. Citizen	Include	A sponsors B
Foreign Born Non U.S. Citizen	U.S. Born	Include	B sponsors A

- If the couple are both U.S.-born, they will be excluded from the calculation;
- If the couple are both foreign-born and neither of them are U.S. citizens, they will be excluded from the calculation;
- If the couple are both foreign-born and one of them is a U.S. citizen, the foreign-born spouse will be considered in the calculation model as being sponsored by a naturalized U.S. citizen;

- If the couple are both naturalized U.S. citizens, then the wife will be considered in the calculation model as sponsored by the husband;
- If the couple contains one U.S.-born partner, then the other (foreign-born) partner will be considered in the calculation model as sponsored by the U.S.-born (citizen) partner.

Table 5-1 illustrates all of these scenarios. Using the USCIS data, we can calculate the total number of foreign-born spouses (US_0) sponsored by U.S. citizens (both U.S.-born and naturalized). Assuming that the rate of U.S.-born citizens sponsoring foreign-born spouses is R_0, we can then calculate the following:

Foreign Spouses of U.S.-Born Citizens (FSUSB) (considered as Principal Immigrants at *Phase 0*):

$$S_0 = US_0 * R_0$$

Spouses of Naturalized U.S. Citizens (FSUSN) (considered as family immigrants of Z_0 at *Phase 3*):

$$S_3 = US_0 * (1-R_0)$$

Family Immigrants

We define all sponsored family immigrants of Principal Immigrants by their classes of admissions under the family reunification category, including those defined by USCIS as "accompanying family members" (spouses and children). In addition to the family members of immigrants, this also includes exempt family members of U.S. citizens (such as spouses, minor children, and parents) and non-exempt family members of U.S. citizens (adult children and siblings of U.S. citizens), as determined by the COA per immigration rules.

Handling COAs

For some reason, some of the COAs (C7P or CNP for Cuban Refugee, or non-Cuban spouse or child of Cuban refugee; and SL1 or SL6 for Juvenile court dependent) provide the standard Principal Immigrants, spouses, and children categories. We will have to regroup immigrants in these COAs, using the following logic:

1. If the age of the immigrant is less than 18, the immigrant will be regrouped as a minor child;

2. If the age is greater or equal to 18 and the gender is female, this immigrant will be regrouped as an accompanying spouse. This assumption is valid, since most of the international migrations are more

likely to begin with a male in the family, although there is increasing evidence that females are playing major roles in migrating independently and internationally.

3.   All of the immigrants remaining in this category will be treated as Principal Immigrants.

Exclusions

● *Adoption*

Since orphans do not have the potential to sponsor any of their family members, the calculations of the Immigration Multipliers will exclude them.

● *Other Exclusions*

We will also exclude immigrants who are categorized by USCIS as *Persons who lost U.S. citizenship.*

Regions and Countries

This study will focus on the regional variations, as well as on some leading countries that contribute to the influx of immigration to the United States. The main focus of the regional variations will be on the *place of birth* of the immigrants. This data is available in both the USCIS and U.S. Census. However, due to the differences in data collection standards and procedures, it is a challenge to find the match of countries and regions between these two data sources.

In IPUMS data, the 5-digit BPL code (Birth Place Code) is used for identifying the country of birth for all foreign-born immigrants.

Most of the countries reported in the USCIS data have been matched successfully to the IPUMS data.

Data on Immigrant Fertility

As discussed in previous chapters, in order to estimate the *IRM*, we will have to:

1.   Calculate the U.S.-born children to immigrant parent(s) using the census data.

2.   Calculate the fertility rate of the immigrant population in the U.S. using the census data.

3.   Apply the calculated immigrant fertility rate to the immigrant population from the USCIS data, and calculate the estimated number of second-generation immigrants (i.e. estimated native-born children).

In the IPUMS Census data, *age* is collected as a variable that was defined as "the person's age in years as of their last birthday prior to or on the day of census date." In this research, I used the 1980, 1990, and 2000 census data to identify all native-born children, and I used the age to estimate the year of birth of second-generation immigrants.

Because the IPUMS 1980 is not weighted and both IPUMS 1990 and IPUMS 2000 are, the calculation processes for these three census years are somewhat different. Weights have been adjusted for all 1990 and 2000 samples.

To identify the U.S.-born children to immigrants, I use the BPL (birthplace code) of the parents identified in the IPUMS. The children's parents are tracked by MOMLOC and POPLOC in IPUMS data sets. IPUMS authors note that these pointers identify the location within the household of each child's mother and father through a set of logic calculations. We will exclude all children whose parents are U.S.-born citizens (with BPL being in the United States), as well as those whose BPL is outside of the United States. The final population should include only those children who were born in the United States who have at least one foreign-born parent.

In the process of calculating the TFRs for further adjustment to the age-gender structure of the immigrant cohort, we will give each parent half weight for each U.S.-born immigrant child.

Based on the age and gender distribution of the non-U.S.-born parents from IPUMS data, we will calculate the TFR for both immigrant women and men by certain categories (year, region, or country). Applying the calculated fertility rates to the immigrant cohort based on the age-gender distribution from the USCIS data for the category in discussion (year, region, or country), we will then have the immigrant fertility rate. Therefore, we can derive the estimated total number of second-generation immigrants.

SPECIAL NOTES ON DATA

Data Limitations

IPUMS Census Data
Although the IPUMS data is an excellent source for this research, it does have the following limitations:

1.   It is available within only a ten-year interval.
2.   The sample size is 5%.
3.   Since the census 1980 is not a weighted sample, while the census data from 1990 and 2000 is, we will need to use a different calculation method. We will adjust each record using a weight at the personal record level for 1980 and 1990.

USCIS Data

The complete data sets on *Immigrants Admitted to the United States* published by the *Citizenship and Immigration Services (1972-2000)* have some limitations:

1.   Although there is much immigration admission related information, there are no naturalization related variables and records in the data sets.

2.   The detailed information on the class of admissions categories, which is crucial in this study, is available in the data sets from only 1972-1998. Somehow, the data sets for 1999 and 2000 do not have the field *class of admissions*. Therefore, I have not used data sets from 1999 and 2000 in part of my research.

3.   The USCIS data sets are published annually, and there are some lags in the reporting and collecting process. The data sets for each year always misreport the records from previous year. For example, only 75% of the data reported in 1999 came from 1999; the other 25% came from 1998 records. Therefore, in this research, I dropped the records from 1998.

4.   The USCIS data is not cohort data, which does not provide the complete history of each individual immigrants.

5.   The data starts at 1972.

Assumptions

It is a challenge to combine these two data sources (USCIS data and the IPUMS Census data) to calculate the Immigration Multipliers, which is the foundation for building the model that replicates the immigration process.

The following assumptions will apply:

1.   Emigration will be omitted, because this research focuses on the international flow of immigration and its chain-migration effect. (See the detailed explanations of this assumption presented in the previous chapter on research method.)

2.   Since undocumented immigrants are not able to sponsor their family members, this population will be involved in only the immigration reproduction process. Therefore, it will not be part of the elements of the family reunification process (See the detailed explanations of this assumption presented in the previous chapter on research method.)

3.   The population represented in the USCIS immigration data is consistent with the foreign-born population in the U.S. Census data.

4.   All Principal Immigrants will sponsor their spouses and all of their children. Therefore, their spouses will not have to sponsor their spouses and their children again.

Special Discussion: Visa Backlogs

It is important to understand that the total number of immigrants admitted under the family preference category is actually the total number of *admitted* family-based immigrants *within the legal limit of the U.S. immigration system.* Citizenship and Immigration Services (USCIS) Data suggests that visa backlogs exist for all of the family-based categories, and that if there were no legal limit, the admission of family-based immigrants would be a lot more. Therefore, we should also explore the visa backlog issue.

Simcox (1988) suggested that there are backlogs for all of the family-based preference categories, and Day (1989) noted that the waiting period for sponsoring siblings of U.S. citizens for some countries is about 20 years. Simcox (1988) suggested that in 1985, 87% of all pending applications for immigrating to the U.S. were family-based, among which 73% were sponsored siblings of U.S. citizens.

Table 5-2 also shows that the backlog is a serious problem for the USCIS, especially for some major immigrant-sending countries (such as Mexico and the Philippines). Since admissions to the United States are numerically limited for most visa categories and the limits are set depending on the country of birth and the family or employment category, USCIS uses a *priority date* to order each immigrant applicant's place in line to be admitted to the United States. Therefore, we can use the *priority date* as a good indicator of the serious extent of backlogs in the USCIS. The rule of thumb is that the earlier the *priority date*, the longer the waiting time, therefore, the larger the USCIS backlog.

Table 5-2 Family Preference Visa Backlog Status

Visa Pref	Other Countries			Mexico			Philippines		
	Dec-02	Nov-04	May-07	Dec-02	Nov-04	May-07	Dec-02	Nov-04	May-07
1st	First: Unmarried Sons and Daughters of Citizens: 23,400 annual visas								
PD	04/08/99	11/01/00	05/15/01	10/15/92	01/01/94	01/01/91	04/01/90	09/15/90	03/22/92
WY	3.65	4.00	5.96	10.13	10.84	16.34	12.68	14.14	15.12
CR		0.82	0.21		0.63	-1.20		0.24	0.61
2A	A. Spouses and Children of Permanent Residents: 77% of 114,200 annual visas								
PD	09/22/97	06/01/00	04/08/02	04/08/95	09/15/97	01/01/01	09/22/97	06/01/00	04/08/02
WY	5.19	4.42	5.07	7.65	7.13	6.33	5.19	4.42	5.07
CR		1.40	0.74		1.27	1.32		1.40	0.74
2B	B. Unmarried Sons and Daughters (21 years of age or older) of Permanent Residents: 23% of 114,200 annual visas								
PD	04/08/94	07/15/95	10/01/97	11/01/91	12/08/91	03/01/92	04/08/94	07/15/95	10/01/96
WY	8.65	9.31	9.59	11.09	12.91	15.18	8.65	9.31	10.59
CR		0.66	0.89		0.05	0.09		0.66	0.49
3rd	Third: Married Sons and Daughters of Citizens: 23,400 annual visas								
PD	12/22/96	11/08/97	04/01/99	11/01/92	06/01/93	02/08/88	12/01/89	05/01/90	01/01/85
WY	5.95	6.99	8.09	10.09	11.43	19.24	13.01	14.52	22.34
CR		0.46	0.56		0.30	-2.13		0.22	-2.14
4th	Fourth: Brothers and Sisters of Adult Citizens: 65,000 annual visas								
PD	12/08/90	09/01/92	05/15/96	11/01/90	09/01/92	07/01/94	12/01/81	07/22/82	01/01/85
WY	11.99	12.18	10.97	12.09	12.18	12.84	21.01	22.30	22.34
CR		0.90	1.48		0.96	0.73		0.33	0.98
Note	• Both China and India have identical priority dates as "Other Countries" for all visa categories, except the 4th. The 4th category's priority date for China is 11/22/1995, and that for India is 1/8/1996. • PD: Priority Dates • WY: Waiting Years, defined as the difference between the Bulletin Date and the Priority Date, divided by 365. • CR: Backlog clearance rate, defined as (Current Bulletin Date and Current Priority Date) divided by (Previous Bulletin Date and Previous Priority Date).								
Source:	U.S. Department of State: Visa Bulletin (http://travel.state.gov/visa/frvi/bulletin/bulletin_1360.html)								

Table 5-2 compares the *priority date* or family preference visas in December 2002, November 2004, and May 2007. It also compares the Waiting Years (WY) and the calculated visa backlog clearance rates (*CR*). It is clear from the calculation results that since May 2007, visa backlogs have been cleared at a very slow pace for most of the family preference categories, except the *spouses and children* category (2A) for Mexican immigrants.[43]

---

[43] Here is the description on the calculation method of the rate of clearing the USCIS backlogs. The Visa Backlog Clearance Rate (CR) is defined as

Within their respective countries of birth, *spouses and children of permanent residents* (2A of 2nd preference as a category), among all family preference categories, have the shortest waiting time for being admitted to the U.S. (about 5 years for all countries, except Mexico, which has 6.33 years). In the case of Mexico, the backlog clearing rates was 1.32 in May 2007. This means that the USCIS' speed of approving applications is faster than the application rate in this category, clearing 132 days worth of cases in 100 days. Using the overall waiting years being 5.07 (without considering the Mexican applicants waiting year 6.33), we can estimate that there are at least 445,825 (5.07 times 114,200 and multiply by 77%, which is the annual cap of this category) applicants waiting to be admitted to the U.S. under the 2A preference category.

At the same time, we notice that siblings of U.S. citizens (4th preference in the family sponsored category) have to wait the longest, while the backlog clearing rate for all countries (except for Mexican and Filipino immigrants) is very fast (at 1.48, or clearing 148 days worth of cases in 100 days). For most countries, these applicants will have to wait about 11 years as of May 2007, decreased from 12 years in 2002 and 2004. At the same time, Mexican applicants have almost 13 years to wait, and the Pilipino applicants have to wait at least 22 years—people from both of these countries have to wait longer because of slower clearing rates that very likely were caused by the increased

$$CR = \frac{current\ \ priority\ \ date - earlier\ \ priority\ \ date}{current\ \ bulletin\ \ date - earlier\ \ bulletin\ \ date}$$

Assume the priority date for a preference category in November 2004 was X and in December 2002 was Y. The rate of clearing the backlog was calculated as: (X-Y)/701, where 701 is the total number of calendar days between December 2002 and November 2004. If CR=1, it means that the USCIS is keeping up its pace of clearing the backlog—there is no impact to the waiting list, and the waiting list is neither lengthened nor shortened. If CR>1, it means that the INS is clearing backlogs at a faster pace than the newly petitioned immigrants in the respective preference category; therefore, the waiting list is shorter. If CR<1, it means that the USCIS is lagging behind in clearing the backlogs, and the newly petitioned immigrants in the respective preference category have made the backlog even worse, or the waiting list longer.

application rates. This implies that the total number of sibling applicants waiting to be admitted to the U.S. is at least 715,000 (11 multiply 65,000—the annual cap of this category) under the 4th visa category for all countries combined, without taking Mexican and Filipino applicants into account.

From Table 5-2, we can also see that Mexico and the Philippines have different kinds of sponsorship patterns: Applicants from the Philippines have longer waiting periods in the 4th preference categories (for siblings) than Mexican applicants, while the Mexican applicants have to wait longer than the Filipino applicants in all other 1st, 2nd, and 3rd preference categories.

These visa backlogs on family immigrants in the current U.S. immigration system show the seriousness of the immigration issue the United States is facing.

CHAPTER 6

Principal Immigrants

THE PRINCIPAL IMMIGRANTS: THE INITIATORS OF MIGRATION CHAINS

Principal Immigrants are those immigrants who come to the United States sponsored by non-family members and/or by their U.S.-born spouses. Examining this group is the key to understanding the *Complete Chain Migration Model* and the *Immigration Multipliers,* because they *start* the migration chains. Without them, there would be no future family-sponsored immigrants, *i.e.* no chain migration. Hence, Principal Immigrant is the most important component of the chain migration process, and it is the core of this study.

According to U.S. Citizenship and Immigration Services (USCIS 2007), the major immigrant categories are:

- Immediate relatives of U.S. citizens
- Special immigrants
- Family-sponsored immigrants
- Employer-sponsored immigrants

Based on our earlier discussion, all family-sponsored immigrants are *derived family immigrants* who are part of the migration chains. Therefore, immigrants who fit the definition of Principal Immigrants will have to be one of the following:

- Immediate Relatives of U.S. Citizens
    - o Spouses of U.S.-born citizens or sponsored by them, as defined by the visa categories. We will define them as *Foreign Spouses of U.S.-Born Citizens* or *FSUSB Principals.*
    - o Note: those who naturalized U.S. citizens sponsored are considered derived family immigrants.
- Special Immigrants

    o   Sponsored by the U.S. government (such as refugees or political asylum-seekers), as defined by the visa categories. We will define them as *Government-Sponsored Principal Immigrants* or *GSI Principals.*

- Employer-sponsored
  - Sponsored by employers, as defined by the visa categories or the Class of Admissions. We will define them as *Employment-Related Principal Immigrants* or *ERI Principals.*

Since the USCIS assigns the Class of Admissions (COA) for each immigrant, we can use the COA not only to separate the Principal Immigrants from the derived family immigrants, but also to group the Principal Immigrants into the above three categories. With 25 years of USCIS data (from 1972-1997[44]), we have some results showing the immigration patterns over the last three decades.

Table 6-1 shows the historical patterns of Principal Immigrants to the U.S. from 1972 through 1997. The most significant pattern is that their volume peaked during the 1970s and then dropped during the 1980s. During the 1990s, the total volume increased again, surpassing the peak level set in the 1970s.

Table 6-1 shows that Government-Sponsored Principal Immigrants (*GSI Principals*) are the greatest contributors to the Principal Immigrant population. They comprised almost half of the total Principal Immigrant population (48.5%) from 1972~1997. At the same time, Foreign Spouses of U.S. Born Citizens (*FSUSB Principals*) make up about one third of the overall Principal Immigrant population (36.7%). Interestingly, about 15% of Principal Immigrants were employment-related (*ERI Principals*) during the same period.

Table 6-2 shows a very different pattern. The ERI Principal is the group that has had the most significant net changes over the last thirty years. The FSUSB Principal also grew, but not as much in relative terms. GSI Principal is the only group that has not grown significantly during the same period.

If we compare the composition of Principal Immigrants admitted to the U.S. each year in terms of the net quantity, as demonstrated in Figure 6-1, we see that FSUSB Principal has contributed the most to

---

[44] Please note that the COA information was available only in the USCIS data sets from 1972~1997 when this research was carried out.

the Principal Immigrants group in the U.S. At the same time, the ERI Principal has been the group that has contributed the least.

Table 6-1 Trend of Principal Immigrants Admitted to the U.S.: 1972-1997

Year	Employment-Related Principal Immigrants	Government-Sponsored Principal Immigrants	Foreign Spouses of U.S.-Born Citizens	Total
Percent	14.84%	48.47%	36.70%	100.00%
Total	741,268	2,421,833	1,833,574	4,996,675
1972	17,784	102,861	47,280	167,925
1973	12,569	97,845	50,011	160,425
1974	16,786	93,375	44,938	155,099
1975	14,683	05,718	40,408	160,809
1976	9,868	84,411	31,213	125,492
1977	13,311	135,044	47,879	196,234
1978	14,920	145,617	52,695	213,232
1979	19,410	47,382	58,818	125,610
1980	21,512	76,683	69,433	167,628
1981	21,608	91,118	70,411	183,137
1982	26,465	90,403	72,932	189,800
1983	25,990	55,216	77,105	158,311
1984	24,622	47,729	80,409	152,760
1985	22,553	60,105	87,789	170,447
1986	24,207	59,555	86,956	170,718
1987	26,235	101,805	85,903	213,943
1988	22,495	96,475	82,721	201,691
1989	24,264	71,296	76,593	172,153
1990	23,091	96,477	76,116	195,684
1991	30,063	97,322	75,254	202,639
1992	55,850	100,071	75,261	231,182
1993	88,530	106,266	81,747	276,543
1994	47,353	101,422	80,220	228,995
1995	37,360	105,430	70,199	212,989
1996	48,585	110,814	90,864	250,263
1997	41,850	85,593	89,945	217,388

If we break this down by region as shown in Table 6-3, we can see that Latin America is the leading region sending Principal Immigrants to the United States (about 37%), while Asia and Europe follow closely as second and third, contributing 29% and 20% respectively. These top three regions, however, have significantly different patterns of sending Principal Immigrants by categories. Latin America is the leading region sending GSI Principals and FSUSB Principals (about 40% for both categories). Asia is the leading region sending ERI Principals (about 50%). Europe, on the other hand, is pretty even in sending Principal Immigrants (about 20% in every category).

Table 6-2 Net Changes of Principal Immigrants to the U.S.: 1972-1997

Year	Employment-Related Principal Immigrants		Government-Sponsored Principal Immigrants		Foreign Spouses of U.S.-Born Citizens		Total	
Percent	Annual Avg	Net Gain	Annual Avg	Net Gain	Annual Avg	Net Gain	Annual Avg	Net Gain
1972 ~1979	14,916		101,532		46,655		163,103	
1980 ~1989	23,995	61%	75,039	-26%	79,025	69%	178,059	9%
1990 ~1997	46,585	94%	100,424	34%	79,951	1%	226,960	27%

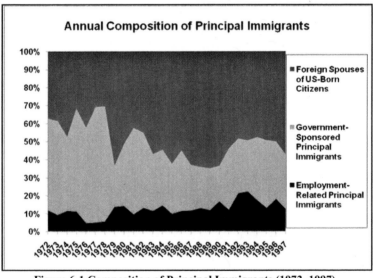

Figure 6-1 Composition of Principal Immigrants (1972~1997)

Table 6-3 Principal Immigrants: Regional Variations

	Total	Employment-Related Principal Immigrants	Government-Sponsored Principal Immigrants	Foreign Spouses of U.S.-Born Citizens
Total	100.00%	100.00%	100.00%	100.00%
Latin America	36.94%	17.13%	39.75%	41.23%
Asia	29.02%	49.87%	29.70%	19.70%
Europe	20.06%	18.63%	21.40%	18.85%
Middle East	5.13%	5.45%	4.14%	6.30%
Africa	4.72%	3.84%	3.62%	6.52%
North America	3.26%	4.07%	1.26%	5.59%
Oceania/Other	0.88%	1.01%	0.14%	1.81%

Since the ERI, GSI, and FSUSB Principals are three very distinct immigrant categories (although they function quite similarly in the chain migration process), I will explore them individually so that we can learn more about their immigration characteristics.

EMPLOYMENT-RELATED PRINCIPAL IMMIGRANTS

Figure 6-2 shows the growth pattern of Employment-Related Principal Immigrants (ERI Principals), which has been consistently on the rise over the last three decades. It shows that the volume of this group actually began to increase in the 1980s, then peaked in the early 1990s.

These dramatic changes in ERI Principals do not coincide with the history of U.S. immigration laws, except in the 1990s. The Immigration and Nationality Act Amendments of 1965, which was in effect until the late 1970s, limited employment-related immigrants to 34,000. The Immigration and Nationality Act Amendments of 1976 set the limit to 20,000 immigrants per country and eliminated preferential treatment for residents of the Western Hemisphere. The Immigration and Nationality Act Amendments of 1978 and the Refugee Act of 1980 increased the limit for employment-related immigrants to 54,000, which capped the flow of employment-related immigrants during the 1980s. Then, the Immigration Act of 1990 revised this limit to 140,000, which has contributed to the surge of employer-sponsored preference immigration.

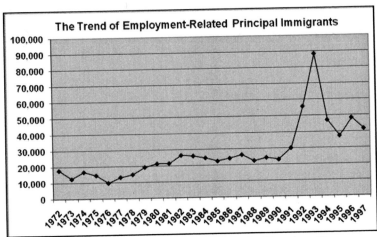

Figure 6-2 Employment-Related Principal Immigrants

Regional Variations

Since the number of ERI Principals has risen between the 1970s and the 1990s, we can further analyze the regional variations to understand the patterns by regions. Tables 6-4 and 6-5 suggest that Asia has taken full advantage of sending ERI Principals to the United States. During the last three decades, the total number from Asia has been consistently higher than from other regions around the world.

Table 6-4 Net Changes of Employment Related Principal Immigrants

Period	Total		Asia		Europe		Latin America	
	Annual Avg	Pct Gain	Annual Avg	Pct Gain	Annual Avg	Pct Gain	Annual Avg	Pct Gain
1972 ~1979	16,079		9,757		3,670		933	
1980 ~1989	23,995	49%	9,240	-5%	4,980	36%	5,608	501%
1990 ~1997	46,541	94%	24,881	169%	7,359	48%	7,926	41%

Table 6-5 Employment Related Principal Immigrants By Region

Year	Total	Asia	Europe	Latin America	Middle East	North America	Africa	Oceania /Other
	100.00%	49.68%	18.55%	17.33%	5.47%	4.11%	3.85%	1.01%
Total	731,613	363,494	135,734	126,795	39,995	30,090	28,147	7,358
1972	17,784	12,390	3,799	357	548	66	486	138
1973	12,569	8,307	3,004	333	408	69	344	104
1974	16,786	11,009	4,164	280	583	47	491	212
1975	14,683	10,496	2,877	230	445	44	438	153
1976	9,868	7,441	1,531	217	279	33	287	80
1977	13,311	7,854	2,914	1,006	536	281	549	171
1978	14,920	7,504	3,794	1,379	593	780	652	218
1979	19,410	7,052	4,980	3,506	1,260	1,306	1,055	251
1980	21,512	6,431	5,455	5,363	1,593	1,326	1,028	316
1981	21,608	7,882	4,630	5,176	1,628	1,158	863	271
1982	26,465	10,558	5,138	6,396	1,934	1,148	1,013	278
1983	25,990	9,982	5,920	5,203	2,330	1,271	1,015	269
1984	24,622	8,968	5,667	5,407	2,075	1,233	984	288
1985	22,553	9,354	4,289	5,381	1,674	891	772	192
1986	24,207	9,377	5,041	5,577	1,920	1,099	980	213
1987	26,235	10,059	5,220	6,652	1,773	1,220	1,084	227
1988	22,495	9,782	4,017	4,907	1,627	896	1,066	200
1989	24,264	10,003	4,423	6,016	1,779	761	1,066	216
1990	23,091	9,880	3,788	5,919	1,598	707	1,021	178
1991	30,063	13,489	4,762	7,565	1,793	988	1,240	226
1992	55,829	27,152	10,138	9,554	3,458	2,521	2,345	661
1993	88,460	63,214	8,584	8,359	2,990	2,665	1,963	685
1994	47,291	25,462	7,664	7,288	1,929	2,523	1,859	566
1995	37,312	17,159	6,735	7,527	1,663	2,226	1,627	375
1996	48,495	21,314	9,723	9,920	2,051	2,795	2,201	491
1997	41,790	21,375	7,477	7,277	1,528	2,036	1,718	379

Table 6-4 shows the rate of gain of these three regions in sending ERI Principals. Asia began with a large base in the 1970s, but experienced a small decrease during the 1980s. During the 1990s, however, its contribution of ERI Principals jumped about 170% percent, feeding the economic boom in the United States. At the same time, the pattern for Europe was quite different in that there was no significant change in the pattern. Europe fed the United States a relatively steady number of immigrants in the ERI Principal category. The net gain of this group from Europe has been at a rate of about 50% per decade. The most significant of all regions is the total number of ERI Principals from Latin American, which jumped from an almost non-existent entity in the 1970s to such a high level that it surpassed

Europe in the 1980s with a net surge of 500%. Moreover, in the 1990s, it continued to increase another 41%, and in the 1990s, it became the number two region sending ERI Principals to the United States.

Table 6-5 shows that, with its significant surge in the early 1990s, Asia accounts for about half of all ERI Principals who were admitted from the 1970s through the 1990s. The data also shows that the total of ERI Principals from Latin America grew from less than 100 in the 1970s to almost 10,000 in the 1990s (the same level as Europe). Latin America, with such astonishing growth of ERI principals, virtually tied with Europe in sending ERI Principals to the U.S. These three regions combined are responsible for sending 86% ERI Principals to the U.S.

Class of Admissions

If we further examine the ERI principals using the class of admissions (COA) categories, we find many different characteristics of the ERI principals. One of these is the level of skills, as defined by COA.

Table 6-6 shows the top group of ERI Principals admitted to the U.S. by regions. Over the last thirty years, the "professional"[45] ("highly skilled" or "professional holding an advanced degrees or of exceptional ability") are the leading categories for Asian immigrants.[46] European ERI Principals experienced a clear transition from the "needed skill/unskilled worker" category in the 1970s to the "professional" in the 1980s. In the 1990s, the immigrants were mainly in the "skilled worker"[47] or "priority worker" (a new term for "professional highly skilled") categories. Although the overall percentage of the "professional" immigrants from Europe is at the same level as those from Asia, it is only about a third in volume compared to Asia. Latin American immigrants also had a transition. The leading employment related category changed from "minister of religion" in the early 1970s to "needed skill/unskilled worker" in the late 1970s. The

---

[45] Professionals are those workers of extraordinary ability or professionals with advanced degrees.

[46] It should be noted that USCIS grouped "Alien covered by Chinese Student Protection Act" as the employment related category, which was the top category in 1993 and 1994.

[47] "Skilled workers" are workers with at least two years of training or experience.

"needed skill/unskilled worker" category dominated the entire 1980s and the majority of the 1990s (the "other worker performing unskilled labor" is at the same level as the "needed skill/unskilled worker"). Yet, in the late 1990s, "skilled worker" started to lead the employment related immigration category.

The top countries by region are China (from Asia), the United Kingdom (from Europe), and Mexico (from Latin America). The data shows that these three countries have immigration patterns that are very similar to the regions they represent.

In the early and mid 1970s, the leading Class of Admissions of ERI Principals from China was the "needed skill/unskilled worker." Since the late 1970s, China has been sending immigrants in the categories of "professional highly skilled" or "professional holding an advanced degree or of exceptional ability" (including Chinese students covered by the Chinese Student Protection Act of 1992).

The United Kingdom has had a very clear immigration pattern during the last three decades. It started with the category of "needed skill/unskilled worker" in the 1970s and then shifted in the 1980s to the category of "professional highly skilled." Finally, in the 1990s, its leading category of employment related immigration became "priority worker—certain multinational executive or manager."

Mexican immigrants also have a very clear pattern. The leading category in the early 1970s was "minister of religion." Then, from 1977 to 1991, it was "needed skill/unskilled worker." Since 1993, "alien who is a skilled worker" has become the major employment related immigration category for Latin Americans..

Other Characteristics of ERI Principals

The ERI Principal is the immigrant group that U.S. immigration policy intends to boost. Most of the immigrants who come to the United States through employers' sponsorship have to demonstrate that their skills and expertise are otherwise unavailable in the domestic workforce. Table 6-7 shows the distribution of occupation categories (defined by the class of admissions) for all ERI Principals from the leading three regions: Asia, Europe, and Latin America. It shows that the majority of ERI Principals from Asia and Europe are "professionals"—both are about 72%—while the majority (about 66%) from Latin America are in the "Labor & Services" category.

Table 6-6 Top Class of Admission of Principal Immigrants by Top Regions

Year	Asia	Europe	Latin America	Major U.S. Immigration Laws
1972	Professional highly skilled	Needed skill / unskilled worker	Minister of religion	*Immigration and Nationality Act, 1965 (in effect during 1969-1977)*
1973				
1974				
1975				
1976				
1977				
1978	Needed skill / unskilled worker			*New Visa System after 1976 and Immigration and Nationality Act Amendments of 1978, Refugee Act of 1980 and Immigration Reform and Control Act of 1986 (in effect during 1978-1991)*
1979				
1980	Professional highly skilled			
1981	Needed skill / unskilled worker	Professional highly skilled	Needed skill / unskilled worker	
1982	Professional highly skilled	Professional highly skilled		
1983				
1984				
1985				
1986				
1987				
1988				
1989				
1990				
1991				
1992	Professional holding an advanced degree or of exceptional ability	Professional holding an advanced degree or of exceptional ability	Alien who is a skilled worker	*Immigration Act of 1990 (in effect Law's Transition Period Since 1992)*
1993	Alien covered by Chinese Student Protection Act	Alien who is a skilled worker	Other worker performing unskilled labor, not of a temporary or seasonal nature, for which qualified	
1994		Priority worker - certain multinational executive or manager		
1995	Alien who is a skilled worker	Alien who is a skilled worker		
1996				
1997	Professional holding an advanced degree or of exceptional ability	Priority worker - certain multinational executive or manager	Alien who is a skilled worker	
1998				

Table 6-7 Employment-Related Principal Immigrants by Region:
Categories by Class of Admissions (COA)

	Total	Asia	Latin America	Europe	Middle East	North America	Africa	Oceania /Other
Total	*100%*	*100%*	*100%*	*100%*	*100%*	*100%*	*100%*	*100%*
Home-makers	*0%*	*0%*	*0%*	*0%*	*0%*	*0%*	*0%*	*0%*
Labor & Services	*26%*	*16%*	*66%*	*26%*	*26%*	*5%*	*15%*	*11%*
No Job/ Retired	*1%*	*1%*	*1%*	*0%*	*0%*	*0%*	*0%*	*0%*
Professional	*66%*	*72%*	*31%*	*72%*	*70%*	*93%*	*82%*	*87%*
Students /Children	*1%*	*2%*	*0%*	*0%*	*0%*	*0%*	*0%*	*0%*
Unknown /Other	*5%*	*8%*	*2%*	*2%*	*4%*	*2%*	*2%*	*2%*

Table 6-8 Gender Patterns of ERI Principals

Gender	TOTAL	Middle East	Europe	Africa	North America	Oceania /Other	Asia	Latin America
Sex Ratio	*200%*	*414%*	*356%*	*284%*	*246%*	*239%*	*193%*	*99%*
Female	*33%*	*19%*	*22%*	*26%*	*29%*	*29%*	*34%*	*50%*
Male	*67%*	*81%*	*78%*	*74%*	*71%*	*71%*	*66%*	*50%*
Total	*100%*	*100%*	*100%*	*100%*	*100%*	*100%*	*100%*	*100%*

As discussed earlier, gender plays a significant role in chain migration, and the gender difference is especially significant among ERI Principals. Table 6-8 illustrates the gender variations among regions.

From the regional gender pattern of ERI Principals, we see that the majority from the Middle East, Europe, Africa, North America, Oceania, and Asia are male. Latin America is the only region that sends fewer male than female ERI Principals (49.75% vs. 50.25%), although the difference is not significant.

With this vast difference in gender percentage, we can anticipate quite different patterns among ERI Principals from these regions in sponsoring their family members. In the later part of this chapter and in the following chapters, I will demonstrate that the Immigration Unification Multiplier effectively measures such pattern variations.

GOVERNMENT-SPONSORED PRINCIPAL IMMIGRANTS

Government-Sponsored Principal Immigrants (GSI Principals) have been granted special permission by the United States government for various reasons. The U.S. Citizenship and Immigration Services (USCIS) defines many different Classes of Admissions (COA) that fit this category. Main COAs include: the Diversity Program, the Refugees, "immigrants who do not qualify under family/employment preferences," "alien born in independent Western Hemisphere," or some special immigrants (which includes employees and dependents of special interest, such as international organizations, U.S. government abroad, minister of religion, diplomats of foreign countries, etc.). Among all of these sub-types of immigrants, the refugee is one of the most significant categories in terms of the total number/quota allowed.

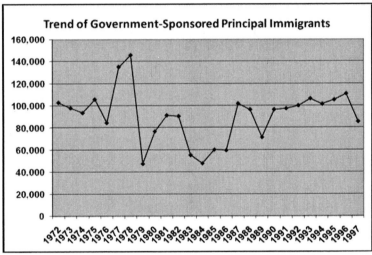

Figure 6-3 Trend of Government Sponsored Principal Immigrants

Figure 6-3 shows that the overall trend of GSI Principals has been down since the early 1980s, and the level was relatively low throughout the rest of that decade. In the 1990s, the number began to increase again to reach a point that is about two-thirds of the peaked volume of the 1970s.

Regional Variations

When we break the immigrants down by region (Table 6-9), we can see that Latin America leads; it has contributed almost half of the GSI Principals to the United States in the last three decades. In second place, Asia is responsible for almost one-third of the GSI Principals during that same period. Over 90% of the GSI Principals came from Latin America, Asia, and Europe.

Table 6-9 Government-Sponsored Principal Immigrants by Region

Year	TOTAL	Latin America	Asia	Europe	Middle East	Africa	North America	Oceania /Other
	100.00%	39.75%	29.70%	21.40%	4.14%	3.62%	1.26%	0.14%
Total	2,421,318	962,444	719,024	518,206	100,179	87,757	30,416	3,292
1972	102,861	65,225	17,062	13,883	2,223	1,700	2,436	332
1973	97,845	65,439	15,146	11,734	1,789	1,480	1,977	280
1974	93,375	66,800	11,187	10,375	2,011	1,410	1,454	138
1975	105,718	77,591	9,796	12,579	2,296	1,460	1,784	212
1976	84,411	62,166	7,071	9,933	2,524	1,033	1,382	302
1977	135,044	111,205	6,148	9,622	1,709	1,259	4,904	197
1978	145,617	70,138	65,543	6,553	674	606	2,062	41
1979	47,382	13,807	24,735	6,745	1,376	475	239	5
1980	76,683	26,713	38,454	8,945	1,273	847	437	14
1981	91,118	33,560	46,575	7,637	1,879	1,278	188	1
1982	90,403	5,256	66,845	13,133	3,429	1,546	183	11
1983	55,216	4,261	37,775	7,527	3,496	2,031	123	3
1984	47,729	4,253	26,466	9,739	5,434	1,702	130	5
1985	60,105	18,075	23,997	8,550	7,086	2,230	166	1
1986	59,555	21,327	23,810	7,278	5,341	1,654	143	2
1987	101,805	60,231	23,789	9,465	5,161	1,809	1,312	38
1988	96,475	55,010	22,367	10,452	5,615	2,095	886	50
1989	71,296	19,593	22,753	18,874	6,103	1,816	2,104	53
1990	96,477	19,598	31,698	30,544	8,050	4,060	2,340	187
1991	97,322	13,513	34,140	38,256	5,862	3,624	1,791	136
1992	100,071	13,125	36,619	43,005	3,792	3,176	320	34
1993	106,265	12,026	29,461	54,004	6,091	3,938	721	24
1994	101,406	14,634	22,383	54,131	5,360	4,285	570	43
1995	105,285	19,700	24,827	41,446	4,169	14,487	283	373
1996	110,634	29,904	25,210	37,601	3,558	13,722	311	328
1997	85,420	25,219	13,800	29,978	2,776	13,062	256	329

Table 6-9 lists the trend of all regions on GSI Principals. If we look closely at the data, we see that the immigrants from Latin American peaked in the 1970s, and then the number dropped significantly during the 1980s and the 1990s. This actually reflects the

Cuban refugee movement that began in the 1960s, when many Cubans fled communist takeover. In the late 1980s, however, the Immigration Reform and Control Act of 1986 (IRCA) contributed a surge of legalized undocumented immigrants, a majority of which came from Latin America.

The number of GSI Principals from Asia is unique because of two distinctive peaks: one in 1978 and another in 1982. Both of them were the result of the waves of refugees from Vietnam and Laos. This flow decreased in the 1990s.

Europe's immigration numbers reflect several events in history, like the collapse of the Soviet Union and other East European countries. The surge of GSI Principals from Europe in the 1990s was due mainly to the immigration of Russian Jews.

The number of GSI Principals from the Middle East is not significant, compared to the top three regions. However, it does have a pattern of its own; the volume peaked during the 1980s when some of the numbers tripled those set in the 1970s. The annual number set in the 1990s has remained relatively high. This could be the direct result of the Soviet invasion of Afghanistan in December 1979, which prompted many to flee (to the U.S.). The Iraqi invasion of Kuwait in 1990 not only made many Kuwaiti citizens and residents refugees of the U.S., but also turned a few thousands Iraqi soldiers (and their family members) into U.S. refugees (because they surrendered to the Allied troops and could not be sent back Iraq).

The total number of GSI Principals from Africa has been relatively small, except for a significant jump in the 1990s (with Ethiopian refugees a major contributor to the increase).

Table 6-10 Net Gains of GSI Principals by Top Regions

Period	Total		Latin America		Asia		Europe	
	Annual Avg	Pct Gain	Annual Avg	Pct Gain	Annual Avg	Pct Gain	Annual Avg	Pct Gain
1972 ~1979	108,507		70,806		21,007		10,955	
1980 ~1989	75,039	-31%	24,828	-65%	33,283	58.44%	10,160	-7%
1990 ~1997	100,360	34%	18,465	-26%	27,267	-18.07%	41,121	305%

Table 6-10 presents a high-level analysis of the growth trends of all regions. If we compare the annual average of each region for the last three decades, we will see that in the 1970s Latin America was the top region sending GSI Principals; in the 1980s, Asia was foremost, and Europe took the lead in the 1990s.

Table 6-11 Top Class of Admissions for GSI Principals by Top Regions

Year	Asia	Europe	Latin America	Major U.S. Immigration Laws
1972 ~1976	Immigrants who do not qualify under family / employment preferences	Immigrants who do not qualify under family / employment preferences	Aliens born in independent Western Hemisphere	*Immigration and Nationality Act, 1965 (in effect during 1969-1977)*
1977			Cuban refugees	
1978	Indochinese refugees		Aliens born in independent Western Hemisphere	
1979			Cuban refugees	*New Visa System after 1976 and Immigration and Nationality Act Amendments of 1978, Refugee Act of 1980 and Immigration Reform and Control Act of 1986 (in effect during 1978-1991*
1980	Refugees paroled into the United States prior to Apr. 1, 1980.	Refugees paroled into the United States prior to Apr. 1, 1980.	Aliens born in independent Western Hemisphere	
1981				
1982 ~1987			Cuban refugees	
1988		Refugees who entered the United States on or after Apr. 1, 1980	Cuban-Haitian entrants	
1989 ~1991			Cuban refugees	
1992 ~1994	Refugees who entered the United States on or after Apr. 1, 1980	Natives of certain adversely affected foreign states (Diversity Transition)		*Immigration Act of 1990 (in effect Law's Transition Period Since 1992)*
1995 ~1998		Refugees who entered the United States on or after Apr. 1, 1980		

This reflects the United States government's changing focus on the global stage and its decision to take in certain types and numbers of refugees to resolve international issues. This pattern coincides with U.S. refugee history: the Cuban crisis in the 1970s, the Vietnam refugee wave of the 1980s, and the arrival of former Soviet Union refugees during the 1990s.

Table 6-12 Top Class of Admissions of GSI Immigrants by Top Countries

Region	Country	Total Immigrants	Leading Class of Admissions (Count & Percentage of the Total)		
Asia	Vietnam	515,864	Refugees who entered the United States on or after Apr. 1, 1980	298,432	58%
	Laos	145,340		87,307	60%
	Cambodia	79,492		62,516	79%
	India	33,338	Immigrants who do not qualify under family / employment preferences	31,247	94%
	China	30,696		15,840	52%
	Korea	19,469		19,255	99%
	Japan	9,740		4,438	46%
	Philippines	9,577	Certain former H1 nonimmigrant registered nurses.	7,361	77%
Europe	Russia	132,368	Refugee who entered the United States on or after Apr. 1, 1980	97,912	74%
	Poland	55,516		24,232	44%
	United Kingdom	20,430	Immigrants who do not qualify under family / employment preferences	13,039	64%
	Germany	7,200		3,558	49%
	Portugal	5,660		5,249	93%
	France	3,155		1,554	49%
	Italy	3,155		1,807	57%
Latin America	Cuba	462,324	Cuban refugees	411,115	89%
	Mexico	348,989	Aliens born in independent Western Hemisphere	344,748	99%
	Dominican Republic	75,068		59,262	79%
	Haiti	69,904	Cuban-Haitian entrants	31,892	46%
	Jamaica	63,847	Aliens born in independent Western Hemisphere	51,577	81%
	Colombia	32,182		23,294	72%
	Guyana	21,822		14,682	67%
	El Salvador	20,343		11,211	55%

Class of Admissions

Now, we examine the top class of admissions for all GSI Principals in the top three regions: Asia, Europe, and Latin America. Table 6-11 shows that the top class of admissions in the 1970s for both Asia and Europe are the categories of "immigrants who do not qualify under family/employment preferences," while the top class of admissions for Latin America is a generic category: "alien born in independent Western Hemisphere."

After the Refugee Act of 1980, a surge of refugees came to the United States, and all three regions show that the leading class of admissions since that time is in the refugee category (see Table 6-12). Asia began with the massive refugee immigration (mainly from Vietnam, Laos, and Cambodia) since 1978, which continued through later years. Since the 1980s, Europe has sent a huge number of refugees from the traditional communist East European countries (such as Russia, Poland). Over the last three decades, Cuba, along with other countries like El Salvador and Haiti, has dominated Latin America, sending a constant flow of refugees.

Other Characteristics of GSI Principals

By examining the occupation distribution (Table 6-13), we notice that GSI Principals (unlike ERI Principals, who are either professionals or skilled labors) have relatively evenly distributed occupation categories. For most regions, most (about 42% average) of the GSI Principals are skilled labors, with Latin American having the highest percentage (52.4%). At the same time, Oceania/Other region has the highest in the professional category (45.86%).

Table 6-13 Occupation Distribution for GSI Principal by Region

	Total	Africa	Asia	Europe	Latin America	Middle East	North America	Oceania /Other
Total	*100%*	*100%*	*100%*	*100%*	*100%*	*100%*	*100%*	*100%*
Home-makers	*13%*	*5%*	*9%*	*6%*	*20%*	*9%*	*21%*	*11%*
Labor/ Services	*42%*	*37%*	*35%*	*36%*	*52%*	*30%*	*19%*	*29%*
No Job /Retired	*14%*	*12%*	*20%*	*20%*	*6%*	*25%*	*8%*	*5%*
Professional	*13%*	*23%*	*12%*	*20%*	*8%*	*19%*	*37%*	*46%*
Students /Children	*9%*	*12%*	*14%*	*6%*	*7%*	*9%*	*8%*	*4%*
Unknown /Other	*8%*	*10%*	*9%*	*11%*	*7%*	*9%*	*6%*	*6%*

Table 6-14 Gender Patterns of GSI Principals by Region

	TOTAL	Middle East	Africa	Asia	Europe	Oceania /Other	North America	Latin America
Sex Ratio	*126%*	*213%*	*200%*	*154%*	*146%*	*103%*	*96%*	*95%*
Female	*44%*	*32%*	*33%*	*39%*	*41%*	*49%*	*51%*	*51%*
Male	*56%*	*68%*	*67%*	*61%*	*59%*	*51%*	*49%*	*49%*
Total	*100%*	*100%*	*100%*	*100%*	*100%*	*100%*	*100%*	*100%*

Examining the gender distribution among GSI Principals (Table 6-14), we conclude that males dominate. This is true for most regions (Middle East, Africa, Asia, Europe, and Oceania/Other). But GSI Principals from both North America and Latin America are more likely to be female. This may be because North America, Latin America, and the United States are located on the same continent; therefore, there are fewer geographic barriers in case people want to move.

FOREIGN SPOUSES OF U.S.-BORN CITIZENS

US-Born Citizens vs. Naturalized Citizens

With the modern transportation, the world has become smaller and smaller. In this research, we have found that more U.S. citizens are sponsoring foreign-born spouses. In this section, we will examine this process and determine the behavior differences between the two types of citizenship: naturalized vs. native U.S.-born.

Using U.S. Census data of 1980, 1990, and 2000, I selected a population pool of all of the couples living in the same household. I identified their places of birth, as well as their citizenship (whether they were naturalized or not). Based on this information, I re-grouped them into the following categories:

- Foreign Born Foreign Nationals
- Foreign Born Naturalized U.S. Citizens
- U.S. Born Citizens

Since this part of the research is on the sponsorship by U.S. citizens, I did some calculations to determine the statistics of all couples comprising at least one person who was a U.S. citizen and one who was foreign-born, and excluding all couples who were U.S.-born.

Some assumptions are:

- If a couple consists of one U.S.-born citizen as the partner, that person is assumed to be the sponsoring party for his/her foreign-born spouse;
- If both parties are both foreign-born, the one with U.S. citizenship (naturalized) is assumed to be the sponsoring party;
- If both parties are naturalized U.S. citizens, we assume the husband is the sponsoring party.

I used the latest U.S. Census data (from 1980 through 2000) to compare the sponsorship of all foreign-born spouses by U.S. citizens. In order to compare the scale of sponsorship by U.S.-born citizens vs. that of naturalized U.S. citizens, I developed a *U/N Ratio* (i.e. U.S. Born/Naturalized Ratio), which is defined as the sponsorship ratio of U.S.-born citizens to naturalized U.S. citizens. As shown in Table 6-18, the calculated data suggests that during the last three decades the U/N ratio gone down. This means that in 1970 twice as many U.S.-born citizens as naturalized U.S. citizens sponsored foreign spouses.

The data (Table 6-15) suggests that the percentage of foreign spouses sponsored by naturalized U.S. citizens increased from the 1970s from less than one third (out of the total sponsorship of foreign-born spouses) to almost one-half in 1990s.

Table 6-15 Trend of Immigrant Spouses of US Citizens: US-Born vs. Naturalized (1980-2000)

	Total Foreign Spouses	Sponsored by Naturalized U.S. Citizens	Sponsored by U.S. Born Citizens	U/N Ratio
1980	100.00%	32.57%	67.43%	2.07
1990	100.00%	36.18%	63.82%	1.76
2000	100.00%	47.77%	52.23%	1.09

Characteristics of FSUSB Principals

There are several interesting characteristics of FSUSB Principals (Foreign Spouses of U.S. Born Citizens). For example, Table 6-16 shows the gender pattern of the FSUSB Principals by region. From the data, we can see that the Middle East, Africa, Latin America, and Europe provide more husbands to U.S. Born citizens, while Asia, Oceania, and North America send more wives to U.S. Born citizens.

Table 6-16 Gender Patterns of FSUSB Principals by Region

Gender	TOTAL	Middle East	Africa	Latin America	Europe	North America	Oceania /Other	Asia
Sex Ratio	124%	538%	306%	170%	113%	85%	84%	42%
Female	45%	16%	25%	37%	47%	54%	54%	71%
Male	55%	84%	75%	63%	53%	46%	46%	29%
Total	100%	100%	100%	100%	100%	100%	100%	100%

Table 6-17 Occupation Distribution of FSUSB Principals By Region

	Total	Africa	Asia	Europe	Latin America	Middle East	North America	Oceania /Other
Total	100%	100%	100%	100%	100%	100%	100%	100%
Home-Makers	23%	9%	42%	20%	20%	9%	18%	17%
Labor & Services	37%	31%	18%	29%	54%	25%	27%	28%
No Job /Retired	12%	16%	14%	15%	9%	18%	12%	14%
Professional	17%	23%	17%	26%	9%	24%	32%	30%
Students/ Children	5%	11%	4%	5%	3%	15%	5%	4%
Unknown /Other	6%	10%	5%	6%	5%	10%	5%	7%

Figure 6-4 Trend of Foreign Spouses of U.S.-Born Citizens by Region

Table 6-18 Trend of FSUSB Principals by Region

	TOTAL	Latin America	Asia	Europe	Middle East	Africa	North America	Oceania /Other
Pct	*100.00%*	*41.23%*	*19.70%*	*18.85%*	*6.30%*	*6.52%*	*5.59%*	*1.81%*
Total	*1,832,905*	*755,665*	*361,002*	*345,571*	*115,481*	*119,505*	*102,424*	*33,257*
1972	*47,280*	*17,358*	*13,358*	*9,717*	*1,812*	*1,251*	*2,877*	*907*
1973	*50,011*	*19,381*	*13,386*	*9,863*	*2,120*	*1,563*	*2,808*	*890*
1974	*44,938*	*18,495*	*11,612*	*8,760*	*1,720*	*1,148*	*2,452*	*751*
1975	*40,408*	*14,878*	*11,027*	*8,387*	*1,542*	*1,327*	*2,506*	*741*
1976	*31,213*	*10,923*	*8,850*	*6,435*	*1,371*	*1,032*	*1,950*	*652*
1977	*47,879*	*18,706*	*10,256*	*9,959*	*2,565*	*2,061*	*3,369*	*963*
1978	*52,695*	*22,147*	*9,822*	*10,276*	*2,874*	*2,502*	*3,940*	*1,134*
1979	*58,818*	*22,877*	*11,363*	*11,126*	*4,869*	*3,466*	*3,958*	*1,159*
1980	*69,433*	*27,246*	*13,533*	*12,587*	*6,690*	*4,507*	*3,790*	*1,080*
1981	*70,411*	*27,652*	*13,841*	*12,971*	*6,764*	*4,490*	*3,546*	*1,147*
1982	*72,932*	*30,260*	*12,981*	*12,763*	*6,839*	*5,084*	*3,838*	*1,167*
1983	*77,105*	*34,549*	*13,021*	*12,764*	*6,290*	*5,316*	*3,917*	*1,248*
1984	*80,409*	*35,852*	*13,422*	*13,227*	*6,547*	*5,938*	*4,160*	*1,263*
1985	*87,789*	*38,957*	*15,187*	*14,416*	*6,994*	*6,420*	*4,449*	*1,366*
1986	*86,956*	*39,374*	*15,223*	*14,624*	*6,065*	*6,017*	*4,308*	*1,345*
1987	*85,903*	*39,327*	*14,654*	*14,326*	*5,404*	*6,684*	*4,218*	*1,290*
1988	*82,721*	*35,760*	*15,060*	*14,866*	*4,886*	*6,450*	*4,248*	*1,451*
1989	*76,593*	*29,989*	*14,921*	*15,295*	*4,855*	*5,639*	*4,327*	*1,567*
1990	*76,116*	*27,179*	*15,577*	*16,001*	*5,129*	*5,818*	*4,679*	*1,733*
1991	*75,254*	*26,732*	*15,123*	*16,530*	*4,677*	*5,769*	*4,737*	*1,686*
1992	*75,217*	*26,680*	*15,344*	*16,465*	*4,465*	*5,670*	*4,946*	*1,647*
1993	*81,625*	*31,953*	*16,235*	*16,506*	*4,452*	*5,829*	*4,885*	*1,765*
1994	*80,087*	*31,596*	*14,997*	*16,857*	*4,167*	*6,027*	*4,869*	*1,574*
1995	*70,077*	*28,155*	*13,344*	*13,943*	*3,629*	*5,625*	*3,994*	*1,387*
1996	*90,727*	*44,290*	*14,964*	*15,024*	*4,012*	*6,902*	*4,096*	*1,439*
1997	*89,834*	*45,781*	*14,692*	*14,028*	*3,635*	*6,465*	*3,759*	*1,474*

As illustrated in Table 6-17, the occupational differences among these Foreign Spouses of U.S. Born Citizens suggest that about 25%-30% of them are low skilled workers, and another 25%-30% are highly skilled professionals. The exceptions are the Asian spouses of U.S.-born citizens (who are most likely to be homemakers—41.73%) and the Latin American spouses of U.S.-born citizens (who are most likely in the category of labor and services—53.86%).

If we examine the regional variations of FSUSB Principals (Figure 6-4 and Table 6-18), we see that the majority of FSUSB Principals come from Latin America. During the last thirty years, about 41% of all FSUSB Principals have come from Latin America.

THE ROLE OF PRINCIPAL IMMIGRANTS IN CHAIN MIGRATION

With the data presented here, we have seen the historical immigration patterns of ERI Principals, GSI principals, and FSUSB Principals. As the starters of all migration chains, we will see in later chapters that these Principal Immigrants will sponsor their family members and produce children in the United States, thus, initiating the migration chains and generating the *Immigration Multiplier Effect*. If the principal immigrants were not allowed to sponsor their family members, there would be no chain migration. The more family members the principal immigrants allowed to sponsor, the stronger the chain migration will be. The strength of the chain migration can be measured using the Yu's Immigration Multiplier.

In the following chapters, I will demonstrate the relationship between the Principal Immigrants and the Immigration Multipliers.

CHAPTER 7

Chain Migration Phase 1: Sponsoring Accompanying Dependents

Principal immigrants initiate the chain migration process when they sponsor their family members (who can later also sponsor other extended family members, and so on). Since the whole chain migration process is quite complicated, we must break these processes down into several different phases (as discussed in Chapter 4). Phase 1 is when immigrants immediately sponsor family members, who migrate with them; Phase 2 is when they delay sponsoring their family members, who will join them a few years later. Phase 3 is when immigrants sponsor immediate family members, including their parents, after they become U.S. citizens; Phase 4 is when they sponsor non-exempt family members (such as siblings and adult children) after they become U.S. citizens.

In this chapter, we will study the chain migration unification phase 1: the sponsorship of immediate family members who migrate with the Principal Immigrants. We define family members sponsored by the Principal Immigrants and granted immigration status at the destination country at the *same* time as the sponsoring Principal Immigrants as *Accompanying Family Members of Principal Immigrants, or AFM Immigrants*. This is, in fact, the first step of the family reunification process of the chain migration. In this chapter, I will explore the sponsorship of these family members, present the method for calculating the *Immigration Unification Multipliers* for them, and measure their immediate impact on chain migration.

IMMIGRATION PATTERN: ACCOMPANYING FAMILY MEMBERS

Now, we examine the accompanying family members, or AFM Immigrants, who came to the United States with either the ERI Principals or GSI Principals.[48] When we look at Figures 7-1 and 7-2 showing the migration patterns of ERI and GSI Principals with their accompanying spouses and children, we see that the volume of accompanying spouses and children has steadily increased over the last three decades.

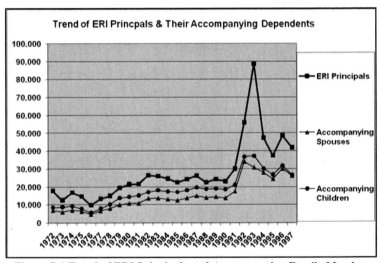

Figure 7-1 Trend of ERI Principals and Accompanying Family Members

The patterns of migration for ERI Principals have been quite consistent, because for the last thirty years the trend of admitted accompanying dependents has matched the trend of admitted ERI Principals. However, the migration patterns for GSI Principals and their accompanying family members are not quite consistent. The data

---

[48] Please note that Foreign Spouses of U.S. Born Citizens (or FSUSB Principals) are a special type of Principal Immigrants because their accompanying dependents are not treated as "Accompanying Family Members," as it is defined here. In fact, their accompanying dependents are categorized and discussed in dependents of U.S. citizens in Chapter 9.

suggests that there were few accompanying spouses during the 1970s, while the number of accompanying children was significant. Beginning in the 1980s, the volume of accompanying spouses of GSI Principals began to pick up. In the 1990s, the migration pattern of accompanying spouses matched the pattern of the GSI Principals and their accompanying children.

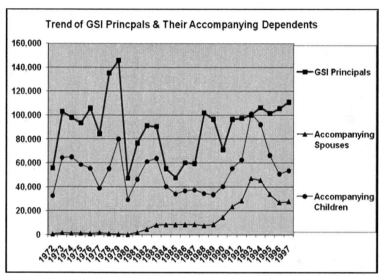

Figure 7-2 GSI Principals and Accompanying Family Members

There is another explanation to this mysterious migration pattern of accompanying spouses of GSI Principals. It is very possible that USCIS did not seriously differentiate the *principal* immigrants and the *Family* dependent immigrants when they issued admission visas to many GSI Principals. This means that many of the admitted GSI Principals are married couples, with both persons in each couple admitted as *Principal Immigrants*, instead of one being admitted as the *Principal Immigrant* and the other one as a *Spouse of Principal Immigrant*.[49]

---

[49] In the later part of this chapter, I will calculate the Immigration Unification Multiplier, using the total number of *Principal Immigrants* as the

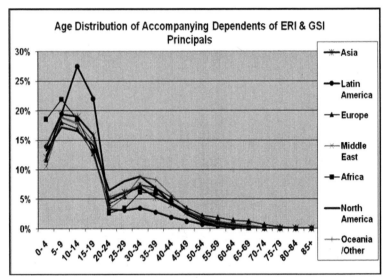

Figure 7-3 AFM Immigrants of ERI & GSI Principals by Region

Regional Variations

The data show (Figure 7-3) that Latin America was once the leading region sending accompanying family members of Principal Immigrants. Asia took the lead in late 1970s and has become the dominant region contributing accompanying family members. In the mid-1990s, Asia and Latin America shared the lead.[50] During this

---

denominator and using the total number of *Spouses of Principal Immigrants* as part of the numerator. If USCIS indeed issued more *Principal Immigrants* visas than it should have, the final results of my *IUM* calculation will smaller than they should be. Even if this is true, it should not be considered a problem because the calculated Immigration Multipliers will strongly suggest the **minimum** multiplier impact to the migration chain. This will also imply that the actual Immigration Multiplier effect should be greater than my calculations.

[50] The surge in the 1990s was mainly related to the Immigration Reform and Control Act (IRCA) of 1986 and the Immigration Act of 1990 (*IM*MACT90). The IRCA of 1986 was aimed at the control of illegal immigration since the early 1970s, while the *IM*MACT90 authorized a

same time, the total number of accompanying family members from Europe quintupled. In fact, in the late 1990s, Europe surpassed Latin America and became the second highest region sending AFM Immigrants.

It is also worth noting that Africa has picked up its total number of AFM Immigrants since the 1990s, although the overall volume is relatively small compared to the three major regions (Asia, Latin America, and Europe).

Age Distributions

Age distribution of AFM Immigrants sheds light on the immigration pattern from a very different angle allowing us to examine the demographic composition of the AFM, ERI, and GSI Principals. Figure 7-4 indicates that Latin America is unique in the age distribution of its AFM Immigrants. It has a significantly large proportion of children, especially ages 10-20, and a significantly small proportion of adults between ages 20-50. It is also significant that AFM Immigrants from Africa have a relatively large proportion of children between ages 0 and 9.

Class of Admissions

If we examine the Class of Admissions categories of these admitted immigrants as AFM Immigrants of ERI and GSI immigrants, we see that the migration patterns vary by region in terms of ERI and GSI immigrants.

Table 7-1 shows that the majority (75%) of AFM Immigrants were accompanying family members of ERI Principals from North America and Oceania. At the same time, most of the AFM Immigrants from Latin America, Europe, Asia, Africa, and the Middle East were accompanying family members of GSI Principals.

---

temporary stay of deportation and work authorization for eligible immediate family members of the IRCA-legalized aliens, and made 55 thousand additional visas available for them annually during fiscal years 1992 to 1994. Therefore, the change in immigration laws had a positive impact on Latin American immigrants who were the main beneficiaries of the IRCA of 1986, and their legalized dependents in the early 1990s.

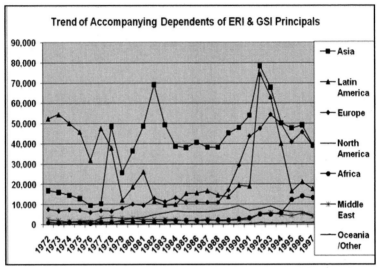

Figure 7-4 Age Distribution of AFM Immigrants of ERI & GSI Principals

Table 7-1 Class of Admission for AFM Immigrants of ERI-GSI Principals

	Total	Asia	Latin America	Europe	Middle East	North America	Africa	Oceania /Other
AFM of ERI	33%	38%	22%	29%	43%	75%	39%	75%
AFM of GSI	67%	62%	78%	71%	57%	25%	61%	25%
Total	100%	100%	100.%	100%	100%	100%	100%	100%

Based on the results we have so far—three different Principal Immigrants (ERI, GSI, and FSUSB Principals) and their accompanying family members (AFM Immigrants)—we can now measure the chain migration process, specifically the *immediate sponsorship* of Principal Immigrants, using the Immigration Unification Multiplier presented in the following section.

Table 7-2 Net Phase 1 Multiplier for ERI Principals by Region

Net IUM	Middle East	Latin America	Africa	Europe	Asia
Total	*1.35*	*1.32*	*1.24*	*1.13*	*1.08*
1972	*0.98*	*1.49*	*0.88*	*0.62*	*0.91*
1973	*0.90*	*1.63*	*0.99*	*0.79*	*1.31*
1974	*0.90*	*1.59*	*0.90*	*0.81*	*1.01*
1975	*1.05*	*1.91*	*0.84*	*0.90*	*0.96*
1976	*1.15*	*1.77*	*0.89*	*0.92*	*1.06*
1977	*1.02*	*1.33*	*1.19*	*0.98*	*1.05*
1978	*1.22*	*1.27*	*1.64*	*1.12*	*1.07*
1979	*1.37*	*1.10*	*1.38*	*1.17*	*1.09*
1980	*1.47*	*0.92*	*1.36*	*1.18*	*1.08*
1981	*1.33*	*1.07*	*1.25*	*1.19*	*1.18*
1982	*1.33*	*1.11*	*1.11*	*1.17*	*1.07*
1983	*1.32*	*1.10*	*1.13*	*1.20*	*1.21*
1984	*1.26*	*1.14*	*1.21*	*1.23*	*1.23*
1985	*1.27*	*1.34*	*1.24*	*1.23*	*1.29*
1986	*1.19*	*1.39*	*1.16*	*1.21*	*1.32*
1987	*1.50*	*1.52*	*1.33*	*1.23*	*1.16*
1988	*1.40*	*1.72*	*1.42*	*1.26*	*1.39*
1989	*1.61*	*1.56*	*1.30*	*1.18*	*1.29*
1990	*1.59*	*1.57*	*1.33*	*1.21*	*1.33*
1991	*1.44*	*1.43*	*1.35*	*1.18*	*1.18*
1992	*1.41*	*1.46*	*1.25*	*1.18*	*1.17*
1993	*1.50*	*1.46*	*1.26*	*1.19*	*0.52*
1994	*1.42*	*1.42*	*1.25*	*1.17*	*1.13*
1995	*1.33*	*1.18*	*1.34*	*1.18*	*1.51*
1996	*1.29*	*1.14*	*1.19*	*1.12*	*1.35*
1997	*1.20*	*1.31*	*1.15*	*1.21*	*1.23*
Notes:	Regions North America and Oceania/Other are not included here because there were not enough data to calculate their Net Phase 1 Multipliers for some of the years.				

MEASURING CHAIN MIGRATION PHASE 1

Chain Migration Phase 1 Multiplier

As discussed in Chapter 4, the Immigration Unification Multiplier (*IUM*) is a new indicator developed to measure the chain migration process. From the discussions so far, we have a general idea of the migration pattern of the Principal Immigrants (ERI, GSI, and FSUSB Principals) and their AFM Immigrants. Adding the *IUM* calculation results will allow us to see the overall picture of the chain migration process.

Table 7-3 Breakdown of Net Phase 1 Multiplier for ERI Principals

	Latin America			Europe			Asia		
Net IUM	SP	CH	All	SP	CH	All	SP	CH	All
Total	*0.49*	*0.83*	*1.32*	*0.54*	*0.59*	*1.13*	*0.54*	*0.54*	*1.08*
1972	*0.48*	*1.01*	*1.49*	*0.31*	*0.31*	*0.62*	*0.41*	*0.50*	*0.91*
1973	*0.48*	*1.15*	*1.63*	*0.37*	*0.41*	*0.79*	*0.52*	*0.79*	*1.31*
1974	*0.53*	*1.06*	*1.59*	*0.39*	*0.42*	*0.81*	*0.43*	*0.58*	*1.01*
1975	*0.65*	*1.27*	*1.91*	*0.43*	*0.47*	*0.90*	*0.43*	*0.52*	*0.96*
1976	*0.61*	*1.16*	*1.77*	*0.43*	*0.49*	*0.92*	*0.49*	*0.56*	*1.06*
1977	*0.51*	*0.82*	*1.33*	*0.47*	*0.52*	*0.98*	*0.51*	*0.53*	*1.05*
1978	*0.48*	*0.79*	*1.27*	*0.54*	*0.59*	*1.12*	*0.51*	*0.56*	*1.07*
1979	*0.40*	*0.70*	*1.10*	*0.56*	*0.61*	*1.17*	*0.51*	*0.58*	*1.09*
1980	*0.33*	*0.58*	*0.92*	*0.56*	*0.63*	*1.18*	*0.53*	*0.55*	*1.08*
1981	*0.40*	*0.68*	*1.07*	*0.55*	*0.64*	*1.19*	*0.53*	*0.65*	*1.18*
1982	*0.40*	*0.71*	*1.11*	*0.54*	*0.63*	*1.17*	*0.55*	*0.52*	*1.07*
1983	*0.38*	*0.72*	*1.10*	*0.55*	*0.65*	*1.20*	*0.57*	*0.64*	*1.21*
1984	*0.39*	*0.75*	*1.14*	*0.57*	*0.66*	*1.23*	*0.58*	*0.65*	*1.23*
1985	*0.48*	*0.85*	*1.34*	*0.57*	*0.66*	*1.23*	*0.58*	*0.72*	*1.29*
1986	*0.51*	*0.88*	*1.39*	*0.58*	*0.64*	*1.21*	*0.61*	*0.71*	*1.32*
1987	*0.55*	*0.97*	*1.52*	*0.56*	*0.67*	*1.23*	*0.58*	*0.58*	*1.16*
1988	*0.62*	*1.09*	*1.72*	*0.58*	*0.68*	*1.26*	*0.65*	*0.74*	*1.39*
1989	*0.54*	*1.02*	*1.56*	*0.57*	*0.62*	*1.18*	*0.64*	*0.65*	*1.29*
1990	*0.52*	*1.05*	*1.57*	*0.57*	*0.63*	*1.21*	*0.66*	*0.68*	*1.33*
1991	*0.49*	*0.94*	*1.43*	*0.56*	*0.62*	*1.18*	*0.64*	*0.53*	*1.18*
1992	*0.55*	*0.91*	*1.46*	*0.57*	*0.61*	*1.18*	*0.66*	*0.51*	*1.17*
1993	*0.54*	*0.91*	*1.46*	*0.57*	*0.62*	*1.19*	*0.26*	*0.26*	*0.52*
1994	*0.54*	*0.88*	*1.42*	*0.56*	*0.61*	*1.17*	*0.62*	*0.52*	*1.13*
1995	*0.48*	*0.69*	*1.18*	*0.58*	*0.60*	*1.18*	*0.79*	*0.72*	*1.51*
1996	*0.49*	*0.65*	*1.14*	*0.56*	*0.57*	*1.12*	*0.72*	*0.63*	*1.35*
1997	*0.55*	*0.77*	*1.31*	*0.58*	*0.63*	*1.21*	*0.68*	*0.55*	*1.23*
Note:	SP =Accompanying Spouses								
	CH = Accompanying Children								

The Phase 1 Multiplier Effect for ERI Principals

In Chapter 4, we learned that the Net Phase 1 Multiplier for ERI is the same as the ERI Principals' sponsorship rate of accompanying family members. That is, the value of the Net Phase 1 Multiplier is the average number AFM Immigrants sponsored by one ERI Principal.

Table 7-2 lists the Net Phase 1 Multiplier values for all regions by year (1972~1997) for ERI Principals. We see that the Middle East,

Latin America, and Africa have the highest Net Phase 1 Multipliers for ERI, on average around 1.3. This means that each ERI Principal from these regions would sponsor and bring about 1.3 accompanying family members to the U.S. with him/her. On the other hand, the Net Phase 1 Multiplier for ERI Principals is the lowest for Asia and Europe, which average 1.1. This implies that about 1.1 AFM immigrants will join each ERI Principal arriving to the U.S.

Table 7-4 Top Countries in Sending Employment-Related Immigrants

Rank	Country	Total
1	China	*271,155*
2	Philippines	*171,470*
3	India	*132,726*
4	USSR/Russia	*126,960*
5	Korea	*93,978*
6	Canada	*87,847*
7	El Salvador	*45,877*
8	Mexico	*44,660*
9	Iran	*39,146*
10	Jamaica	*25,502*
11	Pakistan	*17,840*
12	Colombia	*15,673*
13	Peru	*13,282*
14	Guyana/British Guiana	*12,581*
15	San Marino	*12,001*
16	Haiti	*4,918*
17	Dominican Republic	*4,509*
18	Vietnam	*3,474*
19	Cuba	*1,374*
20	Laos	*295*

The breakdown of the Net Phase 1 Multiplier (Table 7-3) shows that ERI Principals, on average, would sponsor about ½ AFM spouse per ERI Principal, or 1 spouse for every 2 ERI Principals, and this is true for all three top regions (Latin America, Europe, and Asia). The data also suggests that most of the differences in the values of the *Phase 1 net IUM* among these regions are the result of variations in patterns of sponsoring accompanying children. For example, the high volume of accompanying children of Latin American ERI Principals is the contributing factor to its overall high value of Net Phase 1

Multiplier. This data suggests that each Latin American ERI Principal would bring 0.83 accompanying children, while each European ERI Principal would bring 0.59 children. An Asian ERI principal would bring the fewest accompanying children (0.54).

If we rank all countries in terms of the total number of ERI (principals and dependents), we see that China, the Philippines, India, and Russia are the top four ERI-Sending countries (Table 7-4). Table 7-5 shows the calculated Net Phase 1 Multiplier for these countries.

Table 7-5 Net Phase 1 Multiplier for Top ERI-Sending Countries

Net	China			Philippines			India			USSR/Russia		
IUM	**271,155**			**171,470**			**132,726**			**126,960**		
Year	SP	CH	All	SP	CH	All	SP	CH	All	SP	CH	All
Total	*0.50*	*0.43*	*0.93*	*0.53*	*0.82*	*1.35*	*0.59*	*0.32*	*0.91*	*0.56*	*0.71*	*1.26*
1972	*0.47*	*0.53*	*1.01*	*0.35*	*0.47*	*0.83*	*0.53*	*0.45*	*0.98*	*0.38*	*0.54*	*0.91*
1973	*0.48*	*0.56*	*1.05*	*0.56*	*1.05*	*1.61*	*0.44*	*0.38*	*0.82*	*0.47*	*0.63*	*1.10*
1974	*0.45*	*0.32*	*0.76*	*0.45*	*0.75*	*1.20*	*0.36*	*0.30*	*0.66*	*0.47*	*0.64*	*1.11*
1975	*0.49*	*0.37*	*0.86*	*0.44*	*0.68*	*1.13*	*0.34*	*0.25*	*0.59*	*0.53*	*0.70*	*1.23*
1976	*0.51*	*0.40*	*0.90*	*0.50*	*0.71*	*1.21*	*0.43*	*0.34*	*0.77*	*0.59*	*0.76*	*1.35*
1977	*0.52*	*0.39*	*0.91*	*0.57*	*0.76*	*1.33*	*0.52*	*0.39*	*0.90*	*0.57*	*0.76*	*1.33*
1978	*0.58*	*0.41*	*0.98*	*0.45*	*0.67*	*1.12*	*0.53*	*0.41*	*0.94*	*0.60*	*0.79*	*1.38*
1979	*0.58*	*0.48*	*1.06*	*0.52*	*1.00*	*1.52*	*0.49*	*0.41*	*0.90*	*0.62*	*0.78*	*1.40*
1980	*0.60*	*0.60*	*1.20*	*0.65*	*1.45*	*2.10*	*0.48*	*0.35*	*0.84*	*0.59*	*0.79*	*1.38*
1981	*0.62*	*0.52*	*1.14*	*0.53*	*1.09*	*1.61*	*0.46*	*0.35*	*0.81*	*0.58*	*0.78*	*1.36*
1982	*0.61*	*0.44*	*1.04*	*0.63*	*0.74*	*1.37*	*0.49*	*0.36*	*0.85*	*0.55*	*0.76*	*1.32*
1983	*0.59*	*0.51*	*1.10*	*0.60*	*1.01*	*1.60*	*0.54*	*0.46*	*1.00*	*0.57*	*0.75*	*1.32*
1984	*0.63*	*0.49*	*1.12*	*0.54*	*0.96*	*1.50*	*0.55*	*0.44*	*0.99*	*0.58*	*0.78*	*1.35*
1985	*0.63*	*0.68*	*1.31*	*0.59*	*1.19*	*1.78*	*0.47*	*0.36*	*0.82*	*0.58*	*0.80*	*1.38*
1986	*0.67*	*0.66*	*1.33*	*0.64*	*1.23*	*1.87*	*0.53*	*0.36*	*0.89*	*0.61*	*0.76*	*1.37*
1987	*0.66*	*0.59*	*1.25*	*0.60*	*1.03*	*1.63*	*0.55*	*0.33*	*0.87*	*0.56*	*0.76*	*1.33*
1988	*0.67*	*0.56*	*1.23*	*0.66*	*1.30*	*1.96*	*0.58*	*0.43*	*1.00*	*0.57*	*0.76*	*1.33*
1989	*0.70*	*0.55*	*1.24*	*0.63*	*1.21*	*1.84*	*0.56*	*0.28*	*0.84*	*0.55*	*0.69*	*1.24*
1990	*0.69*	*0.57*	*1.26*	*0.60*	*0.99*	*1.59*	*0.65*	*0.46*	*1.11*	*0.55*	*0.70*	*1.25*
1991	*0.66*	*0.36*	*1.03*	*0.65*	*1.16*	*1.81*	*0.61*	*0.26*	*0.87*	*0.55*	*0.66*	*1.21*
1992	*0.68*	*0.43*	*1.11*	*0.66*	*0.95*	*1.61*	*0.64*	*0.27*	*0.91*	*0.56*	*0.66*	*1.21*
1993	*0.13*	*0.15*	*0.28*	*0.65*	*0.94*	*1.59*	*0.68*	*0.26*	*0.94*	*0.55*	*0.67*	*1.22*
1994	*0.58*	*0.45*	*1.02*	*0.62*	*0.80*	*1.42*	*0.73*	*0.30*	*1.03*	*0.52*	*0.59*	*1.11*
1995	*1.22*	*1.22*	*2.44*	*0.50*	*0.56*	*1.06*	*0.74*	*0.30*	*1.04*	*0.54*	*0.59*	*1.13*
1996	*0.94*	*0.85*	*1.79*	*0.44*	*0.55*	*0.98*	*0.75*	*0.27*	*1.02*	*0.51*	*0.56*	*1.07*
1997	*0.80*	*0.66*	*1.46*	*0.40*	*0.52*	*0.92*	*0.75*	*0.26*	*1.01*	*0.55*	*0.64*	*1.19*
Notes:	*SP = Accompanying Spouses*											
	CH = Accompanying Children											

In Table 7-5, we see that China and India have the lowest overall values of the Net Phase 1 Multiplier, at an average of 0.93 and 0.91 respectively. Relatively speaking, both the Philippines and Russia have much higher overall Net Phase 1 Multiplier values (an average of 1.35 and 1.26). Examining the data more carefully, we can identify what is causing these differences: the different values of accompanying children. In the cases of China and India, the Net Phase 1 Multiplier values of accompanying children are very low (0.43 for China, 0.32 for India), while the same indicators for the Philippines and Russia are quite high (9.802 for the Philippines, 0.71 for Russia).

If we look at the trend, the picture is quite different. Both China and India have an upward trend in Net Phase 1 Multiplier values, because the number of their Net Phase 1 Multiplier accompanying spouses has increased over the years, which means that now their ERI Principals are more likely to bring their spouses with them. The data also suggests that the number of accompanying children brought by Chinese ERI Principals has increased over the last thirty years. At the same time, the values of Net Phase 1 Multipliers for both the Philippines and Russia peaked in the 1980s.

The Phase 1 Multiplier Effect for GSI Principals
In this section, we will study the Net Phase 1 Multiplier for GSI Principals, i.e. the average number AFM Immigrants sponsored by GSI Principals.

Table 7-6 lists the values of the Net Phase 1 Multiplier for GSI Principals (which are significantly lower than that for ERI Principals, if we compare this table to Table 7-2). Among all the regions, Asia has the highest Net Phase 1 Multiplier value (0.90). The value of the Net Phase 1 Multiplier for other regions (Africa, Europe, Latin America, and the Middle East) is relatively low (0.63 to 0.72).

Table 7-7, however, shows a very strange pattern. In most years all of the regions have a near-zero Net Phase 1 Multiplier of accompanying spouses for GSI Principals, which implies that GSI Principals sponsored few accompanying spouses. Logically, this just does not make sense, and it may not reflect reality. Since most GSI Principals are refugees and political asylum-seekers, one possible explanation is that the USCIS granted the GSI Principal status to *both* husbands and the wives at the same time they applied for asylum or refugee status (instead of issuing a *GSI Principal* status to one, a *spouse* status to the other).[51]

---

[51] This data issue should have no affect on the calculation of the Immigration Unification Multiplier. Yes, it will increase the value of the denominator (the number of Principal Immigrants) and reduce the value of numerator (the

Table 7-6 Net Phase 1 Multipliers for GSI Principals By Regions

Net IUM	Asia	Europe	Middle East	Latin America	Africa
Total	**0.90**	**0.72**	**0.72**	**0.64**	**0.63**
1972	0.33	0.37	0.36	0.80	0.36
1973	0.34	0.37	0.33	0.82	0.41
1974	0.32	0.39	0.48	0.74	0.49
1975	0.30	0.36	0.56	0.59	0.45
1976	0.23	0.46	0.66	0.51	0.38
1977	0.35	0.42	0.44	0.42	0.40
1978	0.62	0.34	0.53	0.51	0.25
1979	0.73	0.34	0.46	0.60	0.17
1980	0.77	0.42	0.65	0.52	0.23
1981	0.85	0.52	0.72	0.61	0.30
1982	0.86	0.54	0.66	0.86	0.29
1983	0.99	0.56	0.79	0.92	0.33
1984	1.04	0.65	0.74	0.89	0.46
1985	1.09	0.67	0.57	0.45	0.49
1986	1.19	0.69	0.73	0.37	0.52
1987	1.12	0.48	0.72	0.11	0.31
1988	1.10	0.56	0.82	0.11	0.36
1989	1.43	0.63	0.82	0.22	0.43
1990	1.10	0.81	0.85	0.52	0.33
1991	1.12	1.00	0.72	0.60	0.45
1992	1.27	0.83	0.74	**4.61**	0.71
1993	1.18	0.82	0.75	**4.25**	0.65
1994	0.96	0.76	0.76	**2.04**	0.80
1995	0.88	0.80	0.96	0.39	0.70
1996	0.81	0.93	0.99	0.33	0.84
1997	0.94	1.00	0.94	0.32	0.86
Note:	Regions North America and Oceania/Other are not included here, because there were not enough data to calculate their Net Phase 1 Multipliers for some of the years.				

number of sponsored family members), and the subsequent overall value of Immigration Unification Multiplier of Phase 1 for GSI would be smaller than it should. Hence, we can be certain that the Immigration Unification Multiplier will show the **minimum** multiplier effect, or the actual Immigration Multiplier effect would be greater than the value presented here.

Table 7-7 Breakdown of Net Phase 1 Multiplier for GSI Principals

Net	Asia			Europe			Latin America		
IUM	**SP**	**CH**	**All**	**SP**	**CH**	**All**	**SP**	**CH**	**All**
Total	*0.17*	*0.72*	*0.90*	*0.25*	*0.47*	*0.72*	*0.06*	*0.58*	*0.64*
1972	*0.01*	*0.32*	*0.33*	*0.07*	*0.30*	*0.37*	*0.01*	*0.79*	*0.80*
1973	*0.01*	*0.33*	*0.34*	*0.05*	*0.33*	*0.37*	*0.01*	*0.81*	*0.82*
1974	*0.01*	*0.31*	*0.32*	*0.04*	*0.35*	*0.39*	*0.01*	*0.73*	*0.74*
1975	*0.00*	*0.29*	*0.30*	*0.01*	*0.35*	*0.36*	*0.01*	*0.58*	*0.59*
1976	*0.01*	*0.23*	*0.23*	*0.11*	*0.35*	*0.46*	*0.01*	*0.50*	*0.51*
1977	*0.00*	*0.35*	*0.35*	*0.07*	*0.35*	*0.42*	*0.00*	*0.41*	*0.42*
1978	*0.00*	*0.61*	*0.62*	*0.01*	*0.33*	*0.34*	*0.00*	*0.51*	*0.51*
1979	*0.00*	*0.73*	*0.73*	*0.01*	*0.33*	*0.34*	*0.00*	*0.60*	*0.60*
1980	*0.03*	*0.74*	*0.77*	*0.04*	*0.38*	*0.42*	*0.00*	*0.51*	*0.52*
1981	*0.07*	*0.78*	*0.85*	*0.09*	*0.43*	*0.52*	*0.01*	*0.61*	*0.61*
1982	*0.08*	*0.79*	*0.86*	*0.10*	*0.44*	*0.54*	*0.17*	*0.69*	*0.86*
1983	*0.15*	*0.83*	*0.99*	*0.18*	*0.38*	*0.56*	*0.10*	*0.82*	*0.92*
1984	*0.18*	*0.87*	*1.04*	*0.23*	*0.43*	*0.65*	*0.07*	*0.83*	*0.89*
1985	*0.20*	*0.89*	*1.09*	*0.21*	*0.45*	*0.67*	*0.02*	*0.43*	*0.45*
1986	*0.22*	*0.97*	*1.19*	*0.21*	*0.49*	*0.69*	*0.02*	*0.35*	*0.37*
1987	*0.20*	*0.91*	*1.12*	*0.14*	*0.34*	*0.48*	*0.01*	*0.10*	*0.11*
1988	*0.21*	*0.89*	*1.10*	*0.16*	*0.40*	*0.56*	*0.01*	*0.10*	*0.11*
1989	*0.38*	*1.05*	*1.43*	*0.18*	*0.45*	*0.63*	*0.03*	*0.19*	*0.22*
1990	*0.33*	*0.77*	*1.10*	*0.27*	*0.54*	*0.81*	*0.11*	*0.41*	*0.52*
1991	*0.36*	*0.76*	*1.12*	*0.34*	*0.66*	*1.00*	*0.12*	*0.48*	*0.60*
1992	*0.45*	*0.82*	*1.27*	*0.31*	*0.53*	*0.83*	*1.21*	*3.40*	*4.61*
1993	*0.39*	*0.79*	*1.18*	*0.32*	*0.50*	*0.82*	*1.24*	*3.01*	*4.25*
1994	*0.29*	*0.67*	*0.96*	*0.32*	*0.44*	*0.76*	*0.57*	*1.46*	*2.04*
1995	*0.28*	*0.60*	*0.88*	*0.32*	*0.47*	*0.80*	*0.09*	*0.30*	*0.39*
1996	*0.26*	*0.55*	*0.81*	*0.36*	*0.57*	*0.93*	*0.06*	*0.27*	*0.33*
1997	*0.31*	*0.63*	*0.94*	*0.41*	*0.59*	*1.00*	*0.07*	*0.26*	*0.32*
Notes	*SP = Accompanying Spouses*								
	CH = Accompanying Children								

Tables 7-6 and 7-7 also show the impact of the IRCA of 1986 and the Immigration Act of 1990, which have allowed previously undocumented immigrants and their dependents to adjust their status. Table 7-8, which uses Mexican GSI Principals as an example, illustrates such an impact.

Table 7-8 The Impact of IRCA of 1986 and the Immigration Act of 1990 on Net Phase 1 Multiplier for Mexican GSI

Year	Mexican GSI Principals	Mexican GSI Dependents			
		Spouse		Children	
		Total	Net Phase 1 Multiplier	Total	Net Phase 1 Multiplier
1987	11,679	12	0.00	1,991	0.17
1988	29,198	21	0.00	2,159	0.07
1989	9,537	28	0.00	1,430	0.15
1990	3,065	41	0.01	915	0.30
1991	1,723	377	0.22	1,704	0.99
1992	935	10,073	10.77	27,051	28.93
1993	793	11,882	14.98	28,249	35.62
1994	737	7,364	9.99	17,578	23.85
Total	57,667	29,798	0.52	81,077	1.41
Notes	As part of the IRCA of 1986 implementation process, spouses and children of the legalized GSI Principals under the IRCA 1986 act were granted the "accompanying" family member visa status a few years later.				

The Phase 1 Multiplier Effect for FSUSB Principals

The FSUSB Principals is a special group of Principal Immigrants who do not have family members to sponsor in chain migration unification phase 1. To understand this, we must know the family members whom the FSUSB Principals might sponsor:

- Spouses
  Since all FSUSB Principals are considered "Spouses of U.S. Citizens," all of their spouses are sponsors who are also U.S.-born citizens. Therefore, it is *impossible* for any FSUSB Principal to sponsor spouses.
- Minor children, if there are any:
  All minor children of FSUSB Principals, along with all minor children of Foreign Spouses of Naturalized U.S. Citizens (FSUSN Immigrants), are considered as "Minor Children of U.S. Citizens." This, in fact, is Phase 3 of the chain migration process, discussed in Chapter 9.
- Adult Children, if there are any.

All adult children of FSUSB Principals are considered "Adult Children of U.S. Citizens." This is categorized as Phase 4 of the chain migration process that is to be discussed in Chapter 10.

- Parents, if they wish to come to the U.S.
  All parents of FSUSB Principals are considered "Parents of U.S. Citizens," and they do not have a visa limit. Chapter 9 discusses this category in detail as part of the discussion on the Phase 3 of the chain migration process.
- Siblings, if there are any:
  All siblings of FSUSB Principals are considered "Siblings of U.S. Citizens." Since siblings are considered as "non-exempt family members," sponsoring them would be part of Phase 4 of the chain migration process, which is discussed in Chapter 10.

Therefore, the values of Net Phase 1 Multiplier for FSUSB Principals should be zero.

Multiplier Effect in Chain Migration Phase 1:

After reviewing different types of Principal Immigrants (ERI, GSI, and FSUSB), we are ready to study the Principal Immigrants together under the context of Phase 1 of the chain migration process. We will examine the overall Net Phase 1 Multiplier values by comparing all types of Principal Immigrants. Before I present the results, I would like to explore the gender role of the sponsoring spouses of Principal Immigrants and the role they play in the chain migration process.

Sponsoring Spouses: The Gender Differences
As discussed earlier, the sponsorship of spouses is quite consistent across regions, as indicated by the Net Phase 1 Multiplier of spouses for ERI and GSI Principals. Given the existing immigration policies on sponsoring spouses, a proof of marriage is usually required. Therefore, the statistics of the marital status of the Principal Immigrants would be a very good indicator for their potential sponsorship of family members. Table 7-9 shows the percentages of married ERI Principals by region and suggests that the majority of ERI Principals are married. The percentages of those who married are highest for North America (76%) and Latin America (75%), and they are lowest for the Middle East

(64%) and Oceania/Other (65%). It is consistent across all regions that there are more males than females among married ERI Principals.

Table 7-9 ERI Principals: Percentage of Married by Regions

Percent Married	Africa	Asia	Europe	Latin America	Middle East	North America	Oceania /Other
Female Principals	53%	59%	40%	47%	56%	42%	31%
Male Principals	70%	73%	70%	75%	64%	76%	65%
Total	70%	73%	70%	75%	64%	76%	65%

Table 7-10 Net Phase 1 Multiplier for Married ERI Principals by Regions

Net Phase 1 Multiplier	Africa	Asia	Europe	Latin America	Middle East	North America	Oceania /Other
Female Principals	0.80	0.68	0.76	0.64	0.91	0.75	0.69
Male Principals	0.86	0.84	0.86	0.91	0.89	0.97	0.92

At the same, the Net Phase 1 Multiplier values in Table 7-10 show the sponsorship pattern of these married ERI Principals.

For all regions, married male ERI Principals are very likely to bring their family members (accompanying spouses and children combined), while significantly fewer married female ERI Principals would do the same—except those from Africa and the Middle East.

Data shows that North America has the highest Net Phase 1 Multiplier for married male ERI Principals (0.97) and the Middle East has the highest Net Phase 1 Multiplier for female ERI Principals (0.91). This means that each married male ERI Principal from North America would be almost certain to bring his family member(s) with him (0.97 spouses and children combined for each principal), and each married female ERI Principal from the Middle East will very likely have her family member(s) accompany her (0.91 spouses and children combined for each principal).

It is quite interesting to see the different sponsorship patterns among female and male Principal Immigrants across the regions. For married male ERI Principals, the Net Phase 1 Multiplier is consistently high across all regions—the values of all of the regions range from 0.84 to 0.92. This shows the consistency of the sponsorship of male ERI

Principals for their wives and children: each ERI Principal would bring an average of 0.84 to 0.92 family members (spouses and children combined) with them.

At the same time, we see that married female ERI Principals have a much wider range of values of the Net Phase 1 Multiplier across different regions. The values of the Net Phase 1 Multiplier for married female ERI Principals from Africa, Europe, and North America range from 0.80, while those of married female ERI Principals from Asia, Latin America, and Oceania range from 0.64-0.69.

The data also shows that the Middle East is the only region where female ERI Principals have higher Net Phase 1 Multiplier values than their male counterparts (0.91 vs. 0.89). This implies that married ERI Principals (regardless of gender) from the Middle East are more likely than those from other regions to bring their spouses and children to accompany them when they migrate to the U.S.

Overall Chain Migration Phase 1 Multiplier: The Results
Table 7-11 shows all the values of the Net Phase 1 Multiplier for ER, GSI, and FSUSB Principals—and for all of the Principal Immigrants combined. As you can see, the values vary significantly among these different Principal Immigrant types. As demonstrated in the formulas in Chapter 4, we calculated the final overall values of the Net Phase 1 Multiplier by combining all of the Principal Immigrant types.[52]

As shown in Table 7-11, Principal Immigrants from Asia have the highest immediate multiplier value or the largest multiplier effect in the Phase 1 chain migration process—for every Principal Immigrant admitted to the U.S., an additional .72 immigrants will accompany him/her as an AFM Immigrant. The multiplier effect of Principal Immigrants from Europe, the Middle East, and North America in Phase 1 of chain migration (the multiplier ranged from 0.48 to .53) is the next strongest—each Principal Immigrant admitted will bring about .5 AFM Immigrants. At the same time, Principal Immigrants from Africa and Latin America Principal Immigrants have a relatively small multiplier

---

[52] This is a very important concept. As discussed in Chapter 4, we need to evaluate the overall *net IUM* and *IUM* for all Principal Immigrants at different phases. The denominator for the *net IUM* and *IUM* must be standardized to include all Principal Immigrants.

effect in Phase 1 of chain migration, with 0.4 additional AFM immigrants for each principal immigrant. Oceania/Other region has the smallest multiplier effect (0.27 AFM immigrants for each Principal Immigrant).

Table 7-11 Net Phase 1 Multiplier Values of Principal Immigrants By Region

Percent	ERI Principals		GSI Principals		FSUSB Principals		All Principals	
	Pct	Net IUM	Pct	Net IUM	Pct	Net IUM	Pct	Net IUM
Africa	12%	1.24	37%	0.63	51%	0.00	100%	0.38
Asia	25%	1.08	50%	0.90	25%	0.00	100%	0.72
Europe	14%	1.13	52%	0.72	34%	0.00	100%	0.53
Latin America	7%	1.32	52%	0.64	41%	0.00	100%	0.42
Middle East	16%	1.35	39%	0.72	45%	0.00	100%	0.50
North America	18%	1.95	19%	0.65	63%	0.00	100%	0.48
Oceania/ Other	17%	1.20	7%	0.93	76%	0.00	100%	0.27
Total	15%	1.19	48%	0.74	37%	0.00	100%	0.53

Note 1. *Since foreign-born spouses of U.S.-born citizens are a special group of Principal Immigrants whose sponsorship of children and parents are categorized as Phases 3 and 4 in the chain migration process, the Net Phase 1 Multiplier values for this group of immigrants are zero. However, the overall Net Phase 1 Multiplier will still include this group in its denominator so that this overall Net Phase 1 Multiplier could be comparable against net IUMs from Phase 2 through Phase 5 in the following chapters.*

2. *Because of the "0" values of net IUM Values for FSUSB Principals, the higher number of FSUSB Principals would distort the values of net IUM for the region. This is the case for Latin America, which, as shown in Table 6-18 in Chapter 6, contributes almost half of the FSUSB Principals. Therefore, the extreme low value of the Net Phase 1 Multiplier for Latin America is very misleading because the huge volume of FSUSB Principals has effectively lowered its value of Net Phase 1 Multiplier. We should interpret the values of Net Phase 1 Multiplier as the indication of a minimum multiplier effect. The actual multiplier effect should be more significant. In fact, this issue suggests another aspect of chain migration that is not discussed in this book. A portion of U.S.-born citizens, who sponsor Latin American spouses, are actually U.S. citizens of Hispanic origin who are descendents of Latin American immigrants a few generations ago. This type of multiplier effect is beyond the research scope of this book. It can, however, be further explored in the future.*

These results could be very misleading; because one of the contributing factors to this low overall Net Phase 1 Multiplier for some regions is that Latin America's significant volume of FSUSB Principals (about 41%) has effectively lowered the Net Phase 1 Multiplier. As we know, the presence of FSUSB Principals reduces the value of the Net Phase 1 Multiplier, because all AFM Children of FSUSB Principals are to be calculated at Phase 3 as Minor Children of U.S. Citizens. Therefore, the larger the number of the FSUSB Principals, the lower the value of the Net Phase 1 Multiplier.[53]

Figure 7-5 shows the general trend of the Net Phase 1 Multipliers. It seems that the values of the Net Phase 1 Multipliers for ERI and GSI Principals have been moving up over the last three decades. This overall trend has contributed to the slight growth of the overall Net Phase 1 Multipliers for all Principal Immigrants.

Based on the data presented in this chapter, we can see that, during the last three decades, there has been a significant increase of ERI Principals from regions across the world, and the most significant contributing ones are Asia, Europe, and Latin America. The analysis of the class of admissions shows that the patterns of skilled and professional immigrants coming from one top country from each of these regions increased the most in the 1980s, and the trend continued in the 1990s. These patterns coincide with the implementations of U.S. immigration laws during the same period.

It is clear that the Immigration and Nationality Act Amendments of 1965 contributed to the ERI growth until the mid 1970s. Since then, changes in the visa system on hemispheres and the change of the quota in the 1977 and the Refugees Act of 1980, as well as the Immigration Act of 1990, have continued to show significant impact on the ERI

---

[53] We should interpret the values of the Phase 1 *net IUM* as the indication of **minimum** multiplier effect. The actual multiplier effect should be stronger. Since this book does not discuss the Immigration Multiplier effect through multi-immigrant-generations, therefore, the significance of Latin American spouses sponsored by U.S.-born citizens (who are more likely to be descendants of Latin American immigrants), will not be covered in this book. This also suggests that the Immigration Multiplier effect can linger for several generations, and that is part of the nature of chain migration, which can be explored further.

growth patterns for all regions. As we have observed, the ERI growth patterns also have shifted over the last three decades, especially for ERI from Europe (significant decrease) and Latin America (significant increase).

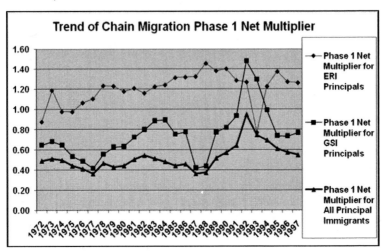

Figure 7-5 Trend of Net Phase 1 Multiplier for Principal Immigrants

At the same time, the volume of GSI (Government-Sponsored Immigrants) fluctuates over time and across regions. It seems that the total number of GSI to the United States is directly tied to the U.S. government's international interest at that time. Although it would be impossible to predict where the next hot spot in the world might be that would prompt the U.S. government to sponsor another round of massive immigration operations, it is still safe to say that the overall trend of government-sponsored immigration is decreasing.

With recent immigration waves to the U.S., the sponsorship of U.S.-born citizens for foreign-born spouses (FSUSB Principals) has increased noticeably over the last three decades. The comparison of the FSUSB Principals across regions leads to the conclusion that most of the FSUSB Principals come from Latin America. More male FSUSB Principals have come from the Middle East, Africa, and Latin America, and more female FSUSB Principals from Asia, Oceania, and North America.

The overall picture of AFM (accompanying family members) Immigrants of the Principal Immigrants (whether ERI or GSI) shows that net gains have dominated the last three decades. There are no surprises in terms what regions lead Asia, Latin America, and Europe continue to lead in this component of the immigration process, with Europe and Latin America gaining the most significant percentages of increase.

The analysis of ERI, GSI, and FSUSB Principals reveals how Principal Immigrants are sponsored and granted permission to enter the United States. It also illustrates the dramatic change in the overall total of combined immigrants in this non-family sponsored category during the last three decades.

The data also demonstrates the variations in the patterns of immigrants who come to the United States from Asia, Latin America, and Europe. While Europe has decreased its contribution to non-family sponsored immigrants (both principal and dependent) over the last three decades, Asia became the top region in this category in the 1980s and remained the top until the late 1990s. Then Latin America surpassed Asia and became the number one region that sent non-family sponsored immigrants to the United States.

Measuring Multiplier Effect in Phase 1 of Chain Migration

As demonstrated in this chapter, there are many different ways to measure the immigration population and its demographic and socioeconomic characteristics. The best way to describe clearly the characteristics of the unification process during the Phase 1 of chain migration is to calculate the *IUM*. The calculations of the Net Phase 1 Multipliers provide us with the insight of the mechanism of migration chain at the Unification *Phase 1* (for sponsoring accompanying family members).

By calculating the Net Phase 1 Multipliers for ERI Principals, we reach the following conclusions:

- North American ERI Principals have the highest multiplier values (1.95, with 0.65 for AFM Spouses and 1.30 for AFM Children).
- Asian ERI Principals have the lowest multiplier values (1.08, with 0.54 for AFM Spouses and 0.54 for AFM Children).
- For all regions:

- o The multiplier values of ERI sponsorship for AFM Spouses are consistent— 0.49 to 0.65.
- o The main cause of the variations of the multiplier values are from the sponsorship of AFM Children, which range from 0.54 to 1.30.

Similarly, the Net Phase 1 Multipliers for GSI Principals reveal the following:

- Asian GSI Principals have the highest multiplier values (0.90)[54] for sponsoring AFM Immigrants.
- Both Europe and the Middle East are top ranked (after Asia) in terms of sponsoring AFM Immigrants.
- Africa, Latin America, and North America ranked last—with the lowest multiplier values (about 0.64).

Since FSUSB Principals would sponsor their dependents at *Phase 3* (for sponsoring exempt family members of U.S. citizens), we performed no calculations on the Chain-Specific *Phase 1 net IUM*s for FSUSB Principals.

As part of the standardization process, we calculated the overall Chain Migration Unification *Phase 1 net IUM* values using the combined total number of ERI, GSI, and FSUSB Principals as the denominator. The final Unification *Phase 1 net IUM* values suggest the following:

- Asia is the top region and has the highest *IUM* at *Chain Migration Unification Phase 1*, with the *net IUM* value of 0.72. This means that each Asian Principal Immigrant is responsible for sponsoring, an average of 0.72 AFM Immigrants.
- The next three top regions are Europe (0.53), the Middle East (0.50), and North America (0.48).
- Latin America's overall *net IUM* value is 0.42, and it is among the lowest.
- In the study of the top countries, we see that several Asian countries (Laos, Vietnam, China, India, Korea, Pakistan, and the Philippines) are among the top in terms of having high *net IUM* values (from 0.52 to 1.01). At the same time, some Latin

---

[54] Although Oceania immigrants have an overall GSI *net IUM* value of 0.92, this region must be excluded because it does not have enough GSI Principal immigrants in most of the calculations (less than 500).

American countries (El Salvador, Jamaica, Mexico) are also on the list, with their *net IUM* values ranging from 0.49 to 0.91). In short, most of the top countries with high *net IUM* values are from either Asia or Latin America.

In the next chapter, I will use *IUM*s to study other phases of the chain migration unification processes so that I can clearly explain the chain migration process.

CHAPTER 8

Chain Migration Phase 2: Reuniting Family Members

The chain migration process begins with the Principal Immigrant, who initiates the migration chain by sponsoring his/her family members, who can also sponsor their family members, and so on. We have discussed the characteristics of the Principal Immigrants (Chapter 6), and later in Chapter 7, we studied their initial sponsorship of their immediate family members by bringing their spouses and children with them as accompanying family members (AFM Immigrants). The Immigration Unification Multiplier, introduced in Chapter 7, made it possible for us to measure such sponsorship (and its multiplier effects) during Phase 1 of the chain migration process. In this chapter, we will study the next phase of sponsorship—the continuing and ongoing sponsorship of family members.

IMMIGRATION PATTERNS: LATER-SPONSORED FAMILY MEMBERS

The *Later-sponsored Family Members of Principal Immigrants* (*LFM Immigrants*) are those family members whom the Principal Immigrants sponsor *after* he or she has migrated to a destination country. This is a common practice, because for various reasons (including, but not limited to, socioeconomic, personal, and/or political reasons), many Principal Immigrants might not be able to bring their family members with them (as AFM Immigrants). Figure 8-1 shows the history data for all LFM Immigrants in the last three decades. The growth pattern indicates that the volume of both LFM spouses and their children increased during this time. It is also clear that the net gain of LFM children outpaced LFM spouses.

149

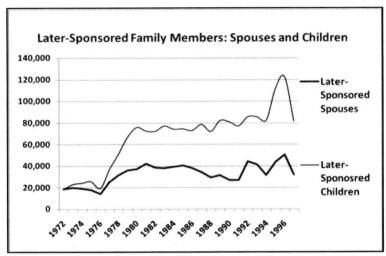

Figure 8-1 Immigration Trend of Later-Sponsored Spouses and Children

Regional Variations

Table 8-1 demonstrates that the growth patterns vary significantly among regions. Latin America tops all regions in sending LFM Immigrants to the U.S. The total number of immigrants from Latin America is about 55.60% of the total number of all of the other regions combined. Asia is second, and its total number is almost one-third of the overall total. The combined total of LFM Immigrants from Latin America and Asia is about 87% of all LFM Immigrants. However, Latin America is the only region that has demonstrated a significant pattern of increase over the last three decades. At the same time, Europe is the only region that has gone in the opposite direction—the total number of LFM Immigrants has decreased during the last thirty years. The average annual number of European LFM Immigrants in 1990s is only about a quarter of its annual number in the early 1970s.

Table 8-2 further illustrates the trend for all of the regions. We clearly see that, in the 1970s, Asia was the leading region in LFM Immigrants. However, in the 1980s, Latin America jumped 338%, while Asia gained only 35.40%. In the 1990s, Latin America gained another 44.52%, while Asia lost 28%. During the last thirty years, the total number of European LFM Immigrants consistently decreased about 50% every ten years.

Table 8-1 Immigration Trend of Later-Sponsored Family Members

Year	TOTAL	Latin America	Asia	Europe	Middle East	Africa	North America	Oceania /Other
	100%	*55.60%*	*31.38%*	*6.36%*	*3.61%*	*1.66%*	*0.99%*	*0.40%*
Total	2,604,593	1,448,044	817,335	165,597	94,037	43,335	25,797	10,448
1972	36,940	756	8,577	7,592	1,095	528	138	135
1973	42,589	1,567	18,415	13,049	2,248	1,008	352	301
1974	43,094	1,861	23,163	12,977	2,872	924	411	381
1975	43,307	1,881	25,530	11,068	2,828	848	479	460
1976	33,348	1,867	27,769	9,480	2,250	865	644	432
1977	61,810	1,260	21,674	6,619	2,236	694	511	354
1978	82,024	11,595	33,593	9,258	3,894	1,552	1,376	542
1979	102,677	38,113	27,008	8,716	4,284	1,500	1,791	612
1980	112,942	54,239	31,293	8,010	4,802	1,743	1,912	678
1981	114,566	58,298	41,990	6,104	3,312	1,454	1,399	385
1982	110,262	57,945	37,189	8,882	5,880	2,166	1,838	666
1983	114,945	60,217	35,715	6,610	3,814	1,814	1,595	497
1984	113,319	65,730	36,736	5,611	3,506	1,702	1,232	428
1985	114,785	68,397	33,844	4,913	2,996	1,638	1,055	476
1986	110,618	62,421	38,892	5,445	4,101	2,124	1,268	534
1987	112,758	63,400	34,686	4,618	4,201	2,108	1,143	462
1988	101,399	61,543	38,382	4,862	4,293	2,053	1,146	479
1989	113,098	58,518	32,005	3,502	4,176	1,779	1,053	366
1990	107,525	62,633	37,864	4,021	4,996	2,081	1,087	416
1991	103,633	61,424	35,237	3,362	4,335	1,791	994	382
1992	129,435	58,464	34,368	3,479	4,386	1,827	824	285
1993	126,562	83,659	34,353	4,077	4,030	2,221	826	269
1994	113,554	88,876	27,779	3,395	3,434	2,121	746	211
1995	154,846	79,688	27,099	2,398	2,037	1,662	522	148
1996	172,555	112,650	33,165	3,250	2,832	2,190	538	221
1997	113,181	136,872	26,483	3,006	3,326	2,073	566	229

If we examine the age distribution of the LFM Immigrants (see Figure 8-2), we see that those who came from most regions (Asia, Europe, the Middle East, Africa, and Oceania) have a high concentration of people between the ages of 15 and 30. Latin America and North America are the only two regions that have a relatively younger LFM immigrant population.

Table 8-2 Later-Sponsored Family Members By Region By Time Period

Region		Annual Average of Later-Sponsored Family Members			
		1972~1979	1980~1989	1990~1997	All
Africa	Annual Average	1,208	1,892	1,844	1,667
	Net Gain		56.65%	-2.52%	
Asia	Annual Average	27,128	36,730	29,126	31,436
	Net Gain		35.40%	-20.70%	
Europe	Annual Average	10,846	5,457	3,033	6,369
	Net Gain		-49.69%	-44.43%	
Latin America	Annual Average	14,142	61,910	89,475	55,694
	Net Gain		337.76%	44.52%	
Middle East	Annual Average	3,314	4,128	3,282	3,617
	Net Gain		24.56%	-20.49%	
North America	Annual Average	952	1,282	671	992
	Net Gain		34.66%	-47.65%	
Oceania /Other	Annual Average	487	471	231	402
	Net Gain		-3.28%	-51.05%	
All Regions	Annual Average	**58,076**	**111,869**	**127,661**	**100,177**
	Net Gain		92.62%	14.12%	

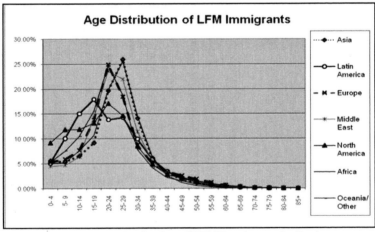

Figure 8-2 Age Distribution of LFM Immigrants by Region

Table 8-3 Top 20 LFM Immigrants-Sending Countries

Top 20 Countries	Annual Average (1972 ~1997)	Distribution				Grand Total	Overall Pct
		1972 ~1979	1980 ~1989	1990 ~1997	All Years		
Mexico	15,500	18%	43%	39%	100%	403,012	15.47%
Dominican Republic	10,742	4%	22%	74%	100%	279,289	10.72%
Philippines	8,047	7%	48%	44%	100%	209,220	8.03%
China	7,752	40%	34%	26%	100%	201,551	7.74%
Jamaica	5,930	22%	49%	29%	100%	154,192	5.92%
India	5,473	10%	62%	29%	100%	142,302	5.46%
Korea	5,365	23%	43%	33%	100%	139,477	5.35%
Haiti	3,883	24%	60%	16%	100%	100,951	3.88%
El Salvador	3,588	6%	49%	46%	100%	93,288	3.58%
Guyana /British Guiana	2,313	4%	37%	59%	100%	60,130	2.31%
Colombia	2,192	7%	59%	33%	100%	56,985	2.19%
Pakistan	1,395	11%	57%	32%	100%	36,280	1.39%
Vietnam	1,257	17%	38%	45%	100%	32,694	1.26%
Iran	1,150	5%	47%	48%	100%	29,888	1.15%
USSR/ Russia	1,075	18%	52%	30%	100%	27,959	1.07%
Peru	1,048	36%	47%	17%	100%	27,244	1.05%
San Marino	794	8%	43%	49%	100%	20,634	0.79%
Canada	525	78%	18%	4%	100%	13,658	0.52%
Cuba	332	28%	54%	18%	100%	8,621	0.33%
Laos	54	9%	64%	26%	100%	1,399	0.05%
Other Countries	21,764	26%	44%	30%	100%	565,874	21.73%
All Countries Combined	100,179	18%	43%	39%	100%	2,604,648	100%

Top Countries

We now examine the top 20 LFM Immigrants-sponsoring countries. The top 10 countries are from either Latin America (6) or Asia (4) (Table 8-3). Mexico and the Dominican Republic are the significant top leading countries. Mexico, the top country, contributes about 15% of the overall LFM Immigrants. When we combine this number with those from Dominican Republic, we see that these countries send 25%

of LFM Immigrants. At the same time, the LFM immigrants from the top two Asian countries (the Philippines and China) are about 8% each.

Table 8-4 Case Study on Latin American Immigrants: Phase 1 and Phase 2 of Chain Migration Process from IRAC 1986 and Immigration Act of 1990

Year	Foreign Spouses of U.S. Born Citizens	Employment-Related Immigrants		Government-Sponsored Immigrants		Phase 2 Chain Migration (Later-Sponsored Family Members)
		Principals	Phase 1 Chain Migration (AFM Immigrants)	Principals	Phase 1 Chain Migration (AFM Immigrants)	
1986	39,374	5,577	7,763	21,327	7,882	62,421
1987	39,327	6,652	10,116	60,231	6,558	63,400
1988	35,760	4,907	8,435	55,010	6,090	61,543
1989	29,989	6,016	9,394	19,593	4,386	58,518
1990	27,179	5,919	9,264	19,598	10,200	62,633
1991	26,732	7,565	10,801	13,513	8,160	61,424
1992	26,680	9,554	13,936	13,125	60,473	58,464
1993	31,953	8,359	12,169	12,026	51,071	83,659
1994	31,596	7,288	10,369	14,634	29,808	88,876
1995	28,155	7,527	8,855	19,700	7,753	79,688
1996	44,290	9,920	11,309	29,904	9,829	112,650
1997	45,781	7,277	9,558	25,219	8,118	136,872

From the overall distribution over the last thirty years, we see that the top three countries (Mexico, the Dominican Republic, and the Philippines) increased in volume mainly in the 1980s and the 1990s, with the Dominican Republic making the largest biggest jump in the 1990s (a 52% increase since the 1980s). The total number of LFM from Mexico and the Dominican Republic in the 1980s and the 1990s may suggest that the surge in their LFM Immigrants during these two periods could be partly because of the IRCA of 1986 and the Immigration Act of 1990, which allowed previously undocumented immigrants and their dependents to adjust their status. Table 8-4 illustrates the impact of these two legislations..

Meanwhile, the LFM Immigrants from China decreased over the last thirty years, with the total in the 1990s being almost half of that in the 1970s. Other Asian countries (India, Korea, Vietnam, Laos, etc.) all increased their volume of LFM immigrants during the same period.

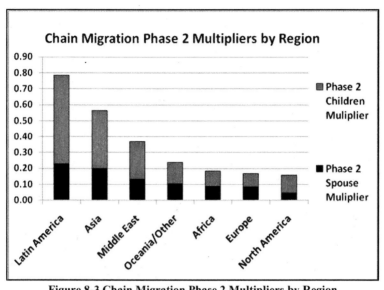

Figure 8-3 Chain Migration Phase 2 Multipliers by Region

Table 8-5 Phase 2 Net IUM Results by Region

Region	Phase 2 Multipliers for Responsible Principal Immigrants Only			Phase 2 Multipliers for All Principal Immigrants		
	Spouse	Children	All	Spouse	Children	All
Africa	0.18	0.19	0.37	0.09	0.10	0.18
Asia	0.26	0.49	0.75	0.20	0.37	0.56
Europe	0.13	0.12	0.25	0.08	0.08	0.17
Latin America	0.38	0.95	1.33	0.23	0.56	0.78
Middle East	0.24	0.43	0.67	0.13	0.24	0.37
North America	0.12	0.30	0.43	0.05	0.11	0.16
Oceania /Other	0.41	0.56	0.97	0.10	0.14	0.24
Total	0.27	0.55	0.82	0.17	0.35	0.52

Note:	The responsible Principal Immigrants are ERI Principals and GSI Principals. By definition, FSUSB Principals are not eligible for sponsoring LFM Immigrants, therefore, not responsible for Phase 2 Multipliers. FSUSB Principals are responsible for Phase 3 and Phase 4 Multipliers.

Table 8-6 Trend of Phase 2 Net IUM for All Principal Immigrants

Year	*Phase 2 Net IUM* for Responsible Principal Immigrants Only			*Phase 2 Net IUM* for All Principal Immigrants		
	Spouse	Children	All	Spouse	Children	All
1972	0.16	0.15	0.31	0.11	0.11	0.22
1973	0.18	0.21	0.39	0.12	0.14	0.27
1974	0.17	0.22	0.39	0.12	0.16	0.28
1975	0.15	0.21	0.36	0.11	0.16	0.27
1976	0.15	0.20	0.35	0.11	0.15	0.27
1977	0.17	0.25	0.42	0.13	0.19	0.31
1978	0.20	0.32	0.51	0.15	0.24	0.38
1979	0.54	1.00	1.54	0.29	0.53	0.82
1980	0.38	0.77	1.15	0.22	0.45	0.67
1981	0.37	0.64	1.02	0.23	0.40	0.63
1982	0.33	0.62	0.94	0.20	0.38	0.58
1983	0.47	0.95	1.42	0.24	0.49	0.73
1984	0.54	1.02	1.57	0.26	0.48	0.74
1985	0.49	0.90	1.39	0.24	0.44	0.67
1986	0.45	0.87	1.32	0.22	0.43	0.65
1987	0.27	0.61	0.88	0.16	0.37	0.53
1988	0.25	0.60	0.85	0.15	0.36	0.50
1989	0.33	0.86	1.18	0.18	0.48	0.66
1990	0.22	0.68	0.90	0.14	0.41	0.55
1991	0.21	0.60	0.81	0.13	0.38	0.51
1992	0.28	0.55	0.83	0.19	0.37	0.56
1993	0.21	0.44	0.65	0.15	0.31	0.46
1994	0.21	0.55	0.76	0.14	0.36	0.50
1995	0.31	0.78	1.08	0.21	0.52	0.73
1996	0.32	0.77	1.08	0.20	0.49	0.69
1997	0.25	0.64	0.89	0.15	0.37	0.52
Total	**0.27**	**0.55**	**0.82**	**0.17**	**0.35**	**0.52**
Note:	The responsible Principal Immigrants are ERI Principals and GSI Principals. By definition, FSUSB Principals are not responsible for the Phase 2 Multiplier because they do not sponsor LFM immigrants. However, they are responsible for Phase 3 and Phase 4 multipliers.					

MULTIPLIER EFFECT IN CHAIN MIGRATION PHASE 2

Table 8-5 shows two different sets of values for Phase 2 net *IUM*: one set for responsible Principal Immigrants (ERI & GSI Principals only), the other for all Principal Immigrants (ERI, GSI, and FSUSB Principals combined). We can see the difference here between the two sets of values of Phase 2 net *IUM*, and it is clear that FSUSB Principals[55] have reduced the values of Phase 2 net *IUM* because they are part of the denominator (all Principal Immigrants).

Figure 8-3 shows the combined (children and spouse) chain migration phase 2 multipliers by region.

The overall patterns for both sets of values still show that Latin America leads the Phase 2 net *IUM* of LFM Immigrants. For Mexican immigrants, each non-FSUSB Principal will sponsor 0.38 LFM spouse and almost one LFM child (0.95), according to the calculated Phase 2 net *IUM* for responsible Principal Immigrants. Using the Phase 2 net *IUM* for all Principal Immigrants, each Mexican Principal Immigrant will bring at least 0.78 additional LFM Immigrants to the U.S.

There are some significant differences among Oceania immigrants. Their Phase 2 net *IUM* values are quite different between the one for responsible Principal Immigrants and the one for all Principal Immigrants. As we previously discussed, the FSUSB Principals is more than 75% of the overall Principal Immigrant population. Therefore, this FSUSB Principal population plays a significant role in reducing the overall values of Phase 2 net *IUM*s.

From Table 8-6, we can see that the trend of the Phase 2 net *IUM* has increased over the last three decades. Such a trend is significant, especially because the net increase in Phase 2 net *IUM* of LFM Children has been faster than that of LFM Spouses. This implies that more family dependents are joining their Principal Immigrants as part of the chain migration process, with the power of the chaining effect. In another words, the multiplier effect of chain migration has increased in strength over the last three decades.

---

[55] Again, this is acceptable for this research because I am looking for the minimum Immigration Multiplier effect. By presenting the diluted values of *Phase 2 net IUM*, we can guarantee the measurement of the minimum impact of chain migration.

CHAPTER 9

Chain Migration Phase 3: Sponsoring Exempt Family Members

Only three types of foreign nationals sponsor immigrants to the United States: non-family sponsorship (employment or government sponsorship), family member sponsorship as "resident aliens" (the official term for "permanent residents" or "Green Card" holders), or U.S. citizen sponsorship. The non-family sponsorship is the source of the migration chain, as discussed in Chapter 6. Chapters 7 and 8 discussed the sponsorship of family members by those Principal Immigrants whose legal status is "resident aliens.' In this chapter, the focus is on the sponsorship patterns of U.S. citizens.

The *exempt family member*, or *immediate relatives of U.S. citizens* (defined by U.S. Citizenship and Immigration Services (USCIS)), are defined as spouses, unmarried children under 21, and parents of U.S. citizens. In this chapter, we will study these three types of exempt family members of U.S. citizens and understand their role in the chain migration process.

FOREIGN SPOUSES OF NATURALIZED U.S. CITIZENS

Characteristics of Foreign Spouses of Naturalized U.S. Citizens (FSUSN Immigrants)

Marrying a U.S. citizen is another way of obtaining permanent residence in the United States, and this group of immigrants would have no quota limit per U.S. immigration law. Those foreign immigrants who are sponsored by U.S. citizens are called *Foreign Spouses of U.S. Citizens.* As we know, there are two different types of U.S. citizens: U.S.-born and naturalized, the latter having been an immigrant to the U.S. As defined in Chapter 6, *Foreign Spouses of U.S. Born Citizens,* or *FSUSB Principals,* are Principal Immigrants. Here, we are introducing another group of foreign spouses: *Foreign Spouses of Naturalized U.S. Citizens,* or *FSUSN Immigrants,* who are actually considered derived family immigrants (instead of *Principal Immigrants*) sponsored by family members who are *naturalized U.S. citizens.*

Figure 9-1 shows the USCIS data on all foreign spouses of naturalized U.S. citizens from 1972 through 1997.

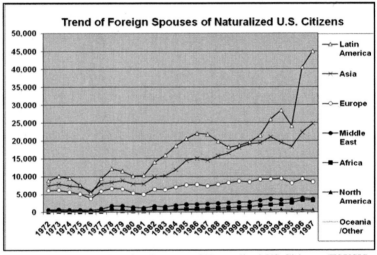

Figure 9-1 Trend of Foreign Spouses of Naturalized US Citizens (FSUSN)

Further calculations show that the total number of foreigners who marry U.S. citizens has been increasing; the average annual number of immigrant spouses of U.S. citizens in 1990s more than doubled the 1970s number, as shown in Table 9-1.

Table 9-1 shows that Latin America sends the most FSUSN immigrants to the U.S. Its total number is almost as large as that of Asia and Europe combined. Asia is sends the next largest number. Latin America and Asia combined account for almost three quarters of all FSUSN immigrants. At the same time, there have been no significant changes in immigrants from Europe and North America.

Table 9-1 Foreign Spouses of Naturalized U.S. Citizens by Region

Year	TOTAL	Latin Am.	Asia	Europe	Middle East	Africa	North Am.	OC
	100.00%	42.77%	31.56%	16.88%	4.82%	2.50%	1.15%	0.32%
Total	1,096,093	468,790	345,942	184,970	52,873	27,367	12,639	3,512
1972	23,444	8,780	7,312	6,070	600	149	448	85
1973	25,497	10,032	7,895	6,174	699	187	420	90
1974	23,537	9,481	7,226	5,624	595	143	384	84
1975	20,995	7,568	7,092	5,096	609	141	405	84
1976	15,812	5,247	5,793	3,843	502	120	260	47
1977	24,743	9,420	7,879	5,902	841	182	436	83
1978	29,969	12,131	8,243	6,616	1,677	552	638	112
1979	29,651	11,494	8,830	6,524	1,681	441	563	118
1980	25,543	10,091	7,876	5,371	1,319	352	443	91
1981	24,987	10,277	7,849	4,991	1,107	283	393	87
1982	32,991	13,994	9,884	6,410	1,595	515	491	102
1983	34,966	15,917	10,152	6,277	1,469	551	474	126
1984	40,568	18,522	11,831	7,028	1,827	693	523	144
1985	46,224	20,534	14,393	7,567	2,105	830	622	173
1986	48,417	22,013	14,995	7,684	2,145	856	557	167
1987	47,329	21,711	14,450	7,300	2,277	908	526	157
1988	47,372	19,774	15,705	7,732	2,395	1,104	486	176
1989	47,327	18,138	16,518	8,203	2,562	1,186	531	189
1990	49,958	18,616	18,013	8,609	2,694	1,323	528	175
1991	51,851	19,603	18,979	8,398	2,765	1,458	499	149
1992	55,653	21,391	19,338	9,153	3,333	1,812	516	110
1993	62,517	25,973	20,969	9,170	3,686	2,036	521	162
1994	63,580	28,481	19,430	9,376	3,380	2,162	574	177
1995	57,235	24,082	18,292	8,115	3,476	2,598	471	201
1996	80,235	40,533	22,285	9,320	3,909	3,444	507	237
1997	85,692	44,987	24,713	8,417	3,625	3,341	423	186
Note	Latin Am = Latin America North Am = North America OC = Oceania and Others							

Figure 9-2 shows the top 10 countries that send FSUSN Immigrants. Mexico ranks number 1, with more than 180,000. The Philippines is second, with more than 140,000. The Dominican Republic, Russia, and China tie for third, with similar totals (between 60,000 and 80,000). The top 10 countries sending FSUSN to the U.S. are mostly Latin American and Asian.

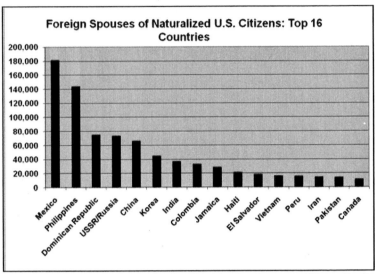

Figure 9-2 Top 16 Countries for Sending Foreign Spouses of Naturalized U.S. Citizens

Phase 3 Multiplier Effect: Foreign Spouses of Naturalized U.S. Citizens

Table 9-2 shows the regional variations of the calculated values of the chain migration unification phase 3 net multiplier of foreign spouses of naturalized U.S. citizens from 1972-1997. There are two different sets of the Phase 3 net multiplier values. One is the original values that are calculated from the only responsible ERI and GSI immigrants; the other is the standardized values that are calculated from all Principal Immigrants combined (including the FSUSB Principals, who are not considered to be responsible for the FSUSN Immigrants). Therefore, as expected, the original Phase 3 net multiplier of FSUSN Immigrants is much higher than the standardized Phase 3 net multiplier of FSUSN immigrants. The FSUSB Principals cause this major difference because they reduce the value of the standard Phase 3 net multiplier (as it does in calculating the standard Phase 1 and 2 net multipliers). Because of this contributing factor, we can conclude that the greater the number of FSUSB principals, the larger the differences between the two values. Therefore, it is obvious that the most significant differences show up for North America and Oceania, because of the existence of the very high volume of FSUSB principals for these two regions.

Table 9-2 Chain Migration Phase 3 Net Multiplier of Foreign Spouses of Naturalized U.S. Citizens by Region

Region	Phase-Specific Net Multiplier of Foreign Spouses of Naturalized U.S. Citizens (Using Responsible Principal Immigrants Only)	Standardized Phase 3 Net Multiplier of Foreign Spouses of Naturalized U.S. Citizens (For All Principal Immigrants)	Differences Between the Two Sets of Multipliers
Latin America	0.43	0.25	0.18
Asia	0.32	0.24	0.08
Middle East	0.38	0.21	0.17
Europe	0.28	0.18	0.10
Africa	0.24	0.12	0.12
Oceania /Other	0.33	0.08	0.25
North America	0.21	0.08	0.13
Total	0.35	0.22	0.13
Note:	*The responsible Principal Immigrants are ERI Principals and GSI Principals. By definition, FSUSB principals (who are sponsored by U.S.-born citizens) are not responsible for Phase 3 FSUSN immigrants. Therefore, we have two sets of multipliers: one calculated using responsible Principal Immigrants, the other using all Principal Immigrants as the standardized calculation.*		
	The differences between these two sets of multiplier values indicate the impact of the total volume of FSUSB immigrants. The smaller the FSUSB principal population is, the less the difference will be (as in the case of Asia). The larger the FSUSB principal population, the larger the differences will be (as in the case of Oceania/Other).		

Comparing all the regions, we can see that Latin America leads in sending FSUSN immigrants to the U.S.—for every two non-FSUSB principal (either ERI or GSI) from Latin America, there will be almost one FSUSN sponsored. For Asia, the Middle East, and Oceania about one FSUSN immigrant will be sponsored for every three non-FSUSB principal. For Africa and Europe, every four non-FSUSB principal will bring about one FSUSN immigrant and one in five non-FSUSB principals will bring a FSUSN immigrant.

Table 9-3 Phase 3 Net Multiplier of Foreign Spouses of Naturalized U.S. Citizens by Top Countries

Year	Phase-Specific Net Multiplier of Foreign Spouses of Naturalized U.S. Citizens (For Responsible Principal Immigrants Only)	Standardized Phase 3 Net Multiplier of Foreign Spouses of Naturalized U.S. Citizens (For All Principal Immigrants)	Multiplier Differences Between the Two Sets of Multipliers
1972	0.19	0.14	0.05
1973	0.23	0.16	0.07
1974	0.21	0.15	0.06
1975	0.17	0.13	0.04
1976	0.17	0.13	0.04
1977	0.17	0.13	0.04
1978	0.19	0.14	0.05
1979	0.44	0.24	0.21
1980	0.26	0.15	0.11
1981	0.22	0.14	0.09
1982	0.28	0.17	0.11
1983	0.43	0.22	0.21
1984	0.56	0.27	0.30
1985	0.56	0.27	0.29
1986	0.58	0.28	0.29
1987	0.37	0.22	0.15
1988	0.40	0.23	0.16
1989	0.50	0.27	0.22
1990	0.42	0.26	0.16
1991	0.41	0.26	0.15
1992	0.36	0.24	0.12
1993	0.32	0.23	0.09
1994	0.43	0.28	0.15
1995	0.40	0.27	0.13
1996	0.50	0.32	0.18
1997	0.67	0.39	0.28
Total	0.35	0.22	0.13
Note	*The responsible Principal Immigrants are ERI Principals and GSI Principals. By definition, FSUSB principals are not responsible for Phase 3 FSUSN immigrants.*		

Table 9-3 shows the historical trend of the Phase 3 net multiplier of foreign spouses of naturalized U.S. citizens from 1972 to 1997. It is noticeable that the phase-specific net multiplier began to increase significantly after the 1980s. This could reflect the lag factor of those immigrants who migrated to the U.S. after the 1965-era, who became

U.S. citizens through naturalization. They settled in the U.S. and wanted to marry and sponsor their foreign-born spouses, who would share the same culture and social values as their own. As more and more immigrants settled in the U.S., the demand for foreign-born spouses picked up. This trend continued in the 1990s.

The third column in Table 9-3, which shows the differences between the phase-specific net multipliers and the standardized net multipliers, confirms this trend and provides some more information. As we know, when the differences are greater, the FSUSM principals have had more impact, and this begins to show in the 1980s. This may have two implications: one is the impact of globalization, which has resulted in an increase in interracial marriage and which brings a greater number of foreign spouses for U.S.-born citizens. Another is the continuing impact of the chain migration multiplier effect, which is the result of migration that took place a few generations before, in which the descendents of immigrant families marry spouses of their own ethnic backgrounds, whom they must sponsor..

MINOR CHILDREN OF U.S. CITIZENS

Characteristics of Minor Children of U.S. Citizens

Table 9-4 shows a strong migration pattern of *Minor Children of U.S. Citizens* (*MC Immigrants*). Latin America and Asia are the two regions that are responsible for sending about 81.5% of the *MC* Immigrants. At the same time, Europe takes about 9.5% of the share, and the remaining 10% comes from the other regions (Africa, the Middle East, North America, and Oceania).

If we examine the top 10 countries sending *MC* Immigrants (See Figure 9-3), we see that Mexico, the Philippines, and the Dominican Republic dominate this category. Among the top three, Mexico contributes about 50,000 more MC than the Philippines, which is in second place. The combined total of all *MC* Immigrants from Mexico, the Philippines, and the Dominican Republic is about three-quarter of the total contribution from the top 10 countries.

We can also see that Jamaica, Canada, and Russia rank 4th, 5th and 6th respectively. They each contributed 20,000 to 28,000. Colombia, Vietnam, Korea, and China each contributed 14,000 to 16,000.

Table 9-4 Trend of Minor Children of U.S. Citizens By Region

Year	TOTAL	Latin Am	Asia	Europe	North Am	Middle East	Africa	OC
	100.00%	54.65%	26.94%	9.43%	3.05%	2.96%	2.35%	0.61%
Total	772,776	422,343	208,221	72,879	23,566	22,898	18,166	4,703
1972	18,651	9,747	5,008	2,629	721	333	73	140
1973	20,519	11,296	5,345	2,634	697	331	106	110
1974	19,700	10,974	5,131	2,568	645	185	91	106
1975	17,158	8,730	5,092	2,147	705	272	91	121
1976	12,280	5,516	4,122	1,682	508	285	84	83
1977	17,109	8,101	4,879	2,557	877	350	156	189
1978	20,003	10,770	4,826	2,581	1,077	378	195	176
1979	21,557	11,578	5,515	2,519	986	574	189	196
1980	21,768	11,858	5,659	2,436	848	572	219	176
1981	21,917	11,424	6,287	2,489	794	558	200	165
1982	22,759	11,846	6,549	2,504	877	565	243	175
1983	23,430	12,239	6,862	2,495	854	549	237	194
1984	24,042	12,231	7,259	2,607	876	605	274	190
1985	27,992	14,017	8,985	2,783	998	703	286	220
1986	30,723	16,122	9,509	2,694	922	832	420	224
1987	30,939	16,689	9,159	2,618	884	876	510	203
1988	31,806	17,087	9,302	2,617	1,001	1,015	559	225
1989	34,420	18,629	9,815	2,789	918	1,346	672	251
1990	39,213	20,762	11,620	3,004	1,073	1,679	831	244
1991	39,214	20,253	12,106	3,273	981	1,395	1,011	195
1992	36,116	17,506	10,841	3,485	1,131	1,785	1,160	208
1993	39,145	20,197	11,351	3,494	1,177	1,400	1,343	183
1994	39,989	23,012	9,710	3,453	1,158	1,063	1,421	172
1995	41,132	24,456	8,963	3,239	947	1,597	1,798	132
1996	55,657	34,862	11,183	3,896	989	1,693	2,824	210
1997	65,537	42,441	13,143	3,686	922	1,957	3,173	215
Note	Latin Am = Latin America North Am = North America OC = Oceania and Others							

Phase 3 Multiplier Effect: Minor Children of U.S. Citizens: The Results

Table 9-5 shows the regional variations of the calculated values of the Phase 3 net multipliers of *MC* Immigrants from 1972-1997. I ranked each region by the values of the Phase 3 net multiplier. As the data shows, Latin America is the top region bringing *MC* Immigrants (i.e. minor children of U.S. citizens). For every four Principal Immigrants from the Latin America region, about one *MC* immigrant will also be admitted. Please note that all Principal Immigrants (whether ERI, GSI or FSUSB) are responsible for *MC* immigrants.

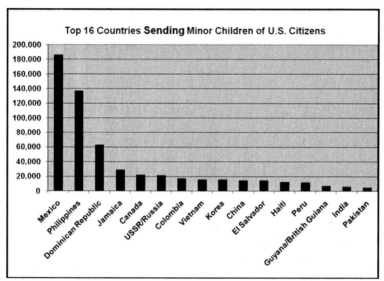

Figure 9-3 Top 16 Countries Sending Minor Children of U.S. Citizens

Table 9-5 Regional Variations of Phase 3 IUM of MC Immigrants

Region	Phase 3 Net Multiplier of Minor Children of U.S. Citizens
Latin America	0.23
North America	0.15
Asia	0.15
Oceania /Other	0.11
Middle East	0.09
Africa	0.08
Europe	0.07
Total	**0.16**

All other regions, except for Latin America, have very low values of Phase 3 net multipliers. For example, the value of the Phase 3 net multiplier of *MC* Immigrants for Asia is 0.15, the same as for North America, which means that one out of every 6 to 7 Asian or North American Principal Immigrants[56] would sponsor one *MC* immigrant (after they acquire the U.S. citizenship).

---

[56] Regardless of the type of Principal Immigrants (ERI, GSI, or FSUSB Principal)

Table 9-6 Trend of Phase 3 IUM of MC Immigrants

Year	Chain Migration Phase 3 Net Multiplier of Minor Children of U.S. Citizens (All Principal Immigrants Are Re)
1972	0.11
1973	0.13
1974	0.13
1975	0.11
1976	0.10
1977	0.09
1978	0.09
1979	0.17
1980	0.13
1981	0.12
1982	0.12
1983	0.15
1984	0.16
1985	0.16
1986	0.18
1987	0.14
1988	0.16
1989	0.20
1990	0.20
1991	0.19
1992	0.16
1993	0.14
1994	0.17
1995	0.19
1996	0.22
1997	0.30
Total	**0.16**
Notes:	*Unlike the case of foreign spouses of naturalized U.S. citizens, the foreign spouses of U.S.-born citizens are also responsible for sponsoring this group of immigrants. Therefore, the phase-specific multiplier is the same as the standardized Phase 3 Multiplier for minor children of U.S. citizens.*

Oceania, the Middle East, Africa, and Europe have even lower net multipliers for *MC* Immigrants. Their values range from 0.07 to 0.11. This suggests that there will be about one *MC* immigrant admitted for at least every 10 Principal Immigrants.

If we examine the trend of *MC* Immigrants (see Table 9-6), we can see that over the last three decades, the values of the Phase 3 net multipliers of *MC* immigrants have steadily increased. The 1997 value (0.30) almost tripled the 1972 value (0.11), and it doubled the 1990 value (0.20). This is significant because this trend implies a steady increase of naturalized U.S. citizens Since there are few scenarios for U.S.-born citizens to sponsor minor children, [57] most of the *MC* Immigrants are indeed the dependents of *naturalized U.S. citizens*, who could be any of the following:

- Original Principal Immigrants (ERI, GSI, or FSUSB Principal) who were naturalized later
- Derived family immigrants (family members of the original Principal Immigrants who later become naturalized U.S. Citizens)

PARENTS OF U.S. CITIZENS

Characteristics of Parents of U.S. Citizens

Over the last three decades, we have seen a steady increase of *Parents of U.S. Citizens* (*PUSC*) who immigrate to the U.S. Figure 9-4 shows such a historical trend. It is quite clear from the chart that the overall total of PUSC Immigrants has increased significantly over the last three decades. In total volume, parents of Asian immigrants dominated all regions in the 1970s, 1980s, and most of the 1990s. At the same time, Latin America sent the second largest number of immigrant parents to the U.S. When its volume increased in later 1996 and 1997, it became the region sending the most immigrant parents.

Now, we break down the immigrants by their sending countries. Table 9-7 lists the total number of PUSC Immigrants from all regions from 1972 to 1997. We can clearly see that Asia leads all regions in sending most PUSC Immigrants to the US. The total number accounts for more than 50% of the total number of all of the other regions combined (52.92%).

At the same time, Latin America is the second region in terms of sending the most PUSC Immigrants. It claims more than one quarter of the total number (27.15%).

Compared to Latin America and Asia, Europe is a distant third. The percentage of parents sent by European countries is only about 9% of the total. All of the other regions account for less than 8 %.

---

[57] As discussed in earlier chapters, this research excludes adoptions.

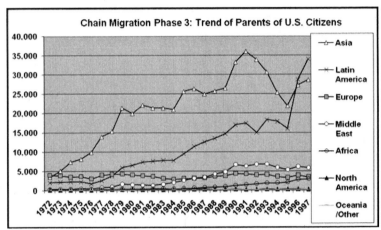

Figure 9-4 Trend of Immigrant Parents Sponsored By U.S. Citizens

Table 9-7 Trend of Parents Sponsored by US Citizens by Region

Year	TOTAL	Asia	Latin Am.	Europe	Middle East	Africa	North Am.	OC
	100.00%	52.92%	27.15%	9.01%	7.73%	2.21%	0.63%	0.34%
Total	1,052,563	557,031	285,736	94,884	81,367	23,310	6,648	3,587
1972	10,040	3,474	2,027	3,917	307	89	180	46
1973	11,655	5,053	2,186	3,812	328	71	141	64
1974	13,758	7,362	2,309	3,461	325	102	144	55
1975	14,789	8,111	2,250	3,630	462	116	149	71
1976	15,302	9,843	1,756	2,960	419	132	134	58
1977	21,696	13,927	2,562	3,946	751	210	228	72
1978	24,951	15,341	3,776	4,154	958	317	291	114
1979	33,908	21,419	5,889	4,181	1,664	382	271	102
1980	32,805	19,965	6,550	4,021	1,541	378	257	93
1981	35,468	22,161	7,366	3,826	1,399	358	245	113
1982	34,701	21,392	7,584	3,612	1,289	437	260	127
1983	34,739	21,419	7,802	3,075	1,631	459	208	145
1984	34,563	20,996	7,754	2,902	2,074	419	263	155
1985	41,723	25,665	9,467	3,021	2,610	510	297	153
1986	45,148	26,381	11,356	3,143	3,176	620	308	164
1987	45,448	24,997	12,547	3,227	3,437	767	306	167
1988	48,513	25,782	13,498	3,581	4,265	891	282	214
1989	51,276	26,539	14,649	3,762	4,847	988	286	205
1990	63,067	33,277	16,986	4,296	6,697	1,297	313	201
1991	65,995	36,080	17,445	4,233	6,300	1,479	268	190
1992	61,793	33,953	15,014	3,949	6,754	1,661	283	179
1993	62,192	30,663	18,294	4,076	6,803	1,878	312	166
1994	55,177	25,408	17,893	3,531	5,961	1,929	289	166
1995	49,147	21,897	16,020	3,258	5,347	2,119	307	199
1996	69,400	27,276	28,742	3,869	6,173	2,811	351	178
1997	75,309	28,650	34,014	3,441	5,849	2,890	275	190

Table 9-8 Net Gain of Parents Sponsored by US Citizens By Region

Time Period	TOTAL		Asia		Latin America		Europe	
	Total	Annual % Gain	Total	Annual % Gain	Total	Annual % Gain	Total	Annual % Gain
1972 ~1979	18,262		10,566		2,844		3,758	
1980 ~1989	40,438	121%	23,530	123%	9,857	247%	3,417	-9%
1990 ~1997	62,760	55%	29,651	26%	20,551	108%	3,832	12%

Now, we will examine the trend of the top regions. As in Table 9-7, we see that, during the last thirty years, Asia has led in sending PUSC Immigrants, and its annual total more than doubled in the 1980s. At the same time, Latin America increased its annual total of the PUSC Immigrants by 246% in the 1980s, and it doubled that number in the 1990s. Comparing Tables 9-7 and 9-8, we see that there was a surge of PUSC Immigrants from Latin America in the late 1990s (1996 and 1997). This could be the indirect result of the IRCA of 1986. The possible scenario here is that those immigrants became naturalized US citizens in the late 1990s so that they could sponsor their parents. As a result, we see the surge.

Meanwhile, there is no significant change in the total of PUSC immigrants from Europe. Over the last three decades, the average annual total of PUSC Immigrants from Europe has been between 3.4 and 3.8 thousand. Since the 1970s, both the Middle East and Africa have dramatically increased their annual totals of PUSC Immigrants, although their combined annual total in the 1990s is less than one-third of Asia's. However, the rates of increase of these two regions have been the most significant: both have increased their annual totals of PUSC Immigrants in the 1990s by tenfold over their annual totals in the 1970s.

Figure 9-5 shows the top countries that sent PUSC Immigrants to the U.S. Among them, we see that Asian and Latin American countries took 8 out of 10 spots—Iran and Russia are the only two other countries on the list.

The Philippines and China sent the most—over the last thirty years, they sent more than 300,000 PUSC Immigrants. Mexico (3rd) and India (4th) sent almost 90,000 PUSC Immigrants. Korea is a close fifth, with a total number of 40,000. The last five countries contributed from 17,000 to 40,000 PUSC Immigrants over the same period.

Here, we can conclude that Asian immigrants are most likely to sponsor their parents once they become naturalized U.S. citizens. However, we would like to measure how likely it would be for that to happen. We would also like to understand how likely it would be for immigrants from other regions to sponsor PUSC Immigrants. The way to measure that is to calculate the chain migration unification phase 3 for PUSC Immigrants. The following discussion will focus on that.

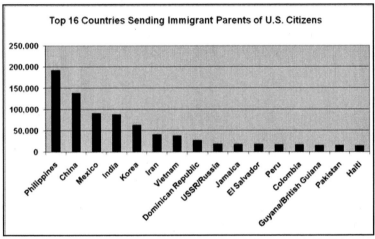

Figure 9-5 Top 16 Countries Sending Immigrant Parents of US Citizens

Phase 3 Net Multiplier Effect: Parents of U.S. Citizens

The calculated values of the Phase 3 net multiplier of parents of U.S. citizens from 1972-1997 are listed in Table 9-9. From the ranking by the values of the Phase 3 net multiplier, we see that Asia and the Middle East are the two top regions in terms of the likelihood of sponsoring their parents once they become U.S. citizens. For every three Principal Immigrants (whether ERI, GSI, or FSUSB) from Asia or the Middle East, about one parent will be sponsored to migrate to the U.S.

Table 9-9 Regional Variations of Phase 3 IUM of PUSC Immigrants

Region	Phase 3 Net Multiplier of Parents of U.S. Citizens
Asia	0.39
Middle East	0.32
Latin America	0.16
Africa	0.10
Europe	0.10
Oceania/Other	0.08
North America	0.04
Total	**0.21**

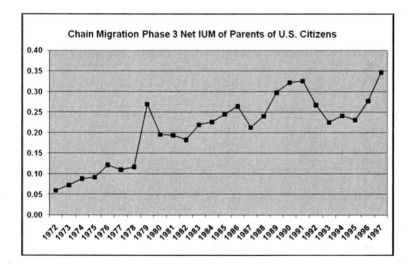

Figure 9-6 Trend of Phase 3 Net Multiplier of Parents of U.S. Citizens

Although it has a very high annual average of PUSC Immigrants, Latin America, ranked only third in its likelihood of sending PUSC Immigrants: each naturalized U.S. citizen on average will sponsor about 0.16 parents.

In the case of Africa or Europe, the ratio of sponsoring parents is about 1 for every 10 Principal Immigrants. For the other two regions (North America and Oceania), the values of the Phase 3 net multiplier are very low (0.04 to 0.08).

It appears that the patterns of the Phase 3 net multiplier of PUSC Immigrants listed here are consistent with our understanding of the cultural differences among these regions. Asia, the Middle East, and Latin America have strong family-oriented cultures, and the norms of these cultures usually favor extended family structures in which children are obligated to take care of parents when they are old. At the same time, Europe, Oceania, and North America represent the Western culture that favors the core family unit, which usually does not include parents.

If we examine the trend (see Figure 9-6), we see that during the last three decades, the overall Phase 3 net multipliers of PUSC Immigrants have steadily increased from 0.06 in 1972 to 0.20 in 1980, to 0.32 in 1990, and to 0.35 in 1997. This is significant, because this implies a steady increase in naturalized U.S. citizenship. This is similar to the case of *MC* Immigrants that we discussed earlier. Since all PUSC Immigrants (Parents of U.S. citizens) are also the dependents of *naturalized U.S. citizens*, they could be any of the following:

- Original Principal Immigrants (ERI, GSI or FSUSB) who were naturalized later;
- Derived family immigrants, who were sponsored by family members, and later became naturalized U.S. citizens.

In next chapter, we will discuss the phase 4 of chain migration, which focuses on sponsoring non-exempt family members of U.S. citizens.

CHAPTER 10

Chain Migration Phase 4: Sponsoring Non-Exempt Family Members

In this chapter, I will study non-exempt family members of U.S. citizens. According to USCIS, we have the following categories:
- Adult Children of U.S. Citizens or AC Immigrants
  - Married Adult Children of U.S. Citizens or MAC Immigrants
  - Unmarried Adult Children of U.S. Citizens or UAC Immigrants
- Siblings of U.S. Citizens or SIB Immigrants

ADULT CHILDREN OF U.S. CITIZENS

Characteristics of Adult Children of U.S. Citizens

As defined by the immigration laws, U.S. citizens can sponsor their children to immigrate to the United States, but the ages of those children are quite important. U.S. immigration laws set aside a special category for minor children of U.S. citizens (in the same group as the spouses or parents of U.S. citizens) so that they can obtain immigration visas without any numeric limit (under the exempt status, see Chapter 9). At the same time, USCIS set up two separate categories for adult children who are over 21: one is for those who are unmarried (Unmarried Adult Children), and the other is for those who are married (Married Adult Children). In most cases, the sponsors are not U.S.-born citizens, but naturalized citizens who immigrated to the United

States some years ago. There are few scenarios in which U.S.-born citizens have children bearing non-U.S. passports. Since the sponsors come from other countries, it is common that they left their children behind when they immigrated to the United States, and it is natural for them to sponsor their children to join them when they have the opportunity. Figure 10-1 shows the historical immigration trend of both married and unmarried children of U.S. citizens.

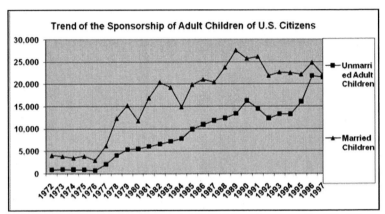

Figure 10-1 Trend of Immigrant Adult Children Sponsored by US Citizens

We can see here that the overall immigration trend of married and unmarried children of US citizens indicates that the volume is steadily increasing. The largest jump was in the 1980s, when the annual average increased to 240% of the number in the 1970s. In the 1990s, the annual average increased another 38% of the total in the 1980s.

Figure 10-2 shows the trend of the AC Immigrants of all regions by year, and Table 10-1 shows the net gain of the average annual total of AC Immigrants over the last three decades for the top regions.[58]

We see that the leading regions sending children of U.S. citizens are Latin America, Asia, and Europe. However, the magnitude of each region is quite different.

Latin America, sending the most, accounts for almost 43% of the total, which is almost all of the AC immigrants from Asia and Europe

---

[58] Table 7-15 omits North America, Africa, and Oceania because their average annual totals were all below 1,000.

combined. If we examine the historical trend for Latin America, we will see that its volume has increased since the late 1970s, and it has maintained its lead for 20 years.

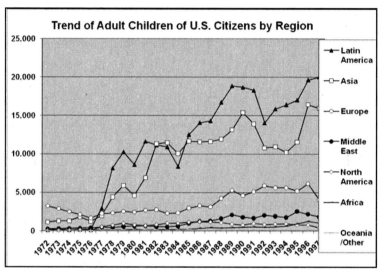

Figure 10-2 Immigrant Adult Children of US Citizens by Region

Table 10-1 Annual Average of Adult Children of U.S. Citizens

	TOTAL		Latin America		Asia		Europe		Middle East	
	100.00%		43.09%		34.05%		13.87%		4.30%	
Total	671,276		289,250		228,589		93,117		28,842	
Year	Annual Avg	% Gain	Annual Avg	% Gain	Annual Avg	% Gain	Annual Avg	% Gain	Annual Avg	% Gain
1972 ~1979	8,438		2,750		2,368		2,433		379	
1980 ~1989	28,701	240%	12,720	363%	10,436	341%	3,135	29%	1,016	168%
1990 ~1997	39,595	38%	17,506	38%	13,161	26%	5,289	69%	1,957	93%

Asia's pattern is similar to Latin America's in terms of its dramatic increase in volume since the late 1970s. If combine the total from Latin America with Asia's (35%), we will see that these two countries claim three-quarters of the total number of AC Immigrants. Further calculations reveal that the net gain for the average annual total of AC from the 1970s to the 1990s is 637% for Latin America and 556% for Asia.

At the same time, Europe has steadily increased its volume of AC Immigrants. In the 1990s, it doubled its average annual 1970s total. Compared to Latin America and Asia, the gain in Europe was not as dramatic, yet it is still remarkable.

The Middle East shows a pattern of increase similar to Latin America and Asia, except that its jump in the 1980s was not as significant as that of Latin America and Asia. Its average annual total of AC Immigrants in the 1990s was more than five-times of its value in the 1970s.

At the same time, Europe steadily increased, yet not as dramatically as we have seen in Latin America and Asia. In the 1990s, it had gained only 218% of its 1970s total.

Mexico, the Philippines, and China are the top three countries sponsoring married and unmarried adult children of U.S. citizens to immigrate to the United States. (See Figure 10-3.) Mexico's total of AC Immigrants exceeded 100,000; the Philippines' total was more than 90,000; and the AC Immigrants from China were about 76,000. The other countries sent fewer than 35,000 AC Immigrants to the United States.

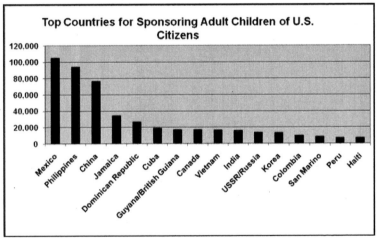

Figure 10-3 Top Countries for Sponsoring Adult Children of U.S. Citizens

Out of the top 16 countries, there are only two Western countries (Canada and Russia). The rest are mainly from Latin America and

Asia. These 16 countries combined contribute a total of almost a half million (0.48 million) AC Immigrants to the United States.

Table 10-2 Phase 4 Net Multiplier for Adult Children of U.S. Citizens

Year of Admission	Chain Migration *Phase 4 Net IUM*		
	Phase 4 Net Multiplier of Unmarried Adult Children of U.S. Citizens	Phase 4 Net Multiplier of Married Adult Children of U.S. Citizens	Phase 4 Net Multiplier of Adult Children of U.S. Citizens (Unmarried and Married Combined)
1972	0.01	0.02	0.03
1973	0.01	0.02	0.03
1974	0.01	0.02	0.03
1975	0.01	0.02	0.03
1976	0.01	0.02	0.03
1977	0.01	0.03	0.04
1978	0.02	0.06	0.08
1979	0.04	0.12	0.16
1980	0.03	0.07	0.10
1981	0.03	0.09	0.12
1982	0.03	0.11	0.14
1983	0.05	0.12	0.17
1984	0.05	0.10	0.15
1985	0.06	0.12	0.17
1986	0.06	0.12	0.19
1987	0.06	0.10	0.15
1988	0.06	0.12	0.18
1989	0.08	0.16	0.24
1990	0.08	0.13	0.21
1991	0.07	0.13	0.20
1992	0.05	0.09	0.15
1993	0.05	0.08	0.13
1994	0.06	0.10	0.16
1995	0.08	0.10	0.18
1996	0.09	0.10	0.19
1997	0.10	0.10	0.20
Total	**0.05**	**0.09**	**0.13**

Phase 4 Net Multiplier Effect: Adult Children of U.S. Citizens

Table 10-2 lists the calculated values of the annual Phase 4 net multiplier of AC immigrants. It is very clear that the unification Phase 4 multiplier effect was insignificant in the early 1970s. However, the effect began to show in the 1980s, because the values of the Phase 4 net multiplier for the adult children of U.S. citizens started to pick up. The value peaked in the late 1980s and 1990s.

Table 10-3 shows the calculated values of the Phase 4 net multiplier of AC immigrants from 1972-1997. Immigrants from Asia and Latin America are the most likely to sponsor AC immigrants. The net multiplier rate for Principal Immigrants (whether ERI, GSI, or FSUSB) from Asia or Latin America is about 0.16

North America, the Middle East, Europe, and Oceania have similar Phase 4 net multiplier values (from 0.08 to 0.12). Africa has the lowest value (0.04).

From the data, we see that all regions (except Africa) have the same sponsorship pattern: the net multipliers of married adult children of U.S. citizens are consistently higher than that of unmarried adult children. In other words, most sponsored adult children are married. This is important, because it implies the potential multiplier effect. Although the actual admitted immigrants in this category include adult children, their spouses, and their children, this pattern suggests that the migration chain does not stop here. These married children, their spouses, and their children can continue to sponsor their relatives. In this sense, the chain migration unification phase 4 net unification multipliers illustrate the ***minimum*** multiplier effect.

Table 10-3 Phase 4 Net Multiplier of Adult Children of U.S. Citizens

Region	Phase 4 Net Multiplier of Unmarried Adult Children of U.S. Citizens	Phase 4 Net Multiplier of Married Adult Children of U.S. Citizens	Phase 4 Net Multiplier of Adult Children of U.S. Citizens (Married & Unmarried Combined)
Asia	0.05	0.11	0.16
Latin America	0.07	0.09	0.16
North America	0.04	0.08	0.12
Middle East	0.03	0.09	0.11
Europe	0.02	0.08	0.09
Oceania/Other	0.01	0.06	0.08
Africa	0.02	0.02	0.04
Total	**0.05**	**0.09**	**0.13**

SIBLINGS OF U.S. CITIZENS

Characteristics of Siblings of U.S. Citizens

Siblings of U.S. Citizens, or *SIB Immigrants,* is another major category in the chain migration process. Similar to adult children of U.S. citizens, siblings are also in the non-exempt category of family members of U.S. citizens. Figure 10-4 shows the historical trend of the total number of immigrants who came to the U.S. as the siblings of U.S. citizens. We can see that the peak was actually in late 1970s and early 1980s.

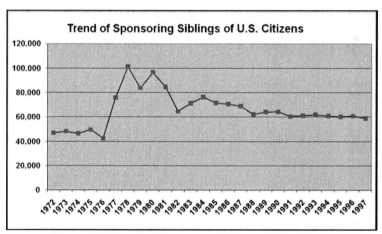

Figure 10-4 Trend of Sponsoring Siblings of U.S. Citizens

Over the last three decades, the average annual number of immigrants in this particular category has not changed much. In fact, the 1990s data is at the same level as it was in the 1970s, and the overall number of sponsored siblings of U.S. citizens has been about 60,000 annually.[59]

---

[59] This could be misleading, because there is a long waiting period for the sponsored siblings to obtain visas. According to the May 2007 Visa Bulletin issued by U.S. State Department (2007), the applications being considered were for those who applied for visas under the 4th preference in 1996 for

Regional comparisons will show the differences among these regions in sponsoring SIB Immigrants. Figure 10-5 shows that Asia sponsors the largest number of SIB immigrants, accounting for about 50% of all siblings admitted to the U.S. during the last three decades. At the same time, Latin America claims one quarter of the overall total number of SIB immigrants. One very interesting observation here is that in the 1970s Europe was the leading region sponsoring SIB immigrants, when the total number of European applicants was well above the total number from all of the other regions combined (1972-1974). In the early 1980s, however, the sponsorship of SIB immigrants from Europe dropped significantly, and it continued to drop to its lowest point ever in the 1990s.

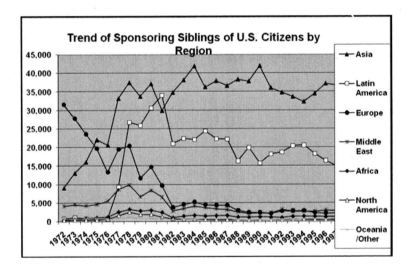

Figure 10-5 Immigrant Siblings Sponsored by US Citizens by Region

most countries. (Hence, the waiting period is about 11 years.) Some countries have longer waiting periods: 12 years for Chinese applicants, 13 years for Mexican applicants, and 22 years for applicants from the Philippines.

Table 10-4 provides quantitative comparisons on regional differences. From the data,[60] we can see that Asia, the leading region sponsoring SIB Immigrants, sponsored a large number in the 1970s, which increased about 60% in 1980s. In the 1990s, the level was almost the same as it was in the 1980s (with an insignificant drop of 2.68%).

Table 10-4 Siblings of U.S. Citizens: Net Gain by Region

	TOTAL		Asia		Latin America		Europe		Middle East	
	100.00%		49.05%		25.91%		14.23%		6.43%	
Total	1,714,977		841,112		444,381		243,993		110,313	
Year	Annual Avg	% Gain	Annual Avg	% Gain	Annual Avg	% Gain	Annual Avg	% Gain	Annual Avg	% Gain
1972 ~1979	61,868		23,160		8,260		20,952		6,038	
1980 ~1989	73,100	18%	36,875	59%	23,523	185%	5,672	-73%	4,032	-33%
1990 ~1997	61,130	-16%	35,886	-3%	17,884	-24%	2,458	-57%	2,711	-33%

Latin America is a very interesting case. It began in the 1970s with a very low annual average (8,260, almost one-third of the Asia counterpart), significantly increased in the 1980s (185%), and then declined in the 1990s (24%).

Over the last three decades, the sponsorship of SIB immigrants from Europe and the Middle East has not increased. Europe had a significant drop in the 1980s (73%), and the annual average total of sponsored SIB immigrants in the 1990s was merely 11.7% of its 1970s total.

With all of the regional variations examined, we can now identify the top countries that sponsor SIB immigrants. Figure 10-6 shows the top 10 countries in this category. Again, three Asian countries (China, India, and Korea) lead the pack. From 1972 to 1997, immigrants from China have sponsored the most *SIB* Immigrants (about 250,000). India, which ranks number two, has contributed about 200,000 *SIB* Immigrants. Korea, which ranks third, sponsored about 180,000 *SIB* Immigrants.

---

[60] Please note that I did not include North America and Oceania, because the annual average total of Siblings of U.S. citizens for these two regions was less than 1,000.

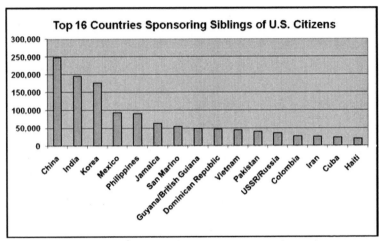

Figure 10-6 Siblings of U.S. Citizens: Top 16 Countries

Mexico and the Philippines, which rank fourth and fifth, respectively, sponsor about 90,000 SIB Immigrants. The other top 10 countries sponsor about 50,000 SIB Immigrants.

As discussed earlier, the net volume does not quite reflect the true migration pattern. In order for us to understand the multiplier effect, we must calculate the multiplier values. In the following section, we will re-examine the sponsorship pattern of the SIB immigrants in terms of multipliers and the multiplier effect.

Phase 4 Multiplier Effect: Siblings of U.S. Citizens

The differences among different regions on the values of the Phase 4 net multiplier are quite significant. From Table 10-5, we can see that Asia, the Middle East, and Oceania rank as the top three regions that send SIB Immigrants to the U.S. For Asian immigrants, the multiplier effect is 0.58, which means that there will be at least one sibling sponsored by every two Asian Principal Immigrants.

In the case of Middle East and Oceania, the multiplier effects are about 0.4. Therefore, there will be about two siblings sponsored for every five Middle Eastern or Oceania Principal Immigrants admitted to the U.S.

Relatively speaking, immigrants from Europe and Latin America have lower sponsorship potentials because their Phase 4 net multiplier of siblings is about 0.25. This implies that about every four European or Latin American Principal Immigrants would potentially sponsor one sibling.

Table 10-5 Phase 4 Net Multiplier of Siblings of U.S. Citizens

Region	Siblings of U.S. Citizens
Asia	0.58
Middle East	0.44
Oceania/Other	0.39
Europe	0.26
Latin America	0.24
Africa	0.17
North America	0.12
Total	**0.35**

Africa and North America rank the lowest, because their net multiplier values are from 0.12 to 0.17. Hence, only one sibling will be sponsored for about every seven African or North American Principal Immigrants admitted to the U.S.

The above illustrations of the regional variations of net multiplier have demonstrated the multiplier effects of the chain migration unification phase 4 for sponsoring the SIB Immigrants.

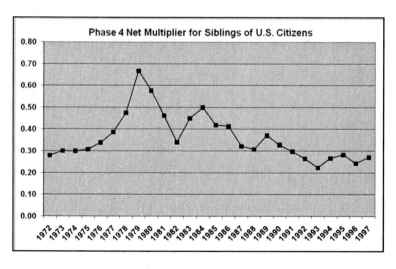

Figure 10-7 Phase 4 of Net Multiplier of Siblings of U.S. Citizens

Figure 10-7 shows the Phase 4 net multiplier for siblings of U.S. citizens, and that chart is very similar to Figure 10-4 (actual numbers). However, this chart is more accurate because it reflects the values of the standardized multipliers. The graph shows the peak in late 1970s and early 1980s at the value of 0.67, the decline during most of the 1980s, then the eventually stabilization at around 0.27 in the 1990s. As discussed in the previous chapters, the demand for sponsoring siblings is real. There have been significant backlogs in processing the sponsorship petitions in USCIS. Such backlogs must have contributed to some of the decline in the values of the net multipliers. Therefore, the net multipliers presented here would only suggest the **minimum** multiplier effect of the chain migration unification phase 4 for sponsoring the SIB immigrants.

Immigration Unification Process Explained

Having studied all phases of the chain migration unification processes (Phases 1-4), we can now examine the complete picture of the chain migration unification process.

Table 11-1 summarizes the immigration distribution of all types of immigrants by year, which will help us understand the distribution trend of the types of immigrants the principals immigrants sponsored over the last three decades.

The distribution patterns suggest that minor children and siblings of U.S. citizens are the top groups in family sponsorship: among the family sponsorships, 18% are for accompanying children (Phase 1), 17% are for later-sponsored minor children, and 16% are for siblings of U.S. citizens (Phase 4). The trends for these three groups, however, are quite different. During the last thirty years, there has been a 64% drop for accompanying children and a decrease of 48% for siblings of U.S. citizens.

Meanwhile, there has been an increase in sponsorship of accompanying spouses, the parents of U.S. citizens, and the adult children of U.S. citizens. There was a 125% increase for accompanying spouses, a 160% jump for parents of U.S. citizens, and a 300% leap for adult children of U.S. citizens over the same period.

Other immigrant spouses (including the later-sponsored spouses and the foreign spouses of naturalized U.S. citizens) did not change significantly during that time.

Table 11-1 Distribution of Family Sponsored Immigrants

Year	Unification Phase 1 Accompanying Family Members		Unification Phase 2 Later-Sponsored Family Members		Unification Phase 3 Exempt Family Members of U.S. Citizens			Unification Phase 4 Non-Exempt Family Members of U.S. Citizens		All Unification Phases Combined All Family Sponsored Immigrants Combined	
	SP	MC	SP	MC	SP	MC	P	AC	SIB	% Total	Number Total
Total	7%	18%	8%	17%	10%	7%	10%	6%	16%	100%	10,513,562
1972	4%	33%	8%	8%	11%	8%	5%	2%	21%	100%	223,007
1973	3%	32%	8%	10%	11%	9%	5%	2%	21%	100%	234,558
1974	4%	30%	8%	11%	10%	9%	6%	2%	20%	100%	227,631
1975	3%	29%	8%	12%	9%	8%	7%	2%	22%	100%	221,066
1976	4%	26%	8%	11%	9%	7%	9%	2%	24%	100%	174,276
1977	3%	23%	9%	13%	9%	6%	8%	3%	27%	100%	280,398
1978	2%	24%	8%	14%	8%	5%	7%	4%	27%	100%	373,876
1979	3%	12%	10%	19%	9%	6%	10%	6%	24%	100%	345,668
1980	3%	16%	10%	20%	7%	6%	9%	5%	25%	100%	380,733
1981	4%	19%	11%	18%	6%	6%	9%	6%	21%	100%	396,576
1982	6%	21%	10%	18%	8%	6%	9%	7%	16%	100%	395,235
1983	6%	15%	10%	20%	9%	6%	9%	7%	18%	100%	386,586
1984	6%	13%	10%	19%	11%	6%	9%	6%	20%	100%	384,795
1985	5%	13%	10%	18%	11%	7%	10%	7%	18%	100%	406,924
1986	5%	13%	9%	18%	12%	7%	11%	8%	17%	100%	415,564
1987	6%	13%	8%	19%	11%	7%	11%	8%	17%	100%	414,871
1988	6%	13%	7%	18%	12%	8%	12%	9%	15%	100%	402,425
1989	7%	14%	7%	19%	11%	8%	12%	9%	15%	100%	439,857
1990	8%	16%	6%	17%	10%	8%	13%	9%	13%	100%	477,592
1991	9%	17%	5%	16%	11%	8%	13%	8%	12%	100%	491,660
1992	14%	23%	7%	14%	9%	6%	10%	6%	10%	100%	597,864
1993	13%	22%	7%	14%	11%	7%	10%	6%	10%	100%	594,474
1994	12%	18%	6%	16%	12%	8%	10%	7%	12%	100%	527,933
1995	10%	15%	8%	21%	11%	8%	9%	7%	11%	100%	530,256
1996	9%	14%	8%	19%	13%	9%	11%	7%	10%	100%	628,721
1997	9%	12%	6%	15%	15%	12%	13%	8%	11%	100%	561,016
Note	SP = Spouses of U.S. Citizens or Legal Immigrants MC = Minor Children of U.S. Citizens or Legal Immigrants PUSC = Parents of U.S. Citizens AC = Adult Children of U.S. Citizens SIB = Siblings of U.S. Citizens										

It is important to understand that the sponsorship of any family member during the chain migration process (as defined in the chain migration model in this study) can be traced back to the Principal Immigrants. This does not mean that the Principal Immigrants are the direct sponsors of all of these family members, except during Phase 1 (for sponsoring accompanying family dependents). All of the family members sponsored during Phases 2, 3, and 4 could be sponsored either by the Principal Immigrants or by other family members (who are relatives of the Principal Immigrants or relatives of other family members, etc.). Therefore, the higher the unification multiplier, the stronger the presence of the migration chain will be.

The sponsorship patterns illustrated in Table 11-2 show the regional variations of all of the different family sponsorship groups. The majority of all family sponsorships from Oceania/Other (31%), the Middle East (22%), and Asia (21%) are for siblings of U.S. citizens. Meanwhile, the majority of family sponsored immigrant groups for Europe (23%), Africa (23%), and North America (31%) are "accompanying children." Latin America is the only region that sponsors a large number of later-sponsored children (25%).

Table 11-2 Distribution of Family Sponsored Immigrants by Region

Year	Unification Phase 1 Accompany-ing Family Members		Unification Phase 2 Later-Sponsored Family Members		Unification Phase 3 Exempt Family Members of U.S. Citizens			Unification Phase 4 Non-Exempt Family Members of U.S. Citizens		All Phases Total
	SP	MC	SP	MC	SP	MC	PUSC	AC	SIB	%
Africa	13%	23%	8%	9%	11%	7%	9%	4%	16%	100%
Asia	8%	18%	7%	13%	9%	5%	14%	6%	21%	100%
Europe	14%	23%	6%	6%	13%	5%	7%	7%	18%	100%
Latin America	3%	16%	10%	25%	11%	10%	7%	7%	11%	100%
Middle East	8%	16%	6%	12%	10%	4%	16%	6%	22%	100%
North America	11%	31%	4%	10%	7%	13%	4%	10%	11%	100%
Oceania /Other	8%	14%	8%	11%	6%	9%	7%	6%	31%	100%
Total	7%	18%	8%	16%	10%	7%	10%	6%	16%	100%
Note	SP = Spouses of U.S. Citizens or Legal Immigrants MC = Minor Children of U.S. Citizens or Legal Immigrants PUSC = Parents of U.S. Citizens AC = Adult Children of U.S. Citizens SIB = Siblings of U.S. Citizens									

With all of these comparisons in percentages, we have a general idea of the distribution of family sponsored immigrants. However, these numbers do not provide us further insight into the mechanism of chain migration. The Immigration Unification Multipliers that I will present next will provide a new look at the same data from a very different angle and give us a real understanding of the chain migration unification process. I want to show that the multiplier effects of the chain migration exist in every phase of the migration process.

CHAIN MIGRATION UNIFICATION PATTERNS: THE TREND

To measure the chain migration family reunification processes clearly, I must calculate the Immigration Unification Multipliers for all four phases so that all of the comparisons will be more meaningful.

Table 11-3 Immigration Unification Multipliers: All Phases Combined

Year	Phase 1 Unification Multiplier — Accompanying Family Immigrants		Phase 2 Unification Multiplier — Later-Sponsored Family Immigrants		Phase 3 Unification Multiplier — Exempt Family Members of U.S. Citizens			Phase 4 Unification Multiplier — Non-Exempt Family Members of U.S. Citizens		Chain Migration Unification Multiplier (All Phases Combined)
	SP	MC	SP	MC	SP	MC	P	AC	SIB	
Total	0.15	0.38	0.17	0.35	0.22	0.16	0.21	0.13	0.35	2.12
1972	0.05	0.44	0.11	0.11	0.14	0.11	0.06	0.03	0.28	1.33
1973	0.05	0.46	0.12	0.14	0.16	0.13	0.07	0.03	0.30	1.46
1974	0.05	0.44	0.12	0.16	0.15	0.13	0.09	0.03	0.30	1.47
1975	0.05	0.39	0.11	0.16	0.13	0.11	0.09	0.03	0.31	1.37
1976	0.05	0.36	0.11	0.15	0.13	0.10	0.12	0.03	0.34	1.39
1977	0.04	0.32	0.13	0.19	0.13	0.09	0.11	0.04	0.39	1.43
1978	0.04	0.42	0.15	0.24	0.14	0.09	0.12	0.08	0.48	1.75
1979	0.08	0.34	0.29	0.53	0.24	0.17	0.27	0.16	0.67	2.75
1980	0.08	0.36	0.22	0.45	0.15	0.13	0.20	0.10	0.58	2.27
1981	0.09	0.42	0.23	0.40	0.14	0.12	0.19	0.12	0.46	2.17
1982	0.12	0.43	0.20	0.38	0.17	0.12	0.18	0.14	0.34	2.08
1983	0.14	0.37	0.24	0.49	0.22	0.15	0.22	0.17	0.45	2.44
1984	0.14	0.34	0.26	0.48	0.27	0.16	0.23	0.15	0.50	2.52
1985	0.12	0.32	0.24	0.44	0.27	0.16	0.24	0.17	0.42	2.39
1986	0.13	0.33	0.22	0.43	0.28	0.18	0.26	0.19	0.41	2.43
1987	0.11	0.25	0.16	0.37	0.22	0.14	0.21	0.15	0.32	1.94
1988	0.11	0.26	0.15	0.36	0.23	0.16	0.24	0.18	0.31	2.00
1989	0.17	0.35	0.18	0.48	0.27	0.20	0.30	0.24	0.37	2.56
1990	0.19	0.38	0.14	0.41	0.26	0.20	0.32	0.21	0.33	2.44
1991	0.23	0.41	0.13	0.38	0.26	0.19	0.33	0.20	0.30	2.43
1992	0.35	0.60	0.19	0.37	0.24	0.16	0.27	0.15	0.26	2.59
1993	0.28	0.47	0.15	0.31	0.23	0.14	0.23	0.13	0.22	2.15
1994	0.27	0.42	0.14	0.36	0.28	0.17	0.24	0.16	0.27	2.31
1995	0.24	0.36	0.21	0.52	0.27	0.19	0.23	0.18	0.28	2.49
1996	0.23	0.34	0.20	0.49	0.32	0.22	0.28	0.19	0.24	2.51
1997	0.23	0.32	0.15	0.37	0.39	0.30	0.35	0.20	0.27	2.58

Note: SP = Spouses of U.S. Citizens or Legal Immigrants
MC = Minor Children of U.S. Citizens or Legal Immigrants
PUSC = Parents of U.S. Citizens
AC = Adult Children of U.S. Citizens
SIB = Siblings of U.S. Citizens

Table 11-3 shows that the overall net unification multipliers have increased from 1.33 in 1972 to 2.58 in 1997. This is significant because this is equivalent to gaining an additional 1.2 family immigrants generated by each Principal Immigrant.

From the detailed listing of values for the net multiplier, we can see that the net multipliers have increased across the board for most of the family sponsored immigrant groups, except for accompanying minor children and siblings of U.S. citizens. Among the groups that have increased the values of the net unification multipliers, parents of U.S. citizens, adult children of U.S. citizens, and accompanying spouses have increased the most significantly. These three groups combined accounted for 0.78 new family immigrants in 1997, a significant jump from the 1972 value (0.14).

The overall pattern suggests that very strong Immigration Multiplier effects can be observed during the chain migration process via sponsoring minor or adult children, parents (of U.S. citizens), and immigrant spouses (including spouses of immigrants, as well as spouses of naturalized U.S. citizens) over the last three decades. It is also clear that since the 1970s for some reason the Immigration Multiplier effect has been weaker for sponsoring siblings of U.S. citizens.[61]

CHAIN MIGRATION UNIFICATION PATTERNS: REGIONAL VARIATIONS

Table 11-4 is important because it ranks all regions in terms of their net unification multiplier values from Phase 1 through Phase 4. It is now possible for us to compare the regional variations using a single indicator.

Asia has the highest value of the net unification multiplier (2.79). This indicates that each Asian Principal Immigrant would be responsible for sponsoring about 2.79 additional immigrants to the U.S., which include 0.66 spouses (0.22+0.20+0.24), 0.94 minor children (0.49+0.37+0.15), 0.16 adult children, 0.39 parents, and 0.58

---

[61] This could be the result of the imposed numerical limit on this visa category, as there is a very long waiting period for anyone who applies for this visa category. The current wait is at least 11 years for most countries, with applicants from some countries waiting longer (e.g., 22 years for the Philippines) (State Department, 2007).

Chain Migration Explained

siblings. Note that the multiplier effects of sponsoring parents of U.S. citizens and siblings of U.S. citizens are the strongest for Asian immigrants. In fact, this sponsorship pattern reflects Asian culture and its traditional family structure.

Table 11-4 Net Immigration Unification Multiplier By Region

Year	Phase 1 Unification Multiplier		Phase 2 Unification Multiplier		Phase 3 Unification Multiplier			Phase 4 Unification Multiplier		Chain Migration Unification Multiplier
	Accompanying Family Immigrants		Later-Sponsored Family Immigrants		Exempt Family Members of U.S. Citizens			Non-Exempt Family Members of U.S. Citizens		(All Unification Phases Combined)
	SP	MC	SP	MC	SP	MC	P	AC	SIB	
Asia	0.22	0.49	0.20	0.37	0.24	0.15	0.39	0.16	0.58	2.79
Latin America	0.06	0.36	0.23	0.56	0.25	0.23	0.16	0.16	0.24	2.25
Middle East	0.17	0.33	0.13	0.24	0.21	0.09	0.32	0.11	0.44	2.03
Europe	0.20	0.33	0.08	0.08	0.18	0.07	0.10	0.09	0.26	1.40
Oceania /Other	0.10	0.18	0.10	0.14	0.08	0.11	0.08	0.08	0.39	1.25
North America	0.12	0.36	0.05	0.11	0.08	0.15	0.04	0.12	0.12	1.14
Africa	0.14	0.24	0.09	0.10	0.12	0.08	0.10	0.04	0.17	1.06
Total	**0.15**	**0.38**	**0.17**	**0.35**	**0.22**	**0.16**	**0.21**	**0.13**	**0.35**	**2.12**
Notes	*SP = Spouses of U.S. Citizens or Legal Immigrants*									
	MC = Minor Children of U.S. Citizens or Legal Immigrants									
	PUSC = Parents of U.S. Citizens									
	AC = Adult Children of U.S. Citizens									
	SIB = Siblings of U.S. Citizens									

Latin America ranks second with its net unification multiplier value being 2.25. The net unification multipliers during most of the chain migration unification phases for Latin American immigrants are very similar to those for Asian immigrants, but Latin America has its own pattern. Some of the phase-specific unification multipliers for Latin American immigrants, in fact, are the highest among all of the regions. These include 1.15 for minor children (0.36+0.56+0.23), 0.48 for later-sponsored spouses and foreign spouses (0.23+0.25), and 0.16 for adult children (This ties with Asian immigrants). It is also significant, however, that Latin American immigrants have much lower sponsorship rates than Asian immigrants in accompanying spouses (0.06), parents of U.S. citizens (0.16), and siblings of U.S. citizens (0.24).

The Middle East ranked third in the overall net unification multipliers. Their sponsorship pattern is quite similar to Asian immigrants, except that the values for all phases are lower than for their Asian counterparts. Middle Eastern culture and family structure are also very well represented here, because the significant portion of the multiplier effects come from sponsoring parents of U.S. citizens (0.32) and siblings of U.S. citizens (0.44).

All other regions (Oceania, Europe, Africa, and North America) have relatively low net unification multiplier values, and this could be translated into the real world context that the overall growth of the immigrant population from these regions has not been as strong as from the other three regions (Asia, Latin America, and the Middle East).

This chapter has covered one of the most important components of the chain migration process: the *Unification of Family Members*. The most important conclusion is the success of using the Immigration Unification Multipliers to measure every single phase of the chain migration process, to calculate the multiplier values for every region, and then to compare them. We have a concrete picture of the unique migration patterns for every region, as well as the sponsorship pattern total over the last three decades. Using the powerful multipliers, we now know many details about chain migration.

Using the power of the Immigration Unification Multipliers, we can conclude that the overall migration pattern for all immigrants shows that each Principal Immigrant would be responsible for 2.12 additional immigrations during the chain migration unification process. The overall multiplier effects are the strongest in sponsoring minor children, parents of U.S. citizens, and siblings of U.S. citizens.

In the next chapter, I will examine the reproduction phase of the chain migration process and present the Immigration Reproduction Multiplier to conclude the *Complete Chain Migration Model*.

CHAPTER 12

Immigration Reproduction Process Explained

In this chapter, I will focus on the immigration reproduction process of the migration chain. I will begin by studying the demographic characteristics of immigrants. Then, I will study the different immigration patterns of Principal Immigrants and family immigrants. At the end of the chapter, I will present the calculation of the Immigration Reproduction Multiplier.

THE IMMIGRANT FERTILITY PATTERNS

When immigrants arrive in the United States, they usually settle down. Since some of them are single or do not have children when they arrive (mostly because of their ages; since most immigrants, especially dependents, they migrate when they are very young), it is quite common for them to produce offspring in the United States in later years.

Since there is no fertility data in the USCIS data sets, I have constructed the data on descendents of immigrants using the U.S. Census 1980, 1990, and 2000 from which I derived the birth data based on children-ever-born to foreign-born parents who have children born in the United States. (See Chapters 4 and 5.) In this calculation, it is important to use the *place of birth* (*POB*) of both the parents and the children to capture the population that meets the following criteria:

- At least one parent is born outside of the United States.
- The child is born in the United States.

With this method, I have successfully collected data on children born to immigrants (at the aggregate level) and matched the high-level categories from the USCIS data.

The data shows that the total number children born to immigrants has increased   during the last three decades; the most significant increase was in the 1990s, when its average annual total doubled the average calculated in the 1970s.

Immigrant Fertility Patterns in the U.S.

We begin the analysis of immigrant fertility patterns in Table 12-1. Using the iPUMS data, we obtain the immigrant fertility rate for both male and female immigrants. As discussed earlier, the calculation of immigrant fertility is based on the U.S.-born children to immigrants, and each immigrant parent is credited for ½ of each child born in the U.S. Hence, the TFR for immigrants is the combined total of TFR for males and the TFR for females. I give the fertility pattern for the U.S. population in general, as a reference.

Table 12-1 Age-Specific Immigrant Fertility Rates by Census Year

Age Group	1980			1990			2000		
	Immigrant		U.S.	Immigrant		US	Immigrant		US
	M	F		M	F		M	F	
15 - 19	4.15	19.04	54.10	4.72	17.70	61.30	2.83	10.23	57.30
20 - 24	35.96	66.21	115.10	25.51	51.58	116.50	17.43	35.17	112.10
25 - 29	67.55	80.37	112.90	46.92	66.49	120.20	34.99	49.74	112.60
30 - 34	68.78	59.30	61.90	53.98	57.76	80.80	44.86	49.06	85.20
35 - 39	44.37	27.65	19.80	42.11	32.67	31.70	33.85	27.75	35.90
40 - 44	21.02	7.73	3.90	20.46	8.80	5.50	17.06	7.76	7.10
45 - 49	8.11	1.42	0.20	8.91	1.82	0.20	7.72	1.84	0.30
50 - 54	3.91			3.70			2.75		
55 - 59	1.25			1.98			1.53		
	1,275	1,308		1,041	1,184		815	907	
TFR	2,584		1,839	2,225		2,081	1,722		2,052
Source:	• *M = Male (half credit calculation method)*								
	F = Female (half credit calculation method)								
	US = U.S. Female (full credit calculation method)								
	• *US Female Fertility Rates are from International Database, U.S. Bureau of the Census.*								
	• *Male & Female Immigrant Fertility Rates are calculated using IPUMS U.S. Census data 1980, 1990, 2000.*								

Comparing the fertility pattern for immigrants against the fertility pattern for the U.S. population, as a whole, some significant differences are noticeable. For example, the census data for both 1980 and 1990 suggest that immigrants have much higher age-specific fertility rates (and TFR) than the U.S. population.[62] In 2000, however, it seems that immigrant fertility is lower than that of the U.S. population. A possible explanation is that the surge of new immigration in late 1980s and early 1990s has produced a relatively large and young immigrant population. Since the immigration population (within the productive age groups) is the denominator of the fertility calculation, this reduces the final calculations. This is important because the children-ever-born method is used to estimate the fertility rates.[63]

Although the U.S. Census uses the *de jure* enumeration to better count the permanent population and household composition of an area, a substantial number of non-immigrants (as well as some undocumented immigrants) have been included in the census data. This implies that non-immigrants have also played a role in the reproduction activities in the United States.[64]

Hence, the immigrant fertility information calculated here actually applies to all members of the foreign-born population, which includes not only immigrants, but also non-immigrants and undocumented immigrants.

---

[62] Higher fertility rates for immigrants in the 1980s were reasonable because most immigrants came from less-developed countries where higher fertilities are the norm.

[63] This should explain the low fertility rate for year 2000 (because of the new arrival of young immigrants, who are less likely to produce children right away. These new immigrants would reduce the fertility rates because they are part of the denominators). This low fertility rate structure would be acceptable for this study because the final outcome of the calculations would be the *Immigration Reproduction Multiplier*. Since I am studying the *minimum multiplier effect* of the chain migration process, *underestimated Immigration Reproduction Multipliers* would guarantee the *minimum impact* of the multiplier effect.

[64] It is, however, not possible to differentiate the immigrants from the non-immigrants in census data. Therefore, we must assume that the reproductive behavior of immigrants and non-immigrants is similar.

Immigrant Fertility Differentials by Regions

Since fertility patterns are mainly affected by socioeconomic and cultural factors, it is very important to examine the regional variations of fertility patterns among immigrants. Using iPUMS data and based on the *place of birth* variable, we can calculate the age-specific fertility rates by region. (See Table 12-2.)

Table 12-2 Immigrant Age-Specific Fertility Rates by Region

Age Group	Africa	Asia	Europe	Latin America	Middle East	North America	Oceania /Other
15 - 19	11.50	8.99	13.01	34.44	15.07	14.29	22.43
20 - 24	52.66	43.71	66.04	101.67	65.75	58.94	54.39
25 - 29	96.76	90.85	102.22	125.53	113.89	102.08	70.21
30 - 34	118.95	113.74	103.72	109.73	124.69	103.87	60.72
35 - 39	91.44	75.05	61.27	69.16	95.70	62.12	41.19
40 - 44	40.76	28.54	21.23	30.49	42.78	23.34	17.06
45 - 49	18.75	8.56	6.49	12.82	14.20	8.74	8.34
50 - 54	5.78	2.69	2.37	4.30	4.77	3.13	2.57
55 - 59	3.59	1.29	0.73	2.70	1.77	1.37	2.12
TFR	2,200.99	1,867.08	1,885.34	2,454.20	2,393.07	1,889.32	1,395.14
Note	• This age-specific fertility rate is the combined rate for both male immigrant and female immigrants. • The calculation is based on data from Census 1980, 1990, and 2000.						

From Table 12-2, we can see that among regions the immigrant fertility differences are quite significant during the same period (from combined census data from 1980, 1990, and 2000). The three regions with highest TFR values are Latin America, the Middle East, and Africa. The TFR values of these countries all exceed 2,200 per 1,000 immigrants (male and female immigrants combined[65]). The TFR value for Latin American immigrants is 2,454.20 per 1,000 immigrants; for Middle Eastern immigrants it is 2,393.07 per 1,000 immigrants; and for African immigrants it is 2,200.99 per 1,000 immigrants.

At the same time, the TFR values for Asia, Europe, and North America are almost the same: all are around 1,880 per 1,000 immigrants. Oceania has the lowest TFR value of 1,400 per 1,000 immigrants.

---

[65] As explained earlier, this study focuses on the reproduction impact of both male and female immigrants. Therefore, all of the fertility data presented here, unless indicated otherwise, are always for both genders, with the logic that each parent is responsible for ½ of each immigrant child.

It is also clear (from Table 12-3) that female immigrants have consistently higher TFR values than their male counterparts.

Table 12-3 Immigrant Age-Specific Fertility Rates by Region by Gender

Age	Africa		Asia		Europe		Latin America		Middle East		North America	
Grp	M	F	M	F	M	F	M	F	M	F	M	F
15 - 19	1.5	10.0	1.4	7.6	2.6	10.5	7.8	26.7	1.3	13.7	2.5	11.8
20 - 24	13.5	39.1	11.3	32.4	21.5	44.5	35.4	66.2	14.2	51.5	19.0	39.9
25 - 29	31.2	65.5	32.8	58.0	45.4	56.8	55.1	70.4	38.1	75.8	43.8	58.3
30 - 34	52.7	66.3	57.1	56.6	53.6	50.1	53.3	56.5	60.3	64.3	51.5	52.4
35 - 39	52.0	39.4	44.3	30.7	37.3	24.0	37.7	31.5	60.1	35.6	34.1	28.0
40 - 44	30.7	10.0	20.7	7.8	16.0	5.2	20.3	10.2	34.2	8.6	15.8	7.6
45 - 49	16.3	2.5	7.2	1.4	5.7	0.8	10.1	2.7	12.9	1.3	7.3	1.5
50 - 54	5.8	0.0	2.7	0.0	2.4	0.0	4.3	0.0	4.8	0.0	3.1	0.0
55 - 59	3.6	0.0	1.3	0.0	0.7	0.0	2.7	0.0	1.8	0.0	1.4	0.0
TFR	1,037	1,164	894	973	926	959	1,134	1,321	1,138	1,255	892	997
	2,201		1,867		1,885		2,454		2,393		1,889	
Note	• M = Male Immigrants F = Female Immigrants • Oceania/other is not included because of its low fertility rates among immigrants.											

Immigrant Fertility Differentials by Top Countries

Table 12-4 shows the TFR values for the top 16 countries (census years 1980, 1990, and 2000 combined) over the last three decades. As indicated in the chart, most of the top countries are in Asia, Latin America, and the Middle East.

Among these, Laos and Mexico lead with very high TFR values, compared to all of the other countries. It is important to note that male immigrants from the top countries (such as Laos, Mexico, Pakistan, Haiti, and El Salvador) have relatively higher TFR values (TFR ≥ 1) than female immigrants from other countries (TFR ≤ 1). This is significant because we can see that male immigrants also play a significant role in producing offspring in the United States.

UNDERSTANDING THE REPRODUCTION PROCESS IN THE MIGRATION CHAIN

Understanding the immigrant fertility patterns is the first step toward the study of the multiplier effect of chain migration. The next section will present the demographic characteristics of second-generation immigrants in the United States.

Table 12-4 Immigrant Total Fertility Rates by Gender: Top 16 Countries

Country	Female TFR	Male TFR	TFR
Laos	1.72	1.65	3.37
Mexico	1.53	1.26	2.79
Pakistan	1.35	1.04	2.39
Haiti	1.20	1.10	2.29
El Salvador	1.19	1.02	2.22
Dominican Republic	1.22	0.99	2.21
Philippines	1.08	0.97	2.05
India	1.03	0.93	1.97
Peru	1.00	0.94	1.94
Cuba	0.95	0.93	1.88
Iran	0.91	0.93	1.84
Canada	0.96	0.86	1.82
Vietnam	0.93	0.85	1.78
Colombia	0.91	0.85	1.77
Guyana/British Guiana	0.86	0.85	1.72
Jamaica	0.89	0.80	1.69

Second-Generation Immigrants in the U.S.

In this research, when we calculate the total number of second-generation immigrants we assume that each parent contributes half of each of their children. (Please refer to the discussions in Chapter 4.) This prevents us from double counting immigrant children and provides fertility information for immigrants of both genders.

Now, let us review the data of the growth of the immigrant second-generation. We know that the immigrant population over the last thirty years has fueled the growth of second-generation immigrants in the United States. Table 12-5 shows the total number of second-generation immigrants (ages 1-10[66]) by census years (1980, 1990, and 2000). It shows a clear pattern of increase in the total number every 10 years, from about 2 million in 1980, to 3 million in 1990, to 5.2 million in 2000. At the same time, it also shows that, along with children who have at least one foreign-born parent, there has been a consistent increase of children with parents who are both foreign-born (from about 59% in 1980, to 62% in 1990, to 69% in 2000).

---

[66] Children of age 0 were excluded to avoid potential data underreporting problems in the census data.

Table 12-5 Children (Age 1 ~10) Born in the U.S. to Foreign Born Parent(s)

Parents' Place of Birth		1980		1990		2000	
Father	Mother	Total	%	Total	%	Total	%
Foreign Born	Foreign Born	1,164,697	58.78%	1,897,718	62.25%	3,606,775	68.83%
Foreign Born	U.S. Born	320,521	16.18%	430,371	14.12%	548,410	10.47%
	Unknown	20,264	1.02%	77,137	2.53%	170,049	3.25%
U.S. Born	Foreign Born	348,322	17.58%	392,285	12.87%	486,614	9.29%
Unknown		127,580	6.44%	251,259	8.24%	427,904	8.17%
Total		1,981,383	100%	3,048,769	100%	5,239,751	100%

It is also important to note that the proportion of single-parent families, in which the parent is foreign-born, have been on the rise (from 7.4% in 1980, to 10.7% in 1990, to 11.4% in 2000). Since we do not have birthplace information for the other parent, we must exclude these parents, and we will not count the ½ children they contribute. We should keep in mind that this exclusion would reduce the overall immigrant fertility because some of the unknown parents are foreign-born. This will lead to an *underestimation* of immigrant fertility, which in turn will produce a lower value of the Immigration Reproduction Multiplier. For the purpose of this research, this is acceptable because we can declare that the multiplier effect demonstrated by the Immigration Reproduction Multiplier is ***minimum***.

If we examine the birth region of the foreign parents, we see quite a different picture. (See Table 12-6.) Latin Americans contribute the most significant portion of second-generation immigrants, and this has increased over the last thirty years (from 44.45% in 1980, to 50.64% in 1990, to 61.48% in 2000). Africa has also contributed second-generation immigrants—1.37% in 1980, 2.28% in 1990, and 2.76% in 2000. Asia has been the second largest contributor of second-generation immigrants during the last three decades. However, its share increased from 15.47% in 1980 to 22.21% in 1990, and then dropped to 19.81% in 2000. The Middle East has a similar pattern. Its contribution of second-generation immigrants dropped (to 3.13%) after an increase from 2.41% in 1980 to 3.46% in 1990. Europe is the third largest contributor of second-generation immigrants. However, it has significantly decreased its share from 26.76% in 1980, to 15.93% in

1990, to 10.46% in 2000. North America and Oceania lost their shares of contributions to the immigrant second-generation.[67]

Table 12-6 Immigrant Children by Census Year by Parents' Birth Region

Census Year	1980			1990			2000		
Region	FF	FM	Total	FF	FM	Total	FF	FM	Total
Africa	54%	46%	27,201	56%	44%	69,544	52%	48%	144,867
Asia	44%	56%	306,459	45%	55%	677,055	46%	54%	1,038,026
Europe	47%	53%	530,172	49%	51%	485,581	49%	51%	547,877
Latin America	48%	52%	880,668	48%	52%	1,543,883	48%	52%	3,221,322
Middle East	57%	43%	47,841	58%	42%	105,340	55%	45%	163,901
North America	42%	58%	80,667	43%	57%	86,403	47%	53%	93,374
Oceania /Other	40%	60%	108,377	44%	56%	80,964	48%	52%	30,385
Total	47%	53%	1,981,383	48%	52%	3,048,769	48%	52%	5,239,751
Note	• FF = Foreign Father FM = Foreign Mother • Children are aged from 1 ~ 10. Age 0 are excluded to avoid double counting. • Data calculated using iPUMs data sets 1980, 1990, and 2000.								

Not surprisingly, female immigrants have played a more significant role in producing immigrant children for their ethnic groups (Asia, Latin America, Europe, North America, and Oceania). They produced more than half of the immigrant children of each respective region.

Africa and the Middle East represent a different pattern. Male immigrants from these two regions contributed more immigrant children than their female counterparts.

The discussion on gender is quite important, because it plays a significant role in migration decision making. It is necessary to demonstrate here (and later) that gender plays a significant role in the chain migration process through second-generation immigrants.

Table 12-7 illustrates a different aspect of the same data. It measures the net gain of the second-generation immigrant population and shows a growth pattern of this population by region. In 2000, Africa had a fastest growth rate (a significant 433% increase since

---

[67] Keep in mind that the total number of second-generation immigrants (children of age 1-10) is derived from the assumption that each parent would contribute only ½ of each of their children. (Refer to the discussion in Chapter 4.)

1980). In 2000, Latin America ranked second (266% since 1980). Asia and the Middle East have similar growth patterns: both regions have gained about 240% since 1980.

Table 12-7 Net Gains in Immigrant Parents (1980 ~ 2000)

Census Year	1980	1990		2000		
Region	Total Children Born to Foreign Parent(s)	Total Children Born to Foreign Parent(s)	Net Gain Since 1980	Total Children Born to Foreign Parent(s)	Net Gain Since 1990	Net Gain Since 1980
Africa	27,201	69,544	155.67%	144,867	108.31%	432.59%
Asia	306,459	677,055	120.93%	1,038,026	53.31%	238.72%
Europe	530,172	485,581	-8.41%	547,877	12.83%	3.34%
Latin America	880,668	1,543,883	75.31%	3,221,322	108.65%	265.78%
Middle East	47,841	105,340	120.19%	163,901	55.59%	242.60%
North America	80,667	86,403	7.11%	93,374	8.07%	15.75%
Oceania /Other	108,377	80,964	-25.29%	30,385	-62.47%	-71.96%
Total	**1,981,383**	**3,048,769**	**53.87%**	**5,239,751**	**71.86%**	**164.45%**

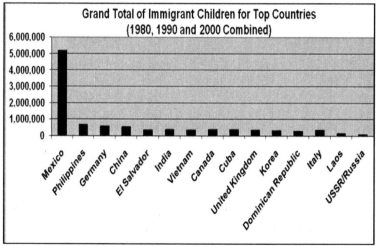

Figure 12-1 Immigrant Children by Top Countries

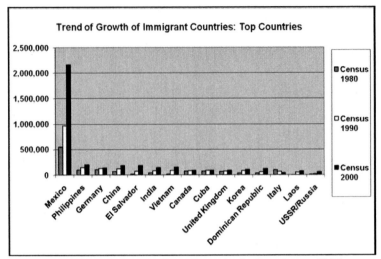

Figure 12-2 Growth Trend of Top Countries for Immigrant Children

Europe and North America have not had a significant gain since 1980 (a mere 3.34% for Europe and 15.75% for North America). Over the last thirty years, Oceania has produced significantly fewer second-generation immigrants.

Combining all regions, we see that over the last three decades, there has been a net gain of 164.45% of second-generation immigrants, and that is significant.

Figure 12-1 shows the top countries that produce immigrant children ranked by age (1-10) (1980, 1990, and 2000 census combined). Mexico is top, producing a total number of 5.1 million. This is significant because it is almost the combined total of all other top 14 countries (5.3 million).

The Philippines, the second top country, produced 0.68 million second-generation immigrants. Germany ranked 3rd (0.6 million) and China produced 0.54 million. The other top countries contributed a range of 200,000-350,000 second-generation immigrants. Both Laos and Russia contributed relatively low numbers, 177,000 and 98,000 respectively.

If we break down the data by census year 1980, 1990 and 2000, we see the growth pattern for these top countries. (See Figure 12-2.) It is clear that immigrants from many of these countries have significantly increased their contributions to the immigrant second-generation. These countries include Mexico, the Philippines, China, El Salvador, India, Vietnam, Korea, the Dominican Republic, Laos, and Russia. In addition, the immigrant population from these countries has significantly grown. (See previous chapters.)

The same illustration shows that immigrants from Western countries have quite a different growth pattern. Immigrants from Germany, Canada, and the United Kingdom have increased their contribution to the second-generation immigrants on a much smaller scale. Italian immigrants have actually decreased their contribution second-generation over the last three decades.

Census data have provided a good tool for measuring the immigrant second-generation. Now, I will use the census data and age structure of the arriving immigrants to estimate the number of future second-generation immigrants.

REPRODUCTION PHASE OF CHAIN MIGRATION: THE IMMIGRATION CHILDREN

In this section, we will apply the immigrant fertility rate (calculated from census data) to the immigrant cohort (from the USCIS data) to estimate the number of second-generation immigrants.

Table 12-8 Immigrant Age-Gender-Specific TFR Values by Gender by Census Year

Age Group	1980		1990		2000	
	Male	Female	Male	Female	Male	Female
0 - 4	1,275.55	1,308.66	1,041.40	1,184.13	815.11	907.81
5 - 9	1,275.55	1,308.66	1,041.40	1,184.13	815.11	907.81
10 - 14	1,275.55	1,308.66	1,041.40	1,184.13	815.11	907.81
15 - 19	1,275.55	1,308.66	1,041.40	1,184.13	815.11	907.81
20 - 24	1,254.82	1,213.45	1,017.78	1,095.65	800.97	856.66
25 - 29	1,075.04	882.39	890.24	837.73	713.84	680.79
30 - 34	737.27	480.52	655.66	505.30	538.88	432.08
35 - 39	393.35	184.01	385.75	216.48	314.57	186.80
40 - 44	171.50	45.75	175.22	53.10	145.32	48.03
45 - 49	66.39	7.10	72.92	9.12	60.00	9.22
50 - 54	25.85	0.00	28.39	0.00	21.41	0.00
55 - 59	6.27	0.00	9.88	0.00	7.67	0.00

It is important to note here that young immigrants (age ≤ 15-19) experience the complete fertility period. The TFR for those who migrate to the U.S. at an older age would be proportional to their remaining fertile years. Table 12-8 shows this TFR structure by age group, which is calculated by census years (1980, 1990, and 2000).

By the same token, age-specific TFR can be calculated for each region with all census years combined. (See Table 12-9.) As discussed earlier, the variations in fertility patterns shown here can produce different multiplier effects for different immigration populations. The combination of higher TFR and younger immigrant cohort can generate a larger second-generation immigrant population.

Table 12-9 Age-Specific TFR Values by Gender by Region

Age Group	Africa	Asia	Europe	Latin America	Middle East	North America	Oceania /Other
0 - 4	2,201	1,867	1,885	2,454	2,393	1,889	1,395
5 - 9	2,201	1,867	1,885	2,454	2,393	1,889	1,395
10 - 14	2,201	1,867	1,885	2,454	2,393	1,889	1,395
15 - 19	2,201	1,867	1,885	2,454	2,393	1,889	1,395
20 - 24	2,143	1,822	1,820	2,282	2,318	1,818	1,283
25 - 29	1,880	1,604	1,490	1,774	1,989	1,523	1,011
30 - 34	1,396	1,149	979	1,146	1,420	1,013	660
35 - 39	802	581	460	597	796	493	356
40 - 44	344	205	154	252	318	183	150
45 - 49	141	63	48	99	104	66	65
50 - 54	47	20	16	35	33	22	23
55 - 59	18	6	4	14	9	7	11

Since the calculated TFR values are based on census data (1980, 1990, and 2000) and since the calculation was for all of the foreign-born population, it is assumed that both immigrants and non-immigrants have similar fertility patterns.[68]

Therefore, the actual total number of second-generation immigrants is the combined total number of children produced by both immigrants and non-immigrants.

Estimating Immigrant Children: the Second Generation

As discussed so far, we can calculate the number of estimated immigrant children by combining the census year TFRs (1980, 1990,

---

[68] See the discussion at the beginning of this chapter.

and 2000) and the USCIS immigration data (1972-1997). (See Table 12-10.) I performed two different calculations. In the first estimate, I applied the ear-specific and age-specific TFR values to the annual admitted immigrants; in the other estimate, I applied the region-specific and age-specific TFR values to admitted immigrants by their sourced regions. Both estimates yielded similar results, with an estimated total of second-generation immigrants of about 10.3-10.8 million or an annual average about 410,000 (from 1972-1997, 26 years in total).[69]

Using census data from 1980, 1990, and 2000, we compare the total number of second-generation immigrant children (ages 1-10), who were born during the last thirty years. The total of all second-generation immigrants is about 10 million or 342,000 annually (30 years in total). Therefore, the actual total number of second-generation immigrants is the combined total of children produced by both immigrants and non-immigrants.

Table 12-10 Estimated Immigrant Second Generation

	Grand Total of Second Generation Immigrants from Census	Estimated Total of Second Generation Immigrants	
	Census Year 1980, 1990 and 2000	Using Age-Specific TFR Values by Year	Using Age-Specific TFR Values by Region
Total	10,269,902	10,837,976	10,339,849
Average Annual Total	342,330	416,845	397,687

Since the actual total number of second-generation immigrants from the census includes both the children of immigrants and non-immigrants and since the estimated total number of second-generation immigrants is for immigrants only, we see that the estimated total is the minimum total number of the potential second-generation immigrants. In the following section, we will use this estimated total to calculate the Immigration Reproduction Multiplier. Since the estimated total number of second-generation immigrants is the minimum total, the *IRM* values to be calculated will measure the ***minimum multiplier effects***.

---

[69] Please note that this research is the study of a synthetic cohort. Therefore, the explanation for this annual total of second-generation immigrants would be contributed by the immigrant cohorts in that year.

Reproduction Multiplier Effect: Immigrant Children

In this section, I will use the method developed earlier to calculate the Immigration Reproduction Multiplier (*IRM*) to measure the multiplier effect of the final phase of chain migration: immigrants' production of second-generation immigrants. For a comprehensive formula in *IRM* calculations, please refer Chapter 4.

If we calculate the net *IRM* using the estimated total number of children born in the U.S. to immigrant parents, i.e. the total number of immigrant second-generation, we have an idea of the general effect of the chain migration multiplier on reproduction. (See Figure 12-3.) From this chart, we can see that in the early 1970s, the net *IRM* was around 0.80, then, it decreased in late 1970s and early 1980s. The net *IRM* jumped back to 0.80 in 1982. However, it has steadily declined ever since. In the late 1990s, it reached a low level of mid 0.50.

The implication on this net *IRM* pattern is quite complicated. The *net IRM* is the ratio of the total number of second-generation immigrants over the total number of immigrants. Since the total number of second-generation immigrants is directly corresponding to the total number of first-generation immigrants,[70] there always is a time lag factor—the time it takes for the first-generation immigrants to produce the second-generation immigrants. Therefore, *any significant changes in the total number of first-generation immigrants would eventually be reflected in the total of second-generation immigrants (through the time lag, or delay)*. If the immigrant population grows (as what we have now), the second-generation immigrant population will also grow accordingly *following a specific fertility pattern with a time lag*. Hence, the net *IRM* in this scenario will usually **underestimate** such a multiplier effect as part of the chain migration process. On the other hand, if the immigrant population decreases, this will eventually be reflected some years later by a decline in fertility of these immigrants, who would in turn produce fewer second-generation

---

[70] As a matter of fact, the relationship between the total second-generation immigrants and the total immigrants is more complicated. The total number of second-generation immigrants is a time lag-function of the total immigrants, because all immigrants are responsible for the immigrant second-generation, and the creation of the second-generation immigrants is completed only after a long period of time (the time lag factor).

immigrants overall. In this case, the net *IRM* will overestimate the multiplier effect.

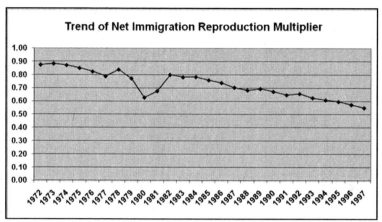

Figure 12-3 Trend of Immigration Reproduction Multiplier

As we know, we are in the era of significant immigration growth, so our calculation of the net IRM would underestimate the multiplier effect. Therefore, the net IRM values will reflect the minimum multiplier effect for immigrants' reproduction as part of chain migration process.[71] The actual multiplier effects would be much greater.

Since the growth of both the first-generation immigrants and the second-generation are time functions, the net *IRM* by year would be more susceptible to period- (year-) specific fluctuations. In the following sections, I will focus on the region-specific and country-

---

[71] Keep in mind that there is another potential factor in underestimation, as discussed earlier in this chapter. The total number of second-generation immigrants estimated here (using *net IRM*, for example) would be only for immigrants. If we were to include non-immigrants, the total number of second-generation immigrants (and the *net IRM* values) would significantly increase. Since this research is to search for the minimum multiplier effect within the chain migration process, it is acceptable to have the minimum multiplier effects measured. This means that the actual multiplier effect would be even greater.

specific multiplier effects. Such calculations will be less susceptible to time factors; therefore, they will more accurately reflect the multiplier effects by region and country.

As discussed earlier, we can also measure the multiplier effects for immigrants by their regions of origin. Table 12-11 shows the regional patterns of net *IRM*. We can see that three regions (Latin America, Africa, and the Middle East) top all other regions in terms of net *IRM* values.

Table 12-11 Immigration Reproduction Multiplier by Region

Region	Net IRM	IRM
Latin America	0.78	1.78
Africa	0.76	1.76
Middle East	0.74	1.74
North America	0.61	1.61
Asia	0.57	1.57
Europe	0.54	1.54
Oceania/Other	0.44	1.44
Total	0.66	1.66

Latin America, which generates the largest immigrant second-generation, has a net *IRM* of 0.78. Africa and the Middle East, the next top two regions, have net *IRMs* of 0.76 and 0.74, respectively. The net *IRM* for North America is 0.61. Asia and Europe are similar, with net *IRMs* in the range of 0.54 and 0.57. Oceania has the lowest net *IRM* value (0.44).

The interpretation of the net *IRM* is simple: immigrants from Latin America, Africa, and the Middle East will generate an average of about 0.76 U.S.-born immigrant children; immigrants from North America, Asia, and Europe will generate around 0.6 U.S.-born immigrant children. Immigrants from Oceania would generate only 0.44 U.S.-born immigrant children.

Using the same method, we can calculate the net *IRM* and *IRM* values for the top countries. (See Table 12-12.) Most countries with high net *IRM* and *IRM* values are from Asia and Latin America. The only countries that are not are Canada (North America), Iran (Middle East), and Russia and San Marino (Europe).

The top country in net *IRM* and *IRM* is Laos from Asia, with net *IRM* value of 1.08. This means that immigrants from Laos would, on average, produce 1.08 U.S.-born immigrant children. Mexican immigrants also have a very high net *IRM* value—0.96 U.S.-born immigrant children per immigrant. The net *IRM* values for immigrants from Pakistan, Haiti, the Dominican Republic, and El Salvador are around high 0.70. The net *IRM* values for the most of the other top countries range from 0.51-0.62. China is not on the list—its net *IRM* value is 0.45.

Table 12-12 Immigration Reproduction Multipliers by Top 16 Countries

Region	Country	*Net IRM*
Asia	Laos	1.08
Latin America	Mexico	0.96
Asia	Pakistan	0.79
Latin America	Haiti	0.77
Latin America	Dominican Republic	0.76
Latin America	El Salvador	0.74
Asia	India	0.62
North America	Canada	0.59
Latin America	Peru	0.59
Asia	Philippines	0.58
Asia	Vietnam	0.58
Latin America	Jamaica	0.57
Latin America	Guyana/British Guiana	0.56
Latin America	Colombia	0.54
Asia	Korea	0.54
Middle East	Iran	0.51

As part of the chain migration model, we have completed the evaluation of the immigrant fertility patterns for all of the regions and for most of the top immigrant-sending countries. Since we want to estimate the future impact of the current immigrant population, we calculated the current fertility patterns of the existing immigrant population in the U.S. and applied that to the incoming immigrant population, assuming that this new population will follow the same fertility patterns. It is important that we have learned that the regions with highest immigrant TFRs also have the highest *IRM* values. Similarly, regions with average TFRs have average *IRM* values. Logically, the region with the lowest TFR is the one the lowest *IRM* values. The relationship between the TFR and *IRM* values is very important. The difference between these two values, however, is that we use the TFRs only for fertility calculations, while we use the *IRM* values to calculate the *reproduction multiplier effect* indicator during the chain migration *reproduction process*.

In the following chapter, we will review the Complete Chain Migration Model and examine the power of both the Immigration Unification Multipliers and the Immigration Reproduction Multiplier.

The Power of the Immigration Multipliers: Chain Migration Process Explained

THE SCOPE OF THE CHAIN MIGRATION PROCESS

In previous chapters, we discussed the Principal Immigrants, the Immigration Unification Multipliers, and the Immigration Reproduction Multiplier during the chain migration processes. In this chapter, I will summarize all of the multipliers and provide an overview of the implications of their effects. I will present these results from a different perspective so that we can understand the scope of the migration chain under the Complete Chain Migration Model.

Unification Phase 1: Multiplier Effect of AFM Immigrants

The scope of chain migration unification phase 1 is limited to the sponsorship of AFM Immigrants (accompanying family members). Figure 13-1 illustrates the flow of *Chain Migration Phase 1* that is responsible for the sponsorship of only accompanying family members.

From the chart, we see that the main multiplier effect in chain migration unification phase 1 comes from the ERI (Employment-Related Principal Immigrants) and the GSI (Government-Sponsored Principal Immigrants), because FSUSB Principals (Foreign Spouses of U.S. Born Citizens) do not participate in the sponsorship of accompanying family members at this level. They are responsible for sponsoring family members during Phases 3 and 4 of the chain migration process.

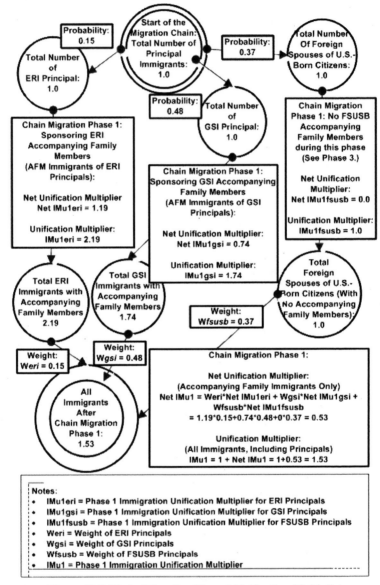

Figure 13-1 Chain Migration Phase 1 Unification Multiplier

As we have learned, the Phase 1 ERI-principal-specific net Immigration Unification Multiplier (*net IUM1eri*) is 1.19, and the Phase 1 GSI-principal-specific net Immigration Unification Multiplier (*net IUM1gsi*) is 0.74. However, we must adjust the standardized Phase 1 net Immigration Unification Multiplier to include the FSUSB principals.[72] Since the proportion of FSUSB Principals is 37%, the standardized value of the Phase 1 net Immigration Unification Multiplier (*net IUM1*) is 0.53 and the standardized Phase 1 Immigration Unification Multiplier (*IUM1*) is 1.53.

Therefore, we can conclude that, on average, *each Principal Immigrant will sponsor 0.53 accompanying family members (spouses and minor children) during Phase 1 of the chain migration process.*

It is important to note here that chain migration unification phase 1 is the only unification phase in which all family members (accompanying spouses and children) are **directly** sponsored by the original Principal Immigrants. Family members sponsored during the other chain migration unification phases are collectively sponsored by both the original Principal Immigrants and by other derived family immigrants (those who were either directly or indirectly sponsored by the original Principal Immigrants). This, in fact, reflects the multiplier effect of the chain migration.

Unification Phase 2: Multiplier Effect of LFM Immigrants

Figure 13-2 illustrates the multiplier effect at Phase 2 of the chain migration process. Due to data limitations, the data does not have the field to differentiate whether ERI or GSI principals sponsored the LFM immigrants (later-sponsored family members). Therefore, I combined these two types of Principal Immigrants in Phase 2. Since the FSUSB principals (*i.e.* the Foreign Spouses of U.S.-Born Citizens) are not responsible for any LFM immigrants during Phase 2, they will be assigned a zero value in their net Immigration Unification Multiplier (i.e. *net IUM2fsusb*=0).

---

[72] As previously discussed, this is for standardization s so that we can compare the *net IUM* values across all levels.

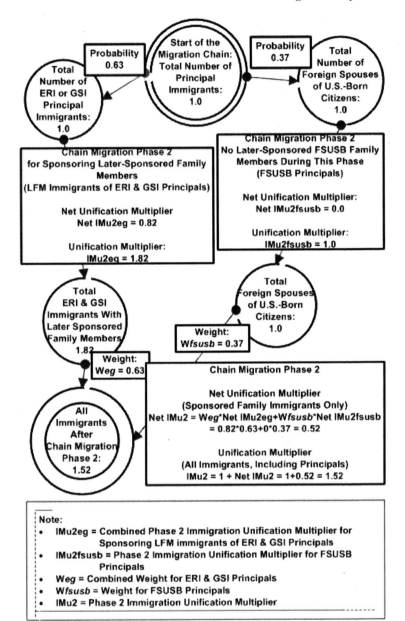

Figure 13-2 Phase 2 Chain Migration Immigration Unification Multiplier

Although the calculated value of the Phase 2 net Immigration Unification Multiplier for ERI and GSI principals (*net IUM2eg*) is 0.82, the standardized Phase 2 net Immigration Unification Multiplier, after the adjustment is made to include the 37% FSUSB principals, is 0.52, and the overall Phase 2 Immigration Unification Multiplier (*IUM2*) is 1.52.

Therefore, we can conclude that, on average, *each Principal Immigrant is responsible for 0.52 later-sponsored family members during Phase 2 of the chain migration process.*

Here, we should understand that the original Principal Immigrants did not sponsor all family members (spouses and minor children) during this phase. Please keep in mind that **all eligible immigrants** can sponsor their spouses and children, regardless of their original visa categories. Therefore, eligible immigrants, who sponsor their family members during this phase, could be either the original Principal Immigrants (ERI or GSI), family members (spouses, parents, children, siblings, etc.) of the original Principal Immigrants or relatives of family members of the Principal Immigrants, etc. This is what we called the *migration chain*.

Unification Phase 3: Multiplier Effect of Exempt Family Members of U.S. Citizens

The scope of Phase 3 chain migration is the sponsorship of exempt family members of U.S. citizens. To measure the Phase 3 Multiplier effect, we must calculate the values of the net Immigration Unification Multiplier for all components of the Phase 3 categories: the *MC* (Minor Children of U.S. Citizens), FSUSN (Foreign Spouses of Naturalized U.S. Citizens), and PUSC immigrants (Parents of U.S. Citizens), as shown in Figure 13-3.

Since only ERI and GSI principals are responsible for the sponsorship of FSUSN immigrants, a special value of the Phase 3 net Immigration Unification Multiplier was calculated for them (*net IUM3fsusn* = 0.35). The standardized net Immigration Unification Multiplier (*net IUM3fs*), which includes FSUSB immigrants, is 0.22. This means that, on average, *each Principal Immigrant is responsible for 0.22 foreign spouses of naturalized U.S. citizens.*

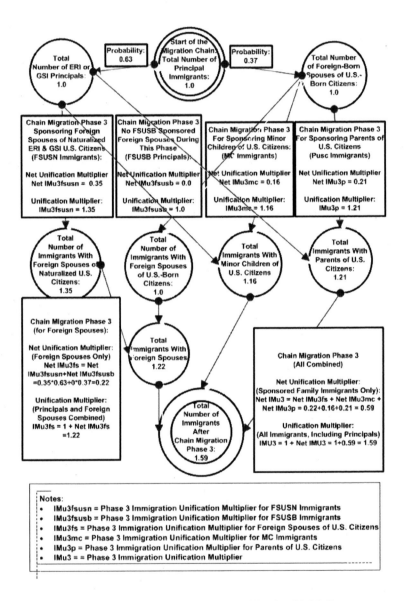

Figure 13-3 Phase 3 Immigration Unification Multiplier

Similarly, the values of net Immigration Unification Multipliers of minor children of U.S. citizens (*net IUM3mc*) and parents of U.S. citizens (*net IUM3p*) were calculated (0.16 and 0.21, respectively).

We now can calculate the standardized value of the net Immigration Unification Multiplier by adding all of these *net IUM3* values together (0.22+0.16+0.21=0.59). Hence, the final Phase 3 net Immigration Unification Multiplier for chain migration (*IUM3*) is 1.59.[73]

Therefore, on average, *each Principal Immigrant is responsible for 0.59 exempt family members of U.S. citizens during Phase 3 of chain migration process.*

As we discussed earlier, foreign spouses of U.S.-born citizens (FSUSB principals) are responsible for some of the *MC* and *PUSC* immigrants (minor children and parents of U.S. citizens) in Phase 3. However, all naturalized U.S. citizens are responsible for the *MC* and *PUSC* immigrants, as well. The naturalized U.S. citizens can also sponsor their spouses (FSUSN immigrants) in this phase. Since all naturalized U.S. citizens can sponsor exempt family members, regardless of their original visa categories, the Immigration Multipliers we calculated here reflect the multiplier effect generated by the original Principal Immigrants, who have contributed the group of immigrants who later become naturalized U.S. citizens.

Unification Phase 4: Multiplier Effect of Non-Exempt Family Members of U.S. Citizens

The scope of Phase 4 chain migration is the sponsorship of non-exempt family members of U.S. citizens, which includes UAC (Unmarried Adult Children of U.S. Citizens), MAC (Married Adult Children of U.S. Citizens), and SIB (Siblings of U.S. Citizens). (See Figure 13-4.)

The calculations for each of these components reveal that the value of the net Immigration Unification Multiplier of UAC immigrants (*net IUM4uac*) is only 0.05, and the value of the Immigration Unification Multiplier of MAC immigrants (*net IUM4mac*) is 0.09. Both of them combined will be (*net IUM4ac*) 0.14. At the same time, the value of the Immigration Unification Multiplier of SIB immigrants (*net*

---

[73] Here, the *net IUM* value is 0.59, and the *IUM* value is 1.59.

IUM4sib) is 0.35; this is significantly higher than that of *AC* Immigrants. By combining these *net IUM4* values, we would arrive at the combined 0.49 as the Phase 4 net Immigration Unification Multiplier (*net IUM4*), or 1.49 as the value of Phase 4 Immigration Unification Multiplier (*IUM4*).

Therefore, we can conclude that, on average, *each Principal Immigrant is responsible 0.49 non-exempt family members of U.S. citizens during Phase 4 of the chain migration process.* It is especially important to note that 0.35 out of the 0.45 (or 71.4% of the sponsorship during Phase 4) is for sponsoring Siblings of U.S. citizens.

Similar to Phase 3, Phase 4 is another unification phase in which all naturalized U.S. citizens can be responsible for all of the sponsored family members, regardless of their original visa categories. Again, the Immigration Multipliers here show the impact of the original Principal Immigrants, who have contributed a group of immigrants who later become naturalized U.S. citizens.

Unification Phases Combined: Multiplier Effect of the Family Reunification Process

If we combine all of the family reunification phases of chain migration, we will have the overall values of the net Immigration Unification Multiplier for measuring the *Family Reunification Process.*

Figure 13-5 shows the values of the net Immigration Unification Multipliers of all four phases of chain migration. Since each phase of sponsorship is independent, mutually exclusive, and standardized, the values of the net Immigration Unification Multipliers can be added together to arrive at the total net Immigration Unification Multiplier for measuring the overall *Unification Multipliers.*

As the chart shows, the final overall value of net Immigration Unification Multiplier (*net IUM*) is 2.12, and the value of Immigration Unification Multiplier (*IUM*) is 3.12. Therefore, we can conclude that on average, *each Principal Immigrant is responsible for 2.12 additional immigrants during the Family Reunification Process.* Among theses, 0.53 are accompanying family members, 0.52 are later-sponsored family members, 0.59 are exempt family members of U.S. citizens, and 0.49 are non-exempt family members of U.S. citizens. Overall, one Principal Immigrant will eventually result in 3.12 immigrants in total because of the multiplier effect.

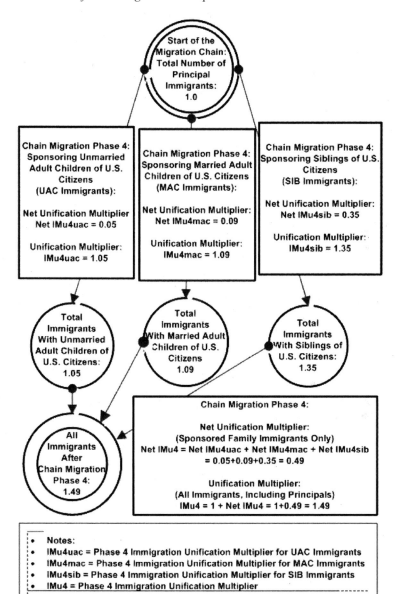

Figure 13-4 Chain Migration Phase 4 Unification Multiplier

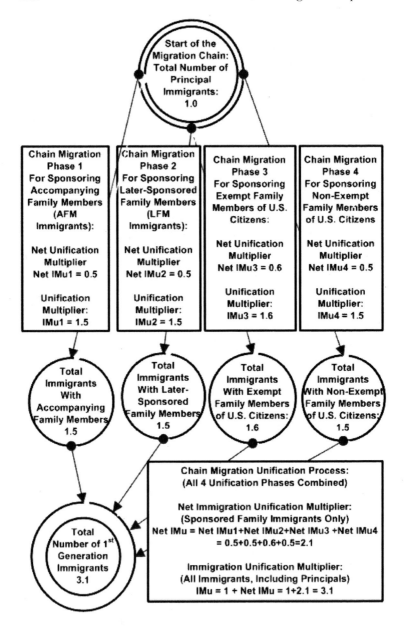

Figure 13-5 Chain Migration Unification Multipliers

Reproduction Phase: Multiplier Effect of Second Generation Immigrants

Previous research on the Immigration Multiplier has tried to include the family reunification process (Jasso and Rosenzweig, 1986, 1989, 1990, and many others). As I demonstrated in previous chapters, the immigration reproduction process is very important in contributing to the significant growth of the immigrant population in the United States. Therefore, I expanded the original Immigration Multiplier concept and added the reproduction component to the chain migration model. My new method includes the immigration reproduction process and provides a new opportunity for us to see and understand the migration process, as a whole, within a complete chain migration model.

As Figure 13-6 illustrates, we see that the compounded multiplier effect becomes quite significant when we combine the Immigration Unification Multiplier (*IUM*) with the Immigration Reproduction Multiplier (*IRM*), because we must *multiply* the *IUM* by the *IRM* to arrive at the final *IM* value.

Using U.S. immigration historical data from 1972 through 1997, we calculated the *IUM* value at 3.12 and the value of *IRM* at 0.7,[74] so the *IM* value for measuring the *Immigration Multiplier Effect* should be 3.12 x 0.7, and the calculated value should be 5.3. The *net IM*, therefore, is 4.3.

We can conclude that, on average, *each Principal Immigrant is responsible for 4.3 family members during the unification and reproduction processes of chain migration.* This result shows the multiplier effect has played a major role in contributing to the growth of the immigrant population in the U.S.

---

[74] The calculated overall *net IRM* for all immigrants using the year-specific and age-specific *TFR* is 0.70, and the calculated overall *net IRM* for all immigrants using the region-specific and age-specific *TFR* is 0.66. Hence, I use the rounded value of the two (0.7) for the generalized presentation of *net IRM*.

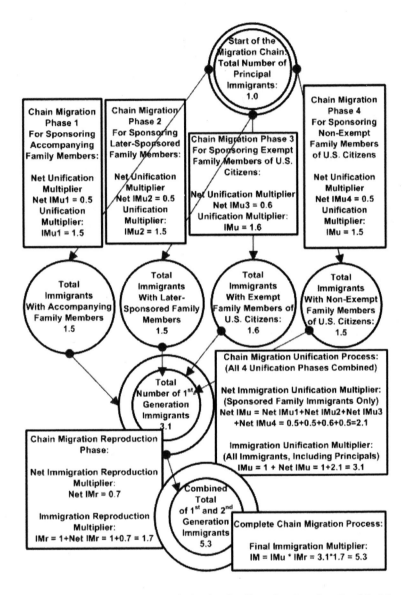

Figure 13-6 Immigration Multiplier for the Complete Immigration Model

MEASURING THE MIGRATION CHAIN USING THE IMMIGRATION MULTIPLIER

Now that we have pieced all of the components together and combined all of the calculations on Immigration Multipliers for each of the unification chains and for the reproduction chain, we have a complete picture of the multiplier effects of migration chains. Using the *IM*, we can now examine the migration chain from several different angles.

Immigration Patten and the Immigration Multiplier

Table 13-1 summarizes all of the values of *IUM* and *IRM* from 1972 through 1997. This table provides an overview of the migration patterns in the United States. For example, the values of net *IUM* increased from 1.33 in 1972 to 2.27 in 1980, to 2.44 in 1990, to 2.58 in 1997. This value refers to the total number of family members who were admitted to the U.S. via sponsorship by Principal Immigrants (including direct and indirect sponsorship). From these net *IUM* values, we can conclude that the chain migration process has a significant *unification multiplier effect.* This means that, on average, *each Principal Immigrant was responsible for bringing 2.12 family members during the unification process.*

The net *IUM* values, however, have a declining trend. As discussed earlier, this may reflect the time-lag factor suggesting that the birth waves have yet not caught up with the immigration waves, especially after the significant increase of immigrant population in the U.S. during the late 1980s and early 1990s. Nevertheless, the net *IRM* values are still significant. They suggest that the reproduction multiplier shows the *theoretical minimum impact.* On average, the net *IRM* is about 0.70. This means that, on average, *each immigrant is responsible for producing 0.70 immigrant U.S.-born children.*

Combining the *IUM* (=3.1) and *IRM* (=1.7) results in the final *IM* value of 5.3. By definition, the *net IM* value is 4.3, which is the overall measurement of the complete migration chain. This implies that each Principal Immigrant will generate on average 4.3 additional immigrants (2.1 of them are derived family members of the original Principal Immigrants, while 2.2 are immigrant children (i.e. the immigrant second-generation) produced by these foreign-born immigrants (*i.e.* 3.1 x 0.7=2.2).

Table 13-1 Immigration Multipliers by Chain Migration Phases by Year

Year	Net IUM1	Net IUM2	Net IUM3	Net IUM4	Net IUM	IUM	Net IRM	IRM	Net IM	IM
1972	0.49	0.22	0.31	0.31	1.33	2.33	0.87	1.87	3.36	4.36
1973	0.51	0.27	0.36	0.33	1.46	2.46	0.88	1.88	3.63	4.63
1974	0.49	0.28	0.37	0.33	1.47	2.47	0.87	1.87	3.61	4.61
1975	0.44	0.27	0.33	0.34	1.37	2.37	0.85	1.85	3.39	4.39
1976	0.41	0.27	0.35	0.37	1.39	2.39	0.82	1.82	3.35	4.35
1977	0.36	0.31	0.32	0.43	1.43	2.43	0.79	1.79	3.34	4.34
1978	0.47	0.38	0.35	0.55	1.75	2.75	0.84	1.84	4.06	5.06
1979	0.43	0.82	0.68	0.83	2.75	3.75	0.77	1.77	5.64	6.64
1980	0.44	0.67	0.48	0.68	2.27	3.27	0.63	1.63	4.32	5.32
1981	0.50	0.63	0.45	0.59	2.17	3.17	0.68	1.68	4.30	5.30
1982	0.54	0.58	0.48	0.48	2.08	3.08	0.80	1.80	4.54	5.54
1983	0.51	0.73	0.59	0.62	2.44	3.44	0.78	1.78	5.13	6.13
1984	0.48	0.74	0.65	0.65	2.52	3.52	0.78	1.78	5.27	6.27
1985	0.44	0.67	0.68	0.59	2.39	3.39	0.76	1.76	4.96	5.96
1986	0.46	0.65	0.73	0.60	2.43	3.43	0.74	1.74	4.97	5.97
1987	0.36	0.53	0.58	0.47	1.94	2.94	0.70	1.70	4.00	5.00
1988	0.37	0.50	0.63	0.49	2.00	3.00	0.68	1.68	4.04	5.04
1989	0.52	0.66	0.77	0.61	2.56	3.56	0.69	1.69	5.02	6.02
1990	0.57	0.55	0.78	0.54	2.44	3.44	0.67	1.67	4.75	5.75
1991	0.64	0.51	0.78	0.50	2.43	3.43	0.65	1.65	4.64	5.64
1992	0.95	0.56	0.66	0.41	2.59	3.59	0.66	1.66	4.94	5.94
1993	0.75	0.46	0.59	0.35	2.15	3.15	0.62	1.62	4.11	5.11
1994	0.69	0.50	0.69	0.42	2.31	3.31	0.61	1.61	4.31	5.31
1995	0.61	0.73	0.69	0.46	2.49	3.49	0.59	1.59	4.57	5.57
1996	0.57	0.69	0.82	0.43	2.51	3.51	0.57	1.57	4.52	5.52
1997	0.55	0.52	1.04	0.47	2.58	3.58	0.55	1.55	4.54	5.54
Total	**0.5**	**0.5**	**0.6**	**0.5**	**2.1**	**3.1**	**0.7**	**1.7**	**4.3**	**5.3**
Notes	*Net IUM1 = Phase 1 Net Immigration Unification Multiplier*									
	Net IUM2 = Phase 2 Net Immigration Unification Multiplier									
	Net IUM3 = Phase 3 Net Immigration Unification Multiplier									
	Net IUM4 = Phase 4 Net Immigration Unification Multiplier									
	Net IUM = Net Immigration Unification Multiplier									
	Net IRM = Net Immigration Reproduction Multiplier									
	IUM = Immigration Unification Multiplier									
	IRM = Immigration Reproduction Multiplier									

To compare the immigration patterns from this period further, we can calculate the *Weighted Immigration Multiplier* or *WIM* (as defined in Chapter 4) by taking the total number of Principal Immigrants (the initiators of the family migration chains) into account. Table 13-2 is the calculation of the weighted *IM* values, which takes the size of the Principal Immigrant population into consideration and illustrates the net chain migration impact and the comparison of the chain migration patterns over the years. The calculation begins with the distribution of 1,000 Principal Immigrants from 1972 through 1997 and measures the multiplier effect over time by calculating the weighted Immigration Multipliers for each year.[75] With all net multiplier impacts calculated from the weighted Principal Immigrants and the corresponding multiplier values calculated for each year, the comparison is standardized. We can determine from the table that the sponsored family immigrants increased in volume since 1977, while the immigrant children began to increase around the same time (the late 1970s). In late 1980s, the number of Principal Immigrants began to increase, while the sponsored family immigrants, along with immigrant children, experienced a significant jump in the early 1990s.

Table 13-2 Complete Chain Migration Model Analysis by Year: Weighted Immigration Multipliers (per 1,000 Principal Immigrants)

Year	Original Total Principal Immigrants	Weighted Principal Immigrants (per 1,000) (*Pw*)	Net IUM	Weighted Sponsored Family Immigrants (Net *IUMw*)	Net IRM	Weighted Immigrant Children (Net *IRMw*)	IM	Grand Total (Weighted Immigration Multiplier) (*IMw*)
1972	167,925	34	1.33	46	0.87	70	4.36	149
1973	160,425	33	1.46	48	0.88	71	4.63	152
1974	155,099	32	1.47	46	0.87	68	4.61	146
1975	160,809	33	1.37	45	0.85	66	4.39	144
1976	125,492	26	1.39	36	0.82	50	4.35	111
1977	196,234	40	1.43	57	0.79	76	4.34	174
1978	213,232	44	1.75	76	0.84	100	5.06	220
1979	125,610	26	2.75	71	0.77	74	6.64	170
1980	167,628	34	2.27	78	0.63	70	5.32	182
1981	183,137	37	2.17	81	0.68	80	5.30	198
1982	189,800	39	2.08	81	0.80	95	5.54	215
1983	158,311	32	2.44	79	0.78	87	6.13	198
1984	152,760	31	2.52	79	0.78	86	6.27	196
1985	170,447	35	2.39	83	0.76	89	5.96	207
1986	170,718	35	2.43	85	0.74	88	5.97	208
1987	213,943	44	1.94	85	0.70	90	5.00	218
1988	201,691	41	2.00	82	0.68	84	5.04	207
1989	172,153	35	2.56	90	0.69	87	6.02	211
1990	195,684	40	2.44	97	0.67	92	5.75	230
1991	202,639	41	2.43	100	0.65	91	5.64	233
1992	231,182	47	2.59	122	0.66	111	5.94	280
1993	276,543	56	2.15	121	0.62	111	5.11	289
1994	228,995	47	2.31	108	0.61	94	5.31	248
1995	212,989	43	2.49	108	0.59	90	5.57	242
1996	250,263	51	2.51	128	0.57	103	5.52	282
1997	217,388	44	2.58	114	0.55	87	5.54	246
Total	4,901,097	1,000	2.15	2,145	0.70	2,211	5.30	5,356

[75] Please see Chapter 4 for more details on the definition and discussion of this method.

The time lag factors are visible in both incidents (1977 and 1987), because most of the family sponsored immigrants arrived in the U.S. a few years after the surge of Principal Immigrants. The same is true for immigrant children.

Regional Variations in Immigration Patterns

We can also calculate the Immigration Multiplier by regions for every phase of the migration chain, as shown in Tables 13-3 and 13-4.[76]

Table 13-3 Complete Immigration Multiplier Comparison By Region

Region	Immigration Multipliers			Immigrants Total			
	IUM	IRM	IM	Principal Immigrants	Unification Immigrants	Second-Generation Immigrants	Grand Total
Latin America	3.25	1.78	5.79	1,845,059	4,145,224	4,692,492	10,682,775
Asia	3.79	1.57	5.95	1,449,523	4,047,146	3,133,058	8,629,727
Europe	2.40	1.54	3.71	1,001,807	1,403,633	1,310,551	3,715,991
Middle East	3.03	1.74	5.29	256,054	519,790	577,545	1,353,389
Africa	2.06	1.76	3.63	235,722	250,740	368,125	854,587
North America	2.14	1.61	3.46	162,973	186,186	214,283	563,442
Oceania /Other	2.25	1.44	3.24	44,002	54,822	43,796	142,620
Total	**3.12**	**1.66**	**5.19**	**4,995,140**	**10,607,541**	**10,339,849**	**25,942,530**

From Tables 13-3 and 13-4, it is clear that Latin America, Asia, and Europe are the top three regions sending immigrants to the United States (in terms of numbers). However, if we examine the values of *IM*, we have a different picture: According to the final values of *IM*, Asia has the highest *IM* value (5.95). This means that each Principal

---

[76] I do want to mention that the overall *net IRM* is 0.66, which is different from the overall *net IRM* value of 0.70 in the previous table of *IRM* by year. The major difference is caused mainly by usages of different *TFR* value sets. In the analysis of *IRM* values by year, the *TFR* values used were from the annual *TFR* values that were derived from the iPUMS data. In the analysis of *IRM* values by region, the *TFR* values used were from the regional analysis of the same iPUMs data, except that the data from every year were collapsed by region. Therefore, this new set of *TFR* values varies slightly in the actual calculation, compared to the calculation using year-specific *TFR*s.

Immigrant will contribute almost five additional immigrants (2.79 of them will be from family reunifications; the rest (4.95-2.79=2.16, or 3.79*0.57=2.16) will be immigrant children born in the U.S). Hence, the growth of Asian immigrants during the last three decades was driven by both the highest unification multiplier effect through the sponsorship of family members and the relative low (Asia is ranked 4th) reproduction multiplier effect of producing immigrant children. We can conclude that the unification multiplier is the key factor that has made Asia the top region in sending immigrants to the U.S.

Table 13-4 Complete Immigration Multiplier Comparison By Region

Region	Net IUM				Net IUM	IUM	Net IRM	IRM	Net IM	IM
	Net IUM1	*Net IUM2*	*Net IUM3*	*Net IUM4*						
Asia	0.72	0.56	0.77	0.74	2.79	3.79	0.57	1.57	4.95	5.95
Latin America	0.42	0.78	0.64	0.40	2.25	3.25	0.78	1.78	4.79	5.79
Middle East	0.50	0.37	0.61	0.55	2.03	3.03	0.74	1.74	4.29	5.29
Europe	0.53	0.17	0.36	0.35	1.40	2.40	0.54	1.54	2.71	3.71
Africa	0.38	0.18	0.29	0.21	1.06	2.06	0.76	1.76	2.63	3.63
North America	0.48	0.16	0.27	0.24	1.14	2.14	0.61	1.61	2.46	3.46
Oceania /Other	0.27	0.24	0.27	0.47	1.25	2.25	0.44	1.44	2.24	3.24
Total	**0.53**	**0.52**	**0.59**	**0.48**	**2.12**	**3.12**	**0.66**	**1.66**	**4.19**	**5.19**

Latin America sends the second highest number of immigrants, and it has very high *IM* values (5.79, only 0.16 less than Asia). Compared to Asian immigrants, however, Latin America has the highest Immigration Reproduction Multiplier (1.78, which is 0.21 higher than Asia's 1.57), and it has the second highest Immigration Unification Multiplier (3.25, which is 0.54 lower than Asia's 3.79). Therefore, Latin American immigrants not only have a relatively strong multiplier effect during the unification process of chain migration (it is ranked number two), but also the strongest multiplier effect during the reproduction process. Hence, the growth of Latin American immigrants during the last three decades was driven by *both* the high multiplier effect through sponsorship (for both Principal Immigrants and their family members) *and* the high multiplier effect through reproduction (for all immigrants combined). Since Latin America has the highest number of Principal Immigrants in the U.S. (about 400,000 more than Asia), the multiplier effects for Latin American immigrants are the most significant; the final total of first and second-generation immigrants from Latin America is higher than any other region (10.7 million, about 2.1 million higher than Asia).

Europe, on the other hand, has a significant size of Principal Immigrants (1 million, which is only 400,000 less than Asia). It ranks fourth in the number of immigrants it sends to the U.S. Because of its very low *IM* values (3.71), the multiplier effect for European immigrants is very weak throughout the chain migration process. During the unification process, the *IUM* for European immigrants is only 2.40. This means that each Principal Immigrant from Europe is responsible for, on average, 1.40 additional family immigrants. During the reproduction process of the chain migration, European immigrants' *IRM* was only 1.54. (It ranked sixth among the seven regions.) This implies that each European immigrant (whether Principal Immigrant or family immigrant) would produce only 0.54 immigrant children. Therefore, for the past three decades, the overall multiplier effect for European immigrants has been among the weakest.

The Middle East, on the other hand, shows a very interesting chain migration pattern. Compared to Asia, Latin America, and Europe, its Principal Immigrant population is only about 0.25 million—about ¼ of the European Principal Immigrant population. However, it ranks surprisingly high in terms of the overall *IM*. Its value of Immigration Multiplier (5.29) is the third highest, following closely behind Asia (5.95) and Latin America (5.79). If we examine its chain migration pattern, we see that Middle Eastern immigrants have a very similar migration pattern to Latin American immigrants with a relatively high *IUM* (3.03, ranking it third among the seven regions), and very high *IRM* (1.74, almost tying it with Latin American immigrants' 1.79). Therefore, the growth of Middle Eastern immigrants during the last three decades was driven by both the relative high multiplier effect through family reunification and the very high multiplier effect through producing immigrant children. This special immigration pattern has caused the Middle East to surpass Europe and become the third highest region that sends immigrants to the U.S.

Meanwhile, Africa has an extremely low Immigration Unification Multiplier *IUM* value (2.06, which means low sponsorship rates for family reunification). The size of the Principal Immigrant population from Africa is similar to the Middle East. It has the second highest *IRM* value (1.76); the overall immigration pattern for African immigrants shows an extremely weak unification multiplier effect during its unification process of the chain migration and an extremely high reproduction multiplier effect during its reproduction process of the chain migration.

The other two regions (North America and Oceania) also have very low *IM* values (3.46 and 3.24). Both are relatively balanced in terms of their *IUM* vs. *IRM* values.

Table 13-5 Complete Chain Migration Model Analysis by Region: Weighted Immigration Multipliers (per 1,000 Principal Immigrants)

Region	Original Total Principal Immigrants	Weighted Principal Immigrants (per 1,000) (Pw)	Net IUM	Weighted Sponsored Family Immigrants (Net IUMw)	Net IRM	Weighted Immigrant Children (Net IRMw)	IM	Grand Total (Weighted Immigration Multiplier) (IMw)
Latin America	1,845,059	369	2.25	830	0.78	939	5.79	2,139
Asia	1,449,523	290	2.79	810	0.57	627	5.95	1,728
Europe	1,001,807	201	1.40	281	0.54	262	3.71	744
Middle East	256,054	51	2.03	104	0.74	116	5.29	271
Africa	235,722	47	1.06	50	0.76	74	3.63	171
North America	162,973	33	1.14	37	0.61	43	3.46	113
Oceania /Other	44,002	9	1.25	11	0.44	9	3.24	29
Total	4,995,140	1,000	2.12	2,124	0.66	2,070	5.19	5,194

Now, we will take into the consideration the Principal Immigrants as part of the Complete Chain Migration Model, as shown in Table 13-5. With the distribution of 1,000 Principal Immigrants among all regions, Latin America, Asia, and Europe have the greatest share of Principal Immigrants (369, 290, and 201 respectively). Relatively speaking, the Middle East, Africa, North America, and Oceania/Other have very small shares of the Principal Immigrant population.

It is important to note, however, that Latin America now has the greatest multiplier effect on chain migration. This is the result of the combined effect of the Principal Immigrants (more than all regions) and the Immigration Multiplier (the second highest). Asia, on the other hand, ranks second in terms of its chain migration multiplier effect, because it has the second largest Principal Immigrant population and the strongest Immigration Multiplier. The low Immigration Multiplier for Europe, whose total of principal immigrants is only 90 less that of Asia, produced far less weighted Immigration Multiplier -- about 1,000 less than that of Asia. This is the case where a weak Immigration Multiplier value has significantly reduced the multiplier effect of chain migration. The Middle East shows the opposite effect: its strong

Immigration Multiplier has made its immigrant population almost one-third that of Europe, while the size of its Principal Immigrants is only one-fourth of its European counterpart.

Immigration Patterns for Top Countries

Immigration multipliers could be used for many purposes. One of the most direct uses is to measure the migration chain for top countries that send immigrants to the United States. Table 13-6 lists the top twenty countries that sent the most immigrants to the United States from 1972-1997.

Table 13-6 Immigrant Population Comparison by Top Countries

Total		Immigration Multipliers			Immigrants Total			
Rank	Country	IUM	IRM	IM	Principals	Family Immigrants	Immigrant Children	Grand Total
1	Mexico	3.08	1.96	6.04	665,825	1,384,185	1,972,532	4,022,542
2	Philippines	5.58	1.58	8.85	213,208	976,829	696,056	1,886,093
3	China	5.15	1.45	7.46	216,242	898,138	499,725	1,614,105
4	Vietnam	2.19	1.58	3.46	427,017	507,891	544,141	1,479,049
5	Dominican Republic	6.83	1.76	12.06	95,147	554,985	497,019	1,147,151
6	India	5.81	1.62	9.41	115,938	557,938	416,777	1,090,653
7	Korea	5.78	1.54	8.90	109,189	521,393	341,189	971,771
8	Cuba	1.43	1.39	1.98	378,547	161,322	210,208	750,077
9	Jamaica	5.44	1.57	8.54	83,462	370,159	259,023	712,644
10	USSR/ Russia	2.60	1.41	3.66	174,733	278,974	185,767	639,474
11	Canada	2.01	1.59	3.21	156,790	159,105	186,889	502,784
12	Haiti	3.71	1.77	6.56	71,645	194,282	204,258	470,185
13	El Salvador	4.94	1.74	8.60	52,686	207,507	192,941	453,134
14	Laos	2.08	2.08	4.32	100,050	108,446	224,216	432,712
15	Iran	2.58	1.51	3.90	106,879	168,523	141,634	417,036
16	Colombia	3.74	1.54	5.77	66,588	182,213	135,228	384,029
17	Guyana /British Guiana	5.54	1.56	8.63	35,765	162,531	110,510	308,806
18	Pakistan	5.15	1.79	9.24	30,993	128,552	126,693	286,238
19	Peru	3.42	1.59	5.42	44,339	107,127	89,041	240,507
20	San Marino	4.30	1.40	6.01	35,956	118,775	61,209	215,940
All Countries		3.12	1.66	5.19	4,995,140	10,607,541	10,339,849	25,942,530
Notes:	All countries = All countries in the data model, including those not on the top list.							

Table 13-7 ranks these countries by their Immigration Multipliers. Here, we use the Immigration Multipliers to examine the immigration patterns of these countries, because we know these multipliers can reveal the immigration patterns of the chain migration process. The following discussion will focus on some top immigrant-sending countries and their chain immigration patterns.

Table 13-7 Immigration Multipliers Comparison by Top Countries

IM Rank	Region	Country	Net IUM1	Net IUM2	Net IUM3	Net IUM4	Net IUM	IUM	IRM	IM
1	Latin America	Dominican Republic	0.40	2.94	1.73	0.77	5.83	6.83	1.76	12.06
2	Asia	India	0.65	1.23	1.11	1.82	4.81	5.81	1.62	9.41
3	Asia	Pakistan	0.53	1.17	1.03	1.42	4.15	5.15	1.79	9.24
4	Asia	Korea	0.63	1.28	1.12	1.75	4.78	5.78	1.54	8.90
5	Asia	Philippines	0.52	0.98	2.22	0.86	4.58	5.58	1.58	8.85
6	Latin America	Guyana /British Guiana	0.45	1.68	0.59	1.82	4.54	5.54	1.56	8.63
7	Latin America	El Salvador	0.91	1.77	0.92	0.34	3.94	4.94	1.74	8.60
8	Latin America	Jamaica	0.54	1.85	0.88	1.16	4.44	5.44	1.57	8.54
9	Asia	China	0.70	0.93	1.01	1.51	4.15	5.15	1.45	7.46
10	Latin America	Haiti	0.29	1.41	0.65	0.37	2.71	3.71	1.77	6.56
11	Latin America	Mexico	0.49	0.61	0.69	0.30	2.08	3.08	1.96	6.04
12	Europe	San Marino	0.24	0.57	0.61	1.88	3.30	4.30	1.40	6.01
13	Latin America	Colombia	0.35	0.86	0.99	0.54	2.74	3.74	1.54	5.77
14	Latin America	Peru	0.33	0.61	0.96	0.51	2.42	3.42	1.59	5.42
15	Asia	Laos	1.01	0.01	0.05	0.01	1.08	2.08	2.08	4.32
16	Middle East	Iran	0.49	0.28	0.54	0.27	1.58	2.58	1.51	3.90
17	Europe	USSR/ Russia	0.51	0.16	0.64	0.28	1.60	2.60	1.41	3.66
18	Asia	Vietnam	0.81	0.08	0.16	0.14	1.19	2.19	1.58	3.46
19	North America	Canada	0.49	0.09	0.23	0.20	1.01	2.01	1.59	3.21
20	Latin America	Cuba	0.24	0.02	0.05	0.11	0.43	1.43	1.39	1.98
	All Countries		**0.53**	**0.52**	**0.59**	**0.48**	**2.12**	**3.12**	**1.66**	**5.19**
	Notes		*All countries = All countries in the data model, including those not on the top list.*							

Mexico

Mexico, which sends the largest number of immigrants to the U.S., has its own unique chain migration pattern. If we check the rankings of its *IM* values, we see that Mexico ranks 11 for *IM*, number 14 for *IUM,* and number 2 for *IRM*. This suggests that the strongest multiplier effect for Mexican immigrants comes from the *reproduction level* of the chain migration process. Relatively speaking, the multiplier effect for Mexican immigrants is not as strong during the *unification level* of the chain migration process (compared to other top countries).

Table 13-8 Complete Chain Migration Model Analysis by Top Countries: Weighted Immigration Multipliers (per 1,000 Principal Immigrants)

Region	Original Total Principal Immigrants	Weighted Principal Immigrants (per 1,000) (Pw)	Net IUM	Weighted Sponsored Family Immigrants (Net IUMw)	Net IRM	Weighted Immigrant Children (Net IRMw)	IM	Grand Total (Weighted Immigration Multiplier) (IMw)
Mexico	665,825	133	2.08	277	0.96	395	6.04	805
Philippines	213,208	43	4.58	196	0.58	139	8.85	378
China	216,242	43	4.15	180	0.45	100	7.46	323
Vietnam	427,017	85	1.19	102	0.58	109	3.46	296
Dominican Republic	95,147	19	5.83	111	0.76	100	12.06	230
India	115,938	23	4.81	112	0.62	83	9.41	218
Korea	109,189	22	4.78	104	0.54	68	8.90	195
Cuba	378,547	76	0.43	32	0.39	42	1.98	150
Jamaica	83,462	17	4.44	74	0.57	52	8.54	143
USSR/Russia	174,733	35	1.60	56	0.41	37	3.66	128
Canada	156,790	31	1.01	32	0.59	37	3.21	101
Haiti	71,645	14	2.71	39	0.77	41	6.56	94
El Salvador	52,686	11	3.94	42	0.74	39	8.60	91
Laos	100,050	20	1.08	22	1.08	45	4.32	87
Iran	106,879	21	1.58	34	0.51	28	3.90	83
Colombia	66,588	13	2.74	36	0.54	27	5.77	77
Guyana/British Guiana	35,765	7	4.54	33	0.56	22	8.63	62
Pakistan	30,993	6	4.15	26	0.79	25	9.24	57
Peru	44,339	9	2.42	21	0.59	18	5.42	48
San Marino	35,956	7	3.30	24	0.40	12	6.01	43
Total	4,995,140	1,000	2.12	2,124	0.66	2,070	5.19	5,194

An examination of the details of the unification process reveals that the strongest unification multiplier effect for Mexican immigrants comes from unification Phase 2 (for sponsoring later-sponsored family members, 0.09 above the average) and unification Phase 3 (for sponsoring exempt family members of U.S. Citizens, 0.10 above the average). Since Mexican immigrants have relatively low *IUM* values for unification Phase 1 (for sponsoring accompanying family members, 0.04 below the average) and unification Phase 4 (for sponsoring non-exempt family members of U.S. citizens, 0.18 below average), the overall net *IUM* for Mexican immigrants for all unification phases is very close to the average of all immigrant countries (3.08, with the average being 3.12).

Since the unification multiplier (which is the highest among all countries) applies to all Mexican Principal Immigrants at all unification phases and the reproduction multiplier applies to all Mexican immigrants at the reproduction phase, the combined multiplier effect produced the highest Mexican immigrant population. In other words, the reason Mexico sends the largest number of immigrants to the U.S. is that it has the largest Principal Immigrant base (0.67 million from 1972-1997), an average unification multiplier (with each Principal Immigrant being responsible for 2.08 additional immigrants), and a very high reproduction multiplier (with each immigrant contributing almost 1 U.S.-born child). Therefore, the aggregate total Mexican immigrant population by 1997 was about 4 million, which topped all other countries.

Compared to other top countries using the standard per 1,000 Principal Immigrants, the Mexican immigration pattern (Please see Table 13-8) shows that 13.3% Mexican Principal Immigrants are responsible for 15.5% all weighted Immigration Multiplier.

This example shows that the number of Principal Immigrants is the foundation of the migration chain. It also demonstrates that multipliers (both unification and reproduction multipliers) are significant contributors to the growth of the immigration population.

The Philippines

The Philippines sends the second highest number of immigrants to the United States. If we examine all of the rankings of different Immigration Multipliers for the Philippines, we see that it has higher rankings for its *IUM* values than for its *IRM* values. The overall total number of immigrants sent by the Philippines is contributed mainly by combined multiplier factors. Comparing the average *IUM, IRM,* and *IM* values, we see that the Philippines has very high *IUM* values—its overall *IUM* is 5.58, which is 2.48 above the average. This means that each principal Filipino immigrant would be responsible for an additional 4.58 immigrants, 0.52 accompanying family members, 0.98 later-sponsored family members, 2.22 exempt family members of U.S. citizens, and 0.86 non-exempt family members of U.S. citizens.

We should also notice that the *IUM3* value for Filipino immigrants is the highest (2.22), which means that they have a tendency to naturalize as U.S. citizens, and then to sponsor a large number of exempt family members (spouses, minor children, and parents). With a relatively large Principal Immigrant population (0.2 million), the multiplier effect has produced a significant total of 1.89 million immigrant population during the last thirty years. Therefore, we can conclude that the strongest growth of Filipino immigrants comes from the unification phase of the chain migration process.

It is also important to note that the Philippines has a smaller size of Principal Immigrants than China (which ranks third), but that its final yield of the immigration population is higher than China's. This suggests that the Immigration Multipliers have played a larger role in contributing to the growth of the Filipino immigrant population.

This case shows that unification multipliers can contribute significantly to the growth of the immigrant population. Since the size of the second-generation immigrant population is the direct result of the multiplier effect through the reproduction multiplier at the reproduction level of the chain migration, the size of the first-generation immigration population (i.e. the combined total of Principal Immigrants and the sponsored family immigrants) that is generated by the unification multiplier is of crucial importance.

China

China is sends the third largest number of immigrants to the United States. Its immigration pattern is quite similar to the Philippines, except that its values of both *IUM* and *IRM* are lower. Therefore, the multiplier effect for Chinese immigrants is not as strong as that for Pilipino immigrants. Although the total number of Principal Immigrants from China is 3,000 more than the Philippines,[77] the final Chinese immigrant population total is actually 27,000 less than the Philippines. This phenomenon can be explained by the effect of the weaker *IM* for Chinese immigrants.

This is a classic example of the multiplier effect in action during the chain migration process. This illustration demonstrates that the migration chain not only exists, but that the Immigration Multipliers (in the form of the immigration unification and Immigration Reproduction Multipliers) also play important roles in the chain migration process. Given the similar size of its Principal Immigrant population (compared

---

[77] The total number of Chinese immigrants was 216,000. The total from the Philippines was 213,000.

to the Philippines), the smaller the values of the Immigration Multipliers, the smaller growth of the immigrant population.

Vietnam

Vietnam has its own place in U.S. immigration history. Since the late 1970s, Vietnamese refugees have flowed into the United States, and it has become one of the top countries sending *Principal Immigrants* to the U.S.—the total number Principal Immigrants is 0.43 million. It ranks second among all other countries (after Mexico, which has 0.67 million).

The immigration pattern for Vietnamese immigrants is unique; however, it has a very low *IUM* value (2.19, compared to the average of 3.12) and a below average *IRM* (1.58, compared to the average of 1.66). Therefore, its overall *IM* value ranks it 18 (out of the top 20 countries). With such a low *IM* value, the multiplier effect for Vietnamese immigrants is very weak. We can illustrate this multiplier effect by comparing Vietnamese immigration patterns with the Philippine immigration pattern.

The Philippines began with half as many Principal Immigrants as Vietnam (0.213 million *vs.* 0.427 million, or 43 *vs.* 85, if we compare the weighted Principal Immigrants P_w). However, with the high values of its *IUM* and *IRM*, the Philippine immigrants sponsored more family immigrants and produced more immigrant children than the Vietnamese immigrants. At the same time, the combined total of the Immigration Multipliers for Vietnam is very low (3.46 *vs.* 8.85 for the Philippines). As a result, the combined total of first-generation and second-generation immigrants for Vietnam is 0.407 million less than that for the Philippines, or the total weighted Immigration Multiplier for Vietnam is only 78% of that of the Philippines, and the total of Principal Immigrants from Vietnam is 50% more than from the Philippines.

This example shows that, although the number of starting Principal Immigrants is important in initiating the migration chain (as in the case of Mexico), size alone is not sufficient without having the strong Immigration Multipliers. Similar to the stronger multiplier effect generated by a larger immigration, a smaller Immigration Multiplier would significantly reduce the multiplier effect. Given a sizable Principal Immigrant population, if the Immigration Multipliers are small (both the Immigration Unification Multipliers and the

Immigration Reproduction Multipliers), then the final growth of this immigrant population will not be as great as other countries with higher values of Immigration Multipliers.

Dominican Republic

Dominican Republic is another unique country whose migration pattern well demonstrates the multiplier effect. Ranked fifth among the top 20 countries in terms of its combined total of immigrant population, it also holds first place in *IUM* and *IM* values, while its *IRM* values rank fifth. These values imply that family reunification plays a larger role in this country's migration pattern.

If we closely examine the *IUM*, *IRM,* and *IM* values, we see that most of the *IUM* values for immigrants from the Dominican Republic are all significantly higher than the reference average. The most significant *IUM* values for immigrants from the Dominican Republic are the net *IUM* values at Phase 2 (for sponsoring later-sponsored family members) and Phase 3 (for sponsoring exempt family members of U.S. citizens). This means that each Principal Immigrant from the Dominican Republic is responsible for, regardless of direct or indirect sponsorship, 2.94 later-sponsored family members, and 1.73 exempt family members of U.S. citizens (foreign-born spouses of naturalized U.S. citizens, minor children, and parents of U.S. citizens).

It is noticeable that the *IRM* values for the immigrants from Dominican Republic is also very high (1.76). (The reference average is 1.66.) This, along with its high *IUM* values, has significantly increased the multiplier effect for immigrants from the Dominican Republic. With all of the multipliers combined, the joined impact of the chain migration process of immigrants from the Dominican Republic has made the country, which began with fewer than 100,000 Principal Immigrants, the fifth highest country for the combined total of first-generation and second-generation immigrants (over 1.1 million).

This example demonstrates that, in the case of a small Principal Immigrant population, the Immigration Multipliers (in the form of the immigration unification and Immigration Reproduction Multipliers) are the most powerful force contributing to the significant growth of this immigrant population.

Conclusion

This is one of the most important chapters of this study. Here, I have presented every aspect of the Immigration Multipliers, including the method, the logic, and the results as part of the Complete Chain Migration Model. As shown in various examples, all of the *IM* values (*net IUM, IUM, net IRM, IRM, IM and net IM*) are interrelated, and they can easily be converted from one to another. For example, we can convert the Phase 1 net *IUM* for ERI and GSI principals to the standardized net *IUM* by using the weight distribution of the Principal Immigrants (ERI, GSI, and FSUSB Principals). From various immigration patterns (from different regions and different countries), we have learned the different roles of Principal Immigrants, Immigration Unification Multipliers, and Immigration Reproduction Multipliers. Different combinations of the total number of Principal Immigrants, the Immigration Unification Multipliers, and the Immigration Reproduction Multiplier can yield different results. All of the examples in this chapter have demonstrated that the Immigration Multipliers are the most powerful force contributing to the significant growth of the immigrant population in the United States.

The next chapter will focus on the study of one of the applications of the Immigration Multiplier: a simulation model. I will attempt to adjust different parameters in the Complete Chain Migration Model to simulate the multiplier effect so that we can estimate the potential impact of Immigration Multipliers.

Understanding Immigration Multipliers: Simulation Results

In this chapter, we will use the Complete Chain Migration Model and the Immigration Multiplier to simulate some of the changes in the chain migration process so that we can observe the multiplier effects. We will calculate the simulations by setting up different, but *controllable,* parameters. This purpose of this chapter is to study the impact and consequences of such adjustments.

SIMULATION ON EMPLOYMENT RELATED IMMIGRANTS

The U.S. government has modified its immigration policies on employment-related immigrants several times over the last three decades. Each time, it increased the annual limit allowed for this particular immigration category to attract more highly skilled professionals, as well as workers that are in high demand in the United States.

ERIs (Employment Related Immigrants) include ERI Principals, who are sponsored by employers in the United States or through other means (those who invest in the U.S.), and derived ERIs, who are dependents and family members of principal ERIs, as well as the descendents of the principal ERIs (first-generation).

The simulation results in Table 14-1 illustrate the historical ERI immigration patterns with the existing annual limits on this immigration category (for selected years). The data shows clearly that both the total number of ERI Principals and the Immigration Multipliers have increased over time, which is the result of increased ERI numerical caps and increased *IM* values. We should note that *IRM* has also been decreasing, which could mean a time-lag factor for the production of second-generation children resulting from a surge of immigrants in the late 1980s and 1990s (increased denominator).

Table 14-1 Simulation on ERIs with Original Data by Selected Years

Actual Data	ERI Principals	IUM	Family Immigrants	IRM	Immigrant Children	IM	Estimated Total Impact
1972	17,784	2.57	28,002	1.87	40,008	4.82	85,793
1980	21,512	3.52	54,194	1.63	47,344	5.72	123,050
1990	23,091	3.88	66,607	1.67	60,265	6.49	149,963
1997	41,850	3.93	122,810	1.55	90,294	6.09	254,954
Note:	*The net IUM for unification Phase 2 calculated here is ERI principal specific net IUM (excluding GSI principals and FSUSB principals).*						

Table 14-2 uses annual Immigration Multipliers to simulate the same initial population of 100,000 ERI Principals to evaluate the comparable impact for selected years. From the simulated results, we can see that the annual total number of ERI immigrants from the same original 100,000 ERI Principals mainly would fluctuate based on the Immigration Multipliers (and the immigration unification and the Immigration Reproduction Multipliers). Since the values of these *IM* values have slowly increased from about 4.82 in 1972 to 6.09 in 1997, the estimated annual total number of ERIs has increased from 0.482 million in 1972 to 0.609 million in 1997.

Table 14-2 Simulation on ERIs with 100,000 Principals by Selected Years

Simulated Results	ERI Principals	IUM	Family Immigrants	IRM	Immigrant Children	IM	Estimated Total Impact
1972	100,000	2.57	157,454	1.87	224,966	4.82	482,420
1980	100,000	3.52	251,926	1.63	220,081	5.72	572,007
1990	100,000	3.88	288,455	1.67	260,988	6.49	649,444
1997	100,000	3.93	293,453	1.55	215,756	6.09	609,209

Now, we can examine the regional variations in Table 14-3. We see that Asia led all regions in sending ERIs over the last three decades. With the total number of about 0.369 million ERI Principals in this category, the final number of ERIs and their family members and the second-generations in this category would eventually reach 2.2 million (with a net impact of 1.8 million, which is the sum of family immigrants and immigrant children, *i.e.*, 1 million plus 0.8 million). The Immigration Multiplier is about 5.98.

Latin America is in second place with about 0.127 million Principal Immigrants in the last three decades. The total ERIs, however, were over 0.8 million (with a net impact of over 0.677 million). It does have a higher Immigration Multiplier, which is about 6.34.

Table 14-3 Simulation on ERIs with Original Data by Regions

Actual Data	ERI Principals	*IUM*	Family Immigrants	*IRM*	Immigrant Children	*IM*	Estimated Total Impact
Asia	369,497	3.81	1,038,709	1.57	802,666	5.98	2,210,872
Latin America	126,950	3.55	324,088	1.78	353,321	6.34	804,358
Europe	138,030	2.89	261,103	1.54	217,459	4.47	616,591
Middle East	40,394	3.61	105,614	1.74	108,689	6.31	254,697
North America	30,133	3.48	74,745	1.61	64,365	5.62	169,243
Africa	28,460	2.78	50,554	1.76	59,793	4.88	138,807
Oceania /Other	7,453	2.98	14,774	1.44	9,850	4.30	32,077

Although Europe had more principal ERIs than Latin America (with 0.138 million principal ERIs, compared to 0.127 million principal ERIs from Latin America), it contributed significantly fewer total ERIs and their derived family immigrants. (The net impact was 0.479 million, compared to 0.677 million of net impact from Latin America.) The reason is the Immigration Multiplier is much lower for Europe (4.47) than for Latin America (6.34)—a difference of 1.87. This implies that for each Principal Immigrant, the European Principal Immigrant would eventually contribute 1.87 family immigrants and/or second-generation immigrants fewer than his/her Latin American counterpart.

This illustrates the effect of Immigration Multiplier. As we have learned, the higher the Immigration Multiplier, the faster the immigrant population grows.

Now we are going to focus on the Immigration Multiplier. By comparing regions with Immigration Multipliers only, we can identify the fastest growing regions in ERIs. In order to make this comparison, we would use 100,000 as the base starting number of Principal Immigrants.

Table 14-4 Simulation on ERIs with 100,000 Principals by Regions

Simulated Results	ERI Principals	IUM	Family Immigrants	IRM	Immigrant Children	IM	Estimated Total Impact
Latin America	100,000	3.55	255,288	1.78	278,315	6.34	633,602
Middle East	100,000	3.61	261,458	1.74	269,073	6.31	630,531
Asia	100,000	3.81	281,114	1.57	217,232	5.98	598,346
North America	100,000	3.48	248,050	1.61	213,602	5.62	561,652
Africa	100,000	2.78	177,632	1.76	210,095	4.88	487,728
Europe	100,000	2.89	189,164	1.54	157,544	4.47	446,708
Oceania /Other	100,000	2.98	198,227	1.44	132,166	4.30	430,393

From the simulation results shown in Table 14-4, we can see that Latin America would be the leading region contributing ERIs, if all of the other regions were to send 100,000 principal ERIs at the same time. This is primarily because Latin America has the highest Immigration Multiplier on ERIs (6.34). This suggests that each ERI from Latin America would contribute an additional 5.34 immigrants (either derived family immigrants or U.S.-born children to immigrant parents, or both) to the U.S. population.

Similarly, we can see that the Middle East would be second in impact of overall total number of immigrants and the number of derived family members it contributes. This is because of the high values of its Immigration Multipliers (IM=6.31, IUM=3.61, IRM=1.74). Asia ranks third, with an IM at the value of 5.98; North America ranks fourth with its IM value being 5.62; and Africa, Europe, and Oceania have the lowest Immigration Multipliers (ranging from 4.30 to 4.88).

We can reach the conclusion that the growth of ERI population directly ties not only to the original size of the Principal Immigrants, but also to the Immigration Multipliers. The higher the Immigration Multiplier, the faster the ERI immigrants would grow.

SIMULATION ON GOVERNMENT SPONSORED IMMIGRANTS

To understand U.S. policy on Government Sponsored Immigrants, we begin with the historical trend of Government Sponsored Immigrants. As we know, Government Sponsored Immigrants (GSI) include immigrants like the Diversity Program, Refugees, "immigrants who do not qualify under family/employment preferences," "aliens born in the independent Western Hemisphere," or special immigrants, which include employees and dependents of special interests (such as international organizations, U.S. government personnel abroad, ministers of religion, diplomats of foreign countries, etc.).

Although some Classes of Admissions (COA) are no longer available, it is still meaningful for us to simulate GSIs so that we understand the immigration pattern better. As we have done so far, we will use the historical data on government-sponsored immigration to complete the simulation calculations.

Table 14-5 is the simulation result of total number of GSIs that come to the United States derived from the GSI Principals based on the USCIS data for selected years. It seems that there has been no overall trend of GSIs over the last three decades: the overall total number of GSIs and their derived family immigrants changed from 0.455 million in 1972, to 0.464 million in 1997. This zero-increase situation mirrors a similar growth pattern in the Immigration Multipliers. If we look into the values of *IM*s (*IUM*s, *IRM*s, and *IM*s), we see that the *IRM* trend has been going down since the 1970s, while the *IUM* values have been going up. However, the net loss of the *IRM* cancelled the net gain of the *IUM*s. Hence, the final *IM* values have experienced no major change.

Table 14-5 Simulation on GSI with Original Data by Selected Years

Actual Data	GSI Principals	*IUM*	Family Immigrants	*IRM*	Immigrant Children	*IM*	Estimated Total Impact
1972	102,861	2.36	139,924	1.87	212,149	4.42	454,934
1980	76,683	3.07	158,375	1.63	146,996	4.98	382,054
1990	96,477	3.37	228,294	1.67	218,201	5.63	542,972
1997	85,593	3.50	213,918	1.55	164,241	5.42	463,752
Note:	The net *IUM* for unification Phase 2 calculated here is GSI principal specific net *IUM* (excluding ERI principals and FSUSB principals).						

Table 14-6 shows the simulation results for 100,000 principal GSIs annually for selected years. We see that the total number of derived family immigrants from the original 100,000 principal GSIs by the end of the 1990s gained a net 100 thousand since the 1970s, and this has contributed mainly by increasing values of the Immigration Multipliers over the last three decades.

Now, we can examine the variations in Table 14-7 to study the regional variations for GSIs. The data in the table show that over the last three decades, Latin America had the highest GSIs volume among all regions. With the total number of almost 1 million GSI Principals in this category, the combined total number of all GSIs from Latin America in this category reached 5.1 million (with almost 4.2 million derived). The Immigration Multiplier for Latin America is about 5.33, which is the second to highest region among all of the regions. Asia is the next biggest region in this category. With 0.7 million principal GSIs over the last three decades, Asia has a total number of 4.1 million GSIs (with 3.4 million derived). The Immigration Multiplier for Asia is the highest, at about 5.74.

Table 14-6 Simulation on GSI with 100,000 Principals by Selected Years

Simulated Results	GSI Principals	IUM	Family Immigrants	IRM	Immigrant Children	IM	Estimated Total Impact
1972	100,000	2.36	136,032	1.87	206,248	4.42	442,280
1980	100,000	3.07	206,532	1.63	191,693	4.98	498,225
1990	100,000	3.37	236,630	1.67	226,169	5.63	562,799
1997	100,000	3.50	249,925	1.55	191,886	5.42	541,811

Table 14-7 Simulation on GSIs with Original Data by Regions

Simulated Results	GSI Principals	IUM	Family Immigrants	IRM	Immigrant Children	IM	Estimated Total Impact
Latin America	962,444	2.99	1,914,246	1.78	2,253,457	5.33	5,130,146
Asia	719,024	3.66	1,909,921	1.57	1,498,478	5.74	4,127,423
Europe	518,206	2.50	776,271	1.54	705,268	3.86	1,999,745
Middle East	100,179	3.04	204,317	1.74	226,670	5.30	531,166
Africa	87,757	2.19	104,724	1.76	145,658	3.85	338,138
North America	30,416	2.22	37,035	1.61	41,396	3.58	108,847
Oceania /Other	3,292	2.72	5,651	1.44	3,963	3.92	12,906

With 518,206 Principal Immigrants, Europe contributed a total number of 2 million GSIs (with 1.5 derived). The Immigration Multiplier for Europe was among the lowest of all regions at 3.86.

The sizes of GSIs from other regions (Middle East, Africa, North America, and Oceania) are relatively small. However, their Immigration Multipliers are quite different. The Immigration

Multiplier for the Middle East (5.30) is very similar to that of Latin America (5.33); therefore, this is region has the potential to grow in the future.

If we focus on the Immigration Multiplier, we should be able to identify the region with the fastest rate of growth or the largest multiplier power through the chain migration process. We accomplish this by simulating all regions with the same 100,000 starting GSI Principals, as in Table 14-8.

Table 14-8 Simulation on GSIs with 100,000 Principals by Regions

Simulated Results	GSI Principals	IUM	Family Immigrants	IRM	Immigrant Children	IM	Estimated Total Impact
Asia	100,000	3.66	265,627	1.57	208,404	5.74	574,031
Latin America	100,000	2.99	198,894	1.78	234,139	5.33	533,033
Middle East	100,000	3.04	203,952	1.74	226,265	5.30	530,217
Oceania /Other	100,000	2.72	171,646	1.44	120,386	3.92	392,032
Europe	100,000	2.50	149,800	1.54	136,098	3.86	385,898
Africa	100,000	2.19	119,334	1.76	165,978	3.85	385,312
North America	100,000	2.22	121,763	1.61	136,099	3.58	357,862

The ranking in Table 14-8 is based completely on the Immigration Multiplier. The top region is the one that multiplies the fastest. In this case, Asia is the top with the highest Immigration Multiplier on GSIs (5.74). With 100,000 principal GSIs, Asia would eventually generate a total number of 0.474 million derived family immigrants in the U.S., which would include 0.266 million sponsored dependents and family members and 0.208 million children born in the U.S. to Asian immigrants.

The Immigration Multipliers for GSIs for regions such as Latin America and the Middle East are similar, ranging from 5.30 to 5.33. However, the patterns are a little different. The *IUM*s for Latin America is lower than that for the Middle East, while the *IRM* for Latin America is higher than that for the Middle East. (In fact, the *IRM* for Latin America is the highest of the seven regions.)

The Immigration Multipliers for GSIs from regions such as Europe, Africa, North America, and Oceania are the lowest, at around 3.58 to 3.92. Their immigration patterns were also similar, except for

Africa. Africa has the lowest *IUM* value (2.19) and the second highest *IRM* value (1.76).

Here, we confirm our earlier conclusion: the growth of GSI population is directly tied not only to the size of the original Principal Immigrant population, but also to the Immigration Multipliers. The higher the Immigration Multiplier, the faster the GSI immigrants will grow.

SIMULATION ON SPONSORING SIBLINGS OF U.S. CITIZENS

"Siblings" is one of the few immigration categories that is beyond the definition of the nuclear family. If we emphasize family reunification using the standard definition of the nuclear family, then we would not consider siblings as a core part of the unification process.

Based on this assumption, we could then simulate the scenario by setting the immigration quota for siblings of U.S. citizens to zero. In such a scenario, we could then calculate the net impact of the magnitude of the reduction caused by such an imaginary policy adjustment. We will provide three comparable results in the simulated model: minimum impact, estimated impact, and maximum impact. These are the following calculation methods we used:

Minimum Impact is the net total number of siblings of U.S. citizens, assuming that there will be no further sponsorship of these siblings.

Estimated Impact is calculated based on the newly modified *IUM*, excluding the total number of siblings sponsored by U.S. citizens. The new estimated impact would then be the difference of the original total number of immigrants and the new total number under this new scenario.[78]

Maximum Impact, however, is derived from the assumption that all of these siblings would behave like Principal Immigrants and start complete new sets of chains to sponsor their family members using the given Immigration Multipliers. Since many of the family members of these siblings have already migrated to the U.S., it is not possible for

---

[78] I will assume that there will be no changes in reproductive behavior and that the age structure of the sibling population is similar to the immigrant population. Therefore, no *IRM* adjustment is necessary.

them to generate a new population with such a hypothetical sponsorship. However, providing this value would help us understand the maximum impact of the sibling population.

To simulate the policy adjustment for sibling immigrants, we must ask a what-if question. If the immigration category for sponsoring siblings of U.S. citizens were to be removed, what impact would that have on the immigration process, as a whole? Here, the policy implication is that, if such adjustment were made, the total number of immigrants would decrease. By how much? Table 14-9 answers this question by presenting the simulated data with minimum impact, estimated impact, and maximum impact, along with the actual data, based on data from census years 1980 and 1990.[79]

Table 14-9 Simulation on Siblings of US Citizens with Original Data by Selected Years

	Scenarios	Principals	Siblings Total	IM	Total Immigrants	Min. Impact	Est. Impact	Max. Impact
1980	Actual	167,628	96,657	5.32	891,284			
	Simulation with no Siblings	167,628	0	4.38	734,182	96,657	157,102	423,341
1990	Actual	195,684	64,373	5.75	1,125,625			
	Simulation with no Siblings	195,684	0	5.20	1,018,002	64,373	107,623	334,886

Table 14-9 shows that there would be a slight decline from 1980 to 1990 in the total net impact of sibling immigrants, if we were to implement the immigration policy of removing the category of sibling sponsorship. The estimated impact is about 157 thousand (ranging from 96,657 to 423,341) in 1980, and dropping to about 108 thousand in 1990 (within the range of 64,373 to 334,886).

Now, we will examine another angle by standardizing the initial Principal Immigrants before we make comparisons. Table 14-10

---

[79] Please note that the calculation of the fertility rates are based on U.S. Census data; therefore, the *IRM* for non-census years are estimated. Hence, I present only census-year data. Since USCIS data for year 2000 does not include detailed Class of Admission data, I could not present immigration data for year 2000.

includes simulations for 1980 and 1990 with the same 100,000 initial Principal Immigrants.

Table 14-10 Simulation on Siblings of US Citizens with 100,000 Principals by Select Years

	Scenarios	PIs	IUM4 for SIB	SIB	IM	Total Immi.	Min. Impact	Est. Impact	Max. Impact
1980	Simulation with Siblings	100,000	0.58	57,662	5.32	531,704			
	Simulation with no Siblings	100,000		0	4.38	437,983	57,662	93,721	252,548
1990	Simulation with Siblings	100,000	0.33	32,896	5.75	575,226			
	Simulation with no Siblings	100,000		0	5.20	520,227	32,896	54,998	171,136
Notes:	*PI = Principal Immigrants*								
	IUM4 for SIB = Phase 4 Immigration Unification Multiplier for Siblings of U.S. Citizens								
	SIB = Total Number of Siblings of U.S. Citizens								
	IM = Immigration Multiplier								
	Total Immi. = Total Immigrants								

We see that, if we begin with a principal population of 100,000 and remove the category of siblings of U.S. citizens, this would have an estimated impact of 93,721 (within the range of 57,662 to 252,548) immigrants in 1980. Then, with the same principal population of 100,000, we would see a decline in the 1990, which would yield about 55 thousand sibling related immigrants (within the range of 32,896 to 171,136).

For regional comparisons, the simulation calculations are similar. Table 14-11 shows the minimum impact, estimated impact, and maximum impact of the adjustment of the sibling sponsorship (i.e. removing the sibling sponsorship category in the immigration process), for all regions, using the original Principal Immigrants for each region as the starting population. We see that Asia topped all regions in terms of the total impact of the adjustment in sibling sponsorship, with an estimated impact of 1.3 million (within the range of 0.8 million to 4.3 million).

Latin America is second in terms of negative impact of the policy adjustment for removing siblings of U.S.-born citizens. The total estimated impact would be 0.677 million (within the range of 0.445 million to 2 million).

Europe is a distant third, with about 0.296 million siblings of U.S. citizens (within the range of 0.257 million to 0.636 million). Compared to Asia and Latin America, the impact of Europe would be relatively small, if the category for siblings was removed.

Table 14-11 Simulation on Siblings of US Citizens with Original Data by Region

Regions	Model	Principals	Siblings Total	*IM*	Total Immi.	Min. Impact	Est. Impact	Max. Impact
Africa	Actual	235,722	38,992	3.63	854,587			
	Sim. with no Siblings	235,722	0	3.33	786,088	38,992	68,499	130,031
Asia	Actual	1,449,523	844,647	5.95	8,629,727			
	Sim. with no Siblings	1,449,523	0	5.04	7,303,638	844,647	1,326,089	4,255,880
Europe	Actual	1,001,807	257,125	2.77	2,773,565			
	Sim. with no Siblings	1,001,807	0	2.47	2,477,090	257,125	296,475	635,773
Latin America	Actual	1,845,059	444,680	4.94	9,123,341			
	Sim. with no Siblings	1,845,059	0	4.58	8,446,083	444,680	677,258	2,035,601
Middle East	Actual	256,054	112,468	4.47	1,143,969			
	Sim. with no Siblings	256,054	0	3.82	978,136	112,468	165,832	429,632
North America	Actual	162,973	19,912	21.37	3,482,217			
	Sim. with no Siblings	162,973	0	20.15	3,283,631	19,912	198,585	401,193
Oceania /Other	Actual	44,002	17,112	10.61	466,949			
	Sim. with no Siblings	44,002	0	8.77	386,093	17,112	80,855	150,148

For the remaining regions, the estimated impacts are all less than 200 thousand. Therefore, the impact for these regions will not be as large as for Asia, Latin America, and Europe.

Now, if we adjust the total Principal Immigrants for each region and perform the simulation again using the 100,000 population as the starting population, we see a different picture. (See Table 14-12.) As we know, this comparison would help us understand the pure Immigration Multiplier without worrying about the impact of the original number of Principal Immigrants.

Here, we would see that Asia continues to lead in terms of the overall impact of removing siblings, with 91,485 (range: 58,271– 293,606). The Middle East and Oceania are second and third, respectively, with the estimated impacts of 776,621 and 56,124 respectively.

Table 14-12 Simulation on Siblings of US Citizens: with 100 Thousand Principal Immigrants by Region

Regions	Model	Principal Immigrants	Siblings Total	IM	Total Immigrants	Min. Impact	Estimated Impact	Max. Impact
Africa	Actual	100,000	16,542	3.63	362,540			
	Simulate with no Siblings	100,000	0	3.33	333,481	16,542	29,059	55,163
Asia	Actual	100,000	58,271	5.95	595,349			
	Simulate. with no Siblings	100,000	0	5.04	503,865	58,271	91,485	293,606
Europe	Actual	100,000	25,666	3.71	370,929			
	Simulate. with no Siblings	100,000	0	3.31	331,279	25,666	39,650	85,026
Latin America	Actual	100,000	24,101	5.79	578,994			
	Simulate. with no Siblings	100,000	0	5.36	536,013	24,101	42,981	129,185
Middle East	Actual	100,000	43,924	5.29	528,556			
	Simulate. with no Siblings	100,000	0	4.52	451,936	43,924	76,621	198,506
North America	Actual	100,000	12,218	3.46	345,727			
	Simulate. with no Siblings	100,000	0	3.26	326,011	12,218	19,716	39,832
Oceania /Other	Actual	100,000	38,889	3.24	324,122			
	Simulate. with no Siblings	100,000	0	2.68	267,998	38,889	56,124	104,222

Latin America ranks fourth. For each 100,000 Principal Immigrants, it would have about 43,000 sibling-derived family immigrants. The impacts of the other regions (Europe, North America, and Africa) are all relatively small (less than 40 thousand).

Visa Backlog and the Simulation

It is very important to know, however, that the simulation presented here does not take into consideration the significant visa backlogs that we discussed in Chapter 5. In fact, the true impact of the elimination of the Siblings of U.S. Citizens category will vary from country to country, because some countries have longer waiting periods for applying for visas under this category. It does suggest that a much greater impact will be observed for immigrants from those countries that have larger visa backlogs (as in the case of for immigrants from Mexico and the Philippines), because of the significant number of pending and new cases.

Since the overall waiting time for most countries is about 11 years, the estimated total immigrants under this visa category is about 0.715 million (11* 0.65 million, where that is the annual cap for this visa category). If we apply the overall Immigration Multiplier based on our calculations from the past thirty years (5.3), we will then have the estimated 3.8 million immigrants (5.3*0.715 million), which would include all immigrants who have applied under this category, plus the family members they will sponsor once they are admitted to the U.S. This number (3.8 million) would be the theoretical ceiling of all potential immigrants in this visa category, assuming that these siblings would be less likely to sponsor other siblings, and that the Immigration Multiplier remains the same in the future.

ESTIMATING UNDOCUMENTED IMMIGRANTS

In the case of simulating the impact of legalized undocumented immigrants, we can assume the following:

- All undocumented immigrants are Principal Immigrants, because no one officially sponsors them.
- All undocumented immigrants came to the US without accompanying family members. This means that level 1 *IUM* would be zero (0).
- The legalized undocumented immigrants would follow the immigrant pattern of their regions.

I will perform the following simulation to estimate their minimum and maximum impact:

Minimum Impact: Assuming that undocumented immigrants would participate only in reproductive level activities, the total number of undocumented immigrants with the standard *IRM* will yield an estimated minimum total number of possible derived family immigrants (immigrant children born in the U.S.).

Maximum Impact: Assuming that undocumented immigrants would be legalized later and that they would sponsor their family members in the same sponsorship patterns, the total number of undocumented immigrants (i.e. the Immigration Multiplier pattern) will yield the estimated maximum total number of possible derived family immigrants (both sponsored family members and immigrant children born in the U.S.).

Making these assumptions, the simulation results using data from year 1980, 1990, and 2000 as illustrated in Table 14-13 show that the simulated minimum impact has declined over the last three decades, because of the declining *IRM* (which was derived from the fertility rate). At the same time, the estimated maximum impact has been increasing over the last three decades, but not as significantly. The data also suggests that legalizing 100,000 undocumented immigrants would add about 0.2 million to 0.5 million immigrants in total.[80]

Table 14-14 shows the simulation results for all regions. It suggests that Asia, Latin America and the Middle East have the highest Immigration Multipliers; therefore, 100,000 legalized Principal Immigrants from these regions would produce 0.5 to 1.5 million new immigrants.

Asia leads in multiplying undocumented immigrants. Legalizing 100,000 undocumented immigrants would actually bring in about 156,999 to 535,081 derived family immigrants.

Similarly, legalizing 100,000 undocumented immigrants from Latin America would generate 178,335 to 492,486 immigrants.

Since the *IM* values for the Middle East are quite similar to those for Latin America, the estimated impact of legalizing 100,000 undocumented immigrants from the Middle East would range from 174,441 to 476,851, which is very similar to that of Latin America.

Table 14-13 Estimating the Impact of 100,000 Undocumented Immigrants Using Multipliers of Selected Years

Est.	UI	*IUM*	Family Immigrants	*IRM*	Immigrant Children	*IM*	Min. Impact	Max. Impact
1972	100,000	1.08	107,734	1.87	181,520	2.02	187,381	389,254
1980	100,000	1.99	198,906	1.63	186,924	3.23	162,536	485,830
1990	100,000	1.98	198,494	1.67	200,547	3.32	167,186	499,041
1997	100,000	1.88	188,499	1.55	158,203	2.92	154,837	446,702
Notes	UI = Undocumented Immigrants							

All other regions (Oceania, Europe, Africa, and North America) would each generate only about 0.144 million to 0.33 million for every 100,000 undocumented immigrants.

---

[80] It is worth noting that the decline of the impact in 1997 is related to the decline of the estimated immigrant fertility rate, which is the combined results of the time-lag factor and the surge of the first-generation immigrants as discussed earlier. Therefore, the true impact should be much higher.

Table 14-14 Estimating the Impact of 100,000 Undocumented Immigrants by Regions

Simulation Results	Undocumented Immigrants	Family Immigrants	Immigrant Children	IM	Min. Impact	Max. Impact
Asia	100,000	240,817	194,263	3.78	156,999	535,081
Latin America	100,000	176,158	216,328	3.14	178,335	492,486
Middle East	100,000	173,360	203,491	3.02	174,441	476,851
Europe	100,000	114,256	116,732	1.77	154,483	330,988
Africa	100,000	87,037	141,538	1.53	175,674	328,575
North America	100,000	91,787	117,702	1.48	161,371	309,489
Oceania/Other	100,000	105,754	91,185	1.53	144,317	296,939

CONCLUSIONS

The simulation models have presented several different scenarios in terms of U.S. citizens' sponsorships, employment related immigration flow, and government and sponsored immigration control, as well as the possible adjustment of the sponsorship policies on siblings of U.S. citizens. We performed different calculations and compared data from different regions and countries. The overall results show that the Immigration Multipliers and the original total number of Principal Immigrants are the determining factors for the final outcomes of the total size of the immigrant population, with derived family immigrants included.

Latin America and Asia are the leading countries in every immigration category (including the Principal Immigrants and the derived family members/dependent immigrants). The size of immigration population and the values of the Immigration Multipliers for both Latin America and Asia demonstrate that the combination of oversized immigrant populations and the strong Immigration Multiplier effect (both the unification multiplier effect and the reproduction multiplier effect) will lead to a fast-growing immigrant population.

All of the results of the simulation models lead us to conclude that, if we control the number of Principal Immigrants, the Immigration Multiplier is the key factor for determining what that will contribute to the growth of any immigrant population.

CHAPTER 15
Conclusions

As we have discussed in this book, chain migration exists within the economic, sociological, demographic, political, and other non socioeconomic frameworks, and the Immigration Multipliers developed under the Complete Chain Migration Model framework can measure and explain the chain immigration process in the U.S. Instead of looking at the chain migration process as a special phenomenon, the Complete Chain Migration Model provides a unifying tool for examining the whole immigration cycle: from the initiation of the migration process by the Principal Immigrants, to the family reunification process that is universal to all immigration processes across the world, to the final settlement and production of second-generation immigrants as the final stage of the immigration process.

Since immigration patterns vary by both region and country, we learned from the Complete Chain Migration Model that the Immigration Multipliers for various regions and countries are quite different. This is determined mainly by the family reunification process (measured by *Immigration Unification Multipliers),* and the family reproduction process (measured by the *Immigration Reproduction Multiplier).*

We also concluded that (1) the selectivity of Principal Immigrants from different regions and different countries is determined by the U.S. immigration policy; (2) the future sponsorship of family members is determined by the combination of U.S. immigration policies and the social and cultural background of the regions and countries from which the immigrants come; and (3) the number of immigrant children is determined by various immigrant fertility patterns. With the standardized Immigration Multipliers, we have compared immigration patterns for immigrants from different regions and countries.

It is important to note that no demographic research on immigration processes has ever combined the immigration unification and the immigration reproduction processes in one complete model. This research is a first attempt to do so. We successfully performed the calculations by combining the immigration data sets with the U.S. Census.

Furthermore, the simulation models that we built and compared helped us understand the implications of real-life situations of different policy changes and adjustments.

The new Immigration Multiplier method introduced in this book has many aspects that other traditional measures do not have. The most important are: *measurable* (for measuring the chain migration process), *complete* (for measuring both the first-generation immigrants and the second-generation), *comparable* (for comparing immigration patterns region-by-region, country-by-country, year-by-year), and *manageable* (for simulating and predicting future immigration patterns).

This research does not stop here. This is actually only the beginning of a long process. Since the actual calculations need census data, we must refresh the data sets every 10 years in order to recalculate the Immigration Multipliers.

With this concept and method of the Immigration Multiplier developed in this book, we know not only how to calculate the Immigration Multiplier, but we also know how to use it to measure the migration chains for any type of immigrant population. Measuring the immigrant population is only the first step. Using this new method and its results, we cannot only determine the different immigration patterns among various immigrant populations, but we can also explain why they are different. We can also use it to measure the migration chains and identify the multiplier effects. This book provides a tool for better understanding the chain migration process by combining the unification process and the reproduction process.

References

Abbasi-Shavazi M.J. and P. McDonald. 2000. Fertility and multiculturalism: Immigrant fertility in Australia, 1977-1991. *International Migration Review* 34 (1): 215-242

Abenaty, F.K. 2003. Family and Social Networks among St Lucian Migrants in Britain: The Birmingham Connection. *Community, Work & Family* 6(1):17-27

Ahlburg, D.A. 1993. The Census Bureau's New Projection of the U.S. Population. *Population and Development Review* 19(1):159-174

Alba, R. and N. Denton. 2004. Old and New Landscapes of Diversity: The Residential Patterns of Immigrant Minorities. In N. Foner and G.M. Fredrickson (eds). *Not Just Black and White: Historical and Contemporary Perspectives on Immigration Race and Ethnicity in the United States.* New York: Russell Sage Foundation

Althaus, F. 1990. Fertility of Immigrants from Asia and Pacific Shifts Towards U.S. Norm. *Family Planning Perspectives* 22(1): 45-46

Andorka, R. 1978. *Determinants of Fertility in Advanced Societies.* New York: The Free Press.

Arnold, F., B.V. Carino, J.T. Fawcett and I.H. Park. 1989. Estimating the Immigration Multiplier: An Analysis of Recent Korean and Filipino Immigration to the United States. *International Migration Review* 23(4):813-838.

Azam, F-I. 1998. International Migration Dynamics in High and Low Migration Districts of Pakistan. In R. Appleyard (ed.) *Emigration Dynamics in Developing Countries, Volume II, South Asia.* Ashgate Publishers, UK.

Bach, R.L. 1981. Migration and Fertility in Malaysia: A Tale of Two Hypotheses. *International Migration Review* 15(3): 502-521.

Banerjee, B. 1983a. The Role of the Informal Sector in the Migration Process: A Test of Probabilistic Migration Models and Labour Market Segmentation for India. *Oxford Economic Papers (New Series)* 35(3).

Banerjee, B. 1983b. Social Networks in the Migration Process: Empirical Evidence on Chain Migration in India. *The Journal of Developing Areas* 17(2):185-96.

Baxter, Kylie. 2006. From Migrants to Citizens: Muslims in Britain 1950s-1990s. *Immigrants & Minorities*. 24 (2): 164 - 192

Bean, F.D. and G. Stevens. 2003. *America's Newcomers and the Dynamics of Diversity*. New York: Russell Sage Foundation.

Bean, F.D. and C.G. Swicegood. 1985. *Mexican American Fertility Patterns*. Austin: University of Texas Press.

Bean, F.D., C.G. Swicegood and R. Berg. 2000. Mexican-Origin Fertility: New Patterns and Interpretations. *Social Science Quarterly* 81(1): 404-420

Bean, F.D., C.G. Swicegood and T.F. Linsley. 1981, Patterns of Fertility Variations among Mexican American and Black Fertility. *Texas Population Research Center Paper* No. 5.018

Becker, G.S. 1981. *A Treatise on the Family*. Cambridge, MA: Harvard University Press

Birrell, R. 1994. Immigration Control in Australia. In M.J. Miller (ed.) *Strategies for Immigration Control: An International Comparison*. Series: *Annals of the American Academy of Political and Social Science* Vol. 534. Thousand Oaks, CA: Sage Periodicals Press

Blau, F.D. 1992. The Fertility of Immigrant Women: Evidence from High-Fertility Source Countries. In G.J. Borjas and R.B. Freeman (eds.) *Immigration and the Work Force: Economic Consequences for the United States and Source Areas*. Chicago: University of Chicago Press

Böcker, A. 1994. Chain Migration over Legally Closed Borders: Settled Immigrants as Bridgeheads and Gatekeepers. *Netherlands' Journal of Social Sciences* 30 (2).

Body-Gendrot, S. 1995. Models of Immigrant Integration in France and the United States: Signs of Convergence? In M.P. Smith and J.R. Feagin (eds) *The Bubbling Cauldron: Race, Ethnicity, and the Urban Crisis*. Minneapolis: University of Minnesota Press.

Bonacich, E. 1973. A Theory of Middleman Minorities. *American Sociological Review* 38(5): 583-594.

Bongaarts, J. and R.A. Bulatao. 1999. Completing the Demographic Transition. *Population and Development Review* 25(3): 515-529

Borjas, G.J. 1989. Economic Theory and International Migration. *International Migration Review* 23(3):457-485.

Borjas, G.J & S.G. Bronars. 1991. Immigration and the Family. *Journal of Labor Economics* 9(2): 123-48.

Boyd, M. 1989, Family and Personal Networks in International Migration: Recent Developments and New Agenda. *International Migration Review* 23(3): 638-670.

Briggs, V.M., Jr. 2003. *Mass Immigration and the National Interest: Policy Directions for the New Century* (3rd ed.). Armonk, NY: M. E. Sharpe:

Brown, D.L. 2002. Migration and Community: Social Networks in a Multilevel World. *Rural Sociology* 67(1): 1-23.

Brown, Lawrence A.., Tamar E. Mott, Edward J. Malecki. 2007. Immigrant Profiles of U.S. Urban Areas and Agents of Resettlement. *The Professional Geographer*. 59 (1), 56–73.

Burnley, I.H. 1988. Population Turnaround and the Peopling of the Countryside – Migration from Sydney to Country Districts of New-South-Wales. *Australian Geographer* 19(2): 268-283.

Carlson, E.C. 1985. The Impact of International Immigration upon the Timing of Marriage and Childbearing. *Demography* 22(1): 61-72

Carter, S.B. and R. Sutch. 1998. Historical Background to Current Immigration Issues. In J.P. Smith and B. Edmonston (eds). *The Immigration Debate: Studies on the Economic, Demographic, and Fiscal Effects of Immigration.* Washing, DC: National Academy Press

Castles, Stephen. 2004. Why Migration Policies Fail. *Ethnic and Racial Studies* 27 (2): 205-227

Castles, Stephen. 2004. The Factors that Make and Unmake Migration Policies. *International Migration Review.* 38 (3): 852-884

Castles, Stephen and Mark J. Miller. 2003. *The Age of Migration: International Population Movements in the Modern World.* Guilford Press.

Cernea, M.M. 2000. Risks, Safeguards, and Reconstruction: A Model for Population Displacement and Resettlement. In M.M. Cernea and C. McDowell (eds) *Risks and Reconstruction: Experiences of Resettlers and Refugees.* Washington, DC: World Bank.

Cerrutti, M. and D.S. Massey. 2001. On the Auspices of Female Migration From Mexico to the United States. *Demography* 38(2): 187-200

Chen, Aimin and Shunfeng Song. 2006. *China's Rural Economy After WTO: Problems And Strategies.* Ashgate Publishing, Ltd.

Choldin, H.M. 1973. Kinship Networks in the Migration Process. *International Migration Review* 7(2): 163-175.

Constant, Amelie and Douglas S. Massey. 2002. Return Migration by German Guestworkers: Neoclassical versus New Economic Theories. *International Migration.* 40(4): 5-38

David, P.A. 1974. Fortune, Risk and Microeconomics of Migration. In P.A. David and M.W. Reder (eds) *Nations and Households in Economic Growth: Essays in Honor of Moses Abramovitz*. New York: Academic Press

Day, R.W. 1989. Current Policy Concerns on Immigration. *International Migration Review* 23(4):900-903.

Dunlevy, J.A. and H.A. Gemery. 1978. Economic Opportunity and the Response of 'Old' and 'New' Migrants to the United States. *The Journal of Economic History* 38(4): 901-917.

Durand, J., E.A. Parrado, and D.S. Massey. 1996. "Migradollars and Development: A Reconsideration of the Mexican Case." *International Migration Review* 30:423-44.

Edmonston, B. (ed.). 1996. *Statistics on U.S. Immigration: An Assessment of Data Needs for Future Research*. Report of the Committee on National Statistics and Committee on Population, National Research Council. Washington DC: National Academic Press

Edmonston, B. and J.S. Passel. 1994. *The Future Immigrant Population of the United States*. In B. Edmonston and J.S. Passel (eds). 1994. *Immigration and Ethnicity: The Integration of America's Newest Arrivals*. Washington, DC: Urban Institute Press.

Enoch, Y. 1994. The Intolerance of a Tolerant People: Ethnic Relations in Denmark. *Ethnic and Racial Studies* 17(2): 282-300

Espenshade T.J. and W. Ye. 1994. Differential Fertility within an Ethnic-Minority --- The Effect of Trying Harder Among Chinese-American Women. *Social Problems* 41(1): 97-113.

Esterlin, R.A. 1987. Fertility. In J. Eatwell, M. Milgate and P. Newman (eds.) *The New Palgrave : A Dictionary of Economics*. New York: Stockton Press

Exter, T.G. 1992. Middle-aging Asians. *American Demographics* 14(11).

Fawcett, J.T. 1989. Networks, Linkages, and Migration Systems. *International Migration Review* 23(3): 671-680

Fix, M. and J.S. Passel. 1994. *Immigration and Immigrants: Setting the Record Straight*. Washington, DC: Urban Institute

Fix, M., W. Zimmermann and J.S. Passel. 2001. *The Integration of Immigrant Families in the United States*. Washington, DC: The Urban Institute Press.

Ford, K. 1990. Duration of Residence in the United States and the Fertility of U.S. Immigrants. *International Migration Review* 24(1): 34-68.

Freeman, G.P. and B. Birrell. 2001. Divergent Paths of Immigration Politics in the United States and Australia. *Population and Development Review* 27(3): 525-551

Friedl, E. 1976. Kinship, Class and Selective Migration. In J. G. Peristiany (ed). *Mediterranean Family Structures.* New York: Cambridge University Press.

Friedlander, D. and C. Goldscheider. 1978. Immigration, Social Change and Cohort Fertility in Israel. *Population Studies* 32(2): 299-317.

Fuller, T.D., P. Kamnuansilpa and P. Lightfoot. 1990. Urban Ties of Rural Thais. *International Migration Review* 24(3):534-562.

General Accounting Office. 1988. *Immigration: The Future Flow of Legal Immigration to the United States.* GAO/PEMD-88-7. Washington, DC: General Printing Office. Jan.

Goering, J.M. 1989. The Explosiveness of Chain Migration - Research and Policy Issues: Introduction and Overview. *International Migration Review* 23(4): 797-812.

Goldscheider, C. 1987. Migration and Social Structure: Analytic Issues and Comparative Perspectives in Developing Nations. *Sociological Forum* 2:674-696

Goldstein, A., White M.J. and S. Goldstein. 1997. Migration, Fertility, and State Policy in Hubei Province, China. *Demography* 34(4): 481-491

Goldstein, S. and A. Goldstein. 1981. The Impact of Migration on Fertility: an 'Own Children' Analysis for Thailand. *Population Studies* 35(2): 265-284.

Gorwaney, N, M.D. Van Arsdol, D.M. Heer and L.A. Schuerman. 1990. Variations in Fertility and Earnings Patterns among Immigrants in the United States, 1970-1980: Assimilation or Disruption? *International Migration* 28(4):451-475

Graham, H.D. 2002. *Collision Course: The Strange Convergence of Affirmative Action and Immigration Policy in America.* Oxford University Press

Grieco, E.M. 1998. The Effects of Migration on the Establishment of Networks: Caste Disintegration and Reformation among the Indians of Fiji. *International Migration Review,* 32 (3): 704-736.

Gualtieri, Sarah. 2004. Gendering the Chain Migration Thesis: Women and Syrian Transatlantic Migration, 1878-1924. *Comparative Studies of South Asia, Africa and the Middle East.* 24 (1): 67-78.

Guiraudon, V. and C. Joppke. 2001. *Controlling a New Migration World.* Routledge: London

Gunatilleke, G. 1991. Sri Lanka. In G. Gunatilleke (ed.) *Migration to the Arab World: Experience of Returning Migrants*. Tokyo, Japan: United Nations University Press.

Gunatilleke, G. 1998. The Role of Networks and Community Structures in International Migration from Sri Lanka. In R. Appleyard (ed.) *Emigration Dynamics in Developing Countries, Volume II, South Asia,*. Ashgate Publishers, UK.

Harris, J.R. and M.P. Todaro. 1970. Migration, Unemployment and Development: A Two-Sector Analysis. *American Economic Review* 22(2): 226-242.

Heer, David M. 1996. *Immigration in America's future: Social Science Findings and the Policy Debate*. Boulder, CO: Westview Press.

Hein J. 1993. Refugees, Immigrants, and the Sate. *Annual Review of Sociology*. 19: 43-59 1993

Helmenstein C. and Yegorov Y., 2000. The Dynamics of Migration in the Presence of Chains. *Journal of Economic Dynamics & Control* 24 (2): 307-323

Hollifield, J. F. 1994. Immigration and Republicanism in France. In W.A. Cornelius, P. L. Martin and J. F. Hollifield (eds) *Controlling Immigration: A Global Perspective*. Stanford, CA: Stanford University Press.

Hotz, V.J., J.A. Klerman and R.J. Willis. 1997. The Economics of Fertility in Developed Countries. In M.R. Rosenzweig and O. Stark (eds). *Handbook of population and family economics*. Amsterdam; New York: Elsevier

Hugo, G.J. 1981. Village-Community Ties, Village Norms, and Ethnic and Social Networks. In G.F. De Jong and R.W. Gardner (eds.) *Migration Decision Making: Multidisciplinary Approaches to Microlevel Studies in Developed and Developing Countries*. New York: Pergamon Press.

Hugo, G.J. 1995. International Labor Migration and the Family: Some Observations from Indonesia. *Asian and Pacific Migration Journal* 4(2-3): 273-301

Jasso, G. and M.R. Rosenzweig. 1986. Family Reunification and the Immigration Multiplier: U.S. Immigration Law, Origin-Country Conditions, and the Reproduction of Immigrants. *Demography* 23(3): 291-311.

Jasso, G. and M.R. Rosenzweig. 1987. Using National Recording Systems for the Measurement and Analysis of Immigration to the United States. *International Migration Review* 21(4): 1212-1244.

Jasso, G. and M.R. Rosenzweig. 1989. Sponsors, Sponsorship Rates and the Immigration Multiplier. *International Migration Review* 23(4): 856-888.

Jasso, G. and M.R. Rosenzweig. 1990. The New Chosen People: Immigrants in the United States. *The Population of the United States in the 1980: A Census Monograph Series.* New York: Russell Sage Foundation

Jasso, G. and M.R. Rosenzweig. 1995. Do Immigrants Screened for Skills do Better Than Family Reunification Immigrants? *International Migration Review* 29(1): 85-111

Jennissen R. 2003. Economic Determinants of Net International Migration in Western Europe. *European Journal of Population* 19(2): 171-198

Jensen, E.R. and D.A. Ahlburg. 2004. Why Does Migration Decrease Fertility? Evidence from Philippines. *Population Studies* 58(2): 219-231

Johnston, Ron; Trlin, Andrew; Henderson, Anne and North, Nicola. 2006. Sustaining and Creating Migration Chains among Skilled Immigrant Groups: Chinese, Indians and South Africans in New Zealand. *Journal of Ethnic and Migration Studies.* 32 (7): 1227-1250

Joly, D. 2002. Odyssean and Rubicon Refugees: Toward a Typology of Refugees in the Land of Exile. *International Migration* 40(6): 3-23

Kahn, J.R. 1988. Immigrant Selectivity and Fertility Adaptation in the United States. *Social Forces* 67:108-28

Kahn, J.R. 1994. Immigrant and Native Fertility during the 1980s: Adaptation and Expectations for the Future. *International Migration Review* 28:501-19

Khoo, S.-E. 2001. The Context of Spouse Migration to Australia. *International Migration* 39(1): 111-132.

Kobrin, F.E. and A. Speare, Jr., 1983. Out-Migration and Ethnic Communities. *International Migration Review* 17(3): 425-444.

Kofman, Eleonore. 2004. Family-Related Migration: A Critical Review of European Studies. *Journal of Ethnic and Migration Studies*, 30 (2): 243 - 262Krafft, S. 1994. Hide-and-seek with illegal aliens. *American Demographics* (16) 7:10

Kurthen, H. 1995. Germany at the Crossroads: National Identity and the Challenge of Immigration. *International Migration Review* 29(4): 914-938.

Lee, B.S. and L.G. Pol. 1993. The Influence of Rural-Urban Migration on Migrants Fertility in Korea, Mexico and Cameroon. *Population Research and Policy Review* 12 (1): 3-26

Lever-Tracy, C. and R. Holton. 2001. Social Exchange, Reciprocity and Amoral Familism: Aspects of Italian Chain Migration to Australia. *Journal of Ethnic and Migration Studies* 27(1): 81-99

Lindquist, B. A. 1993 Migration Networks: A Case Study in Philippines. *Asian and Pacific Migration Journal* 2(1).

Lindstrom, D.P. 1996. Economic Opportunity in Mexico and return Migration from the United States. *Demography* 33:357-374

Lindstrom, D.P. 2003. Rural-urban Migration and Reproductive Behavior in Guatemala. *Population Research and Policy Review* 22(4): 351-372

Lindstrom, D.P. and S.G. Saucedo. 2002. The Short- and Long-Term Effects of U.S. Migration Experience on Mexican Woman's Fertility. *Social Forces* 80(4): 1341-1368

Liu, J.M., P.M. Ong and C. Rosenstein. 1991. Dual Chain Migration: Post-1965 Filipino Immigration to the United States. *International Migration Review* 25(3): 487-513

Luk, Chiu M. and Mai B. Phan. 2005. Ethnic Enclave Reconfiguration: A 'new' Chinatown in the Making. *GeoJournal.* 64 (1): 17 - 30

Mahmood, R. A. 1991. Bangladesh Return Migrants from the Middle East: Process, Achievement, and Adjustment. In G. Gunatilleke (ed.). *Migration to the Arab World: Experience of Returning Migrants.* Tokyo, Japan: United Nations University Press.

Massey, D.S. 1990. The Social and Economic Origins of Immigration. In S.H. Preston (ed.) *World Population: Approaching the Year 2000.* Series: *Annals of the American Academy of Political and Social Science*, Vol. 510:60-72. Newbury Park, CA: Sage Periodicals Press

Massey, D.S. 1995. The New Immigration and Ethnicity in the United States. *Population and Development Review* 21(3): 631-652.

Massey, D.S. 1999. Why Does Immigration Occur? A Theoretical Synthesis. In C. Hirschman, P. Kasinitz and J. DeWind (eds.) *The Handbook of International Migration: the American Experience.* New York: Russell Sage Foundation.

Massey, D.S., R. Alarcon, J. Durand and H. Gonzalez. 1987. *Return to Aztlan: The Social Process of International Migration from Western Mexico.* University of California Press.

Massey, D.S., J. Arango, G. Hugo, A. Kouaouci, A. Pellegrino and J.E. Taylor. 1993. Theories of International Migration: A Review and Appraisal. *Population and Development Review* 19(3): 431-466.

Massey, D.S., J. Arango, G. Hugo, A. Kouaouci, A. Pellegrino and J.E. Taylor. 1994. An Evaluation of International Migration Theory: The North American Case. *Population and Development Review* 20(4): 699-751.

Massey, D.S., J. Arango, A. Kouaouci, A. Pelligrino and J.E. Taylor. 1998. *Worlds in Motion: Understanding International Migration at the End of*

Millennium. International Studies in Demography. New York: Oxford University Press.

Massey, D.S., J. Durand and N.J. Malone. 2002. *Beyond Smoke and Mirrors: Mexican Immigration in an Era of Economic Integration.* New York: Russell Sage Foundation.

Massey, D.S. and K.E. Espinosa, 1997. What's Driving Mexico-U.S. Migration? A Theoretical, Empirical, and Policy Analysis. *The American Journal of Sociology* 102(4): 939-999.

Massey, D.S. and G. Espana. 1987. The Social Process of International Migration. *Science* 237: 733-738.

Massey, D.S., L.P. Goldring and J. Durand. 1994. Continuities in Transnational Migration: An Analysis of Nineteen Mexican Communities. *American Journal of Sociology* 99:1491-1533

Massey, D.S. and B.P. Mullan. 1984. A Demonstration of the Effect of Seasonal Migration on Fertility. *Demography* 21(4):501-517

Massey, D.S. and A. Singer. 1995. New Estimates of Undocumented Mexican Migration and the Probability of Apprehension. *Demography* 32(2): 203-13.

Mayer, Jochen and Regina T. Riphahn. 2000. Fertility Assimilation of Immigrants: Evidence from Count Data Models. *Journal of Population Economics* 13 (2): 241-261

McDonald, J.S. and L.D. McDonald. 1964. Chain Migration, Ethnic Neighborhood Formation, and Social Networks, *Milbank Memorial Fund Quarterly* 42(1)

McDonald, J.S. and L.D. McDonald. 1974. Chain Migration, Ethnic Neighborhood Formation, and Social Networks, In C. Tilly (ed.) *An Urban World.* Boston: Little, Brown.

Menon, R. 1988. How Malaysian Migrants Pre-Arrange Employment. *Sociology and Social Research* 73(4): 257-259.

Meyer, E. 2004. *International Immigration Policy: A Theoretical and Comparative Analysis.* Palgrave MacMillan: New York

Moch, Leslie Page. 2003. *Moving Europeans: migration in Western Europe since 1650.* Indiana University Press

Ng, E. and F. Nault. 1997. Fertility Among Recent Immigrant Women to Canada, 1991: An Examination of the Disruption Hypothesis. *International Migration* 35 (4): 559-580

Palloni, A., D.S. Massey, M. Cebrallos, K. Espinosa, and M. Spittal. 2001. Social Capital and International Migration: A Test Using Information on Family Networks. *American Journal of Sociology* 106:1262-1298.

Passel, J.S. and K.A. Woodrow. 1987. Change in the Undocumented Alien Population in the United States, 1979-1983. *International Migration Review* 21(4): 1304-1334.

Petersen, W. 1964. *The Politics of Population*. Garden City, N.Y. Doubleday

Phillips, J.A. and D.S. Massey. 1999. The New Labor Market: Immigrants and Wages after IRCA (in Consequences of Policy Shifts and Political Change). *Demography* 36(2): 233-246.

Piore, M.J. 1979. *Birds of Passage: Migrant Labor in Industrial Societies*. Cambridge; New York: Cambridge University Press.

Portes, A. 1995. Children of Immigrants: Segmented Assimilation and Its Determinants. In A. Portes (ed.) *The Economic Sociology of Immigration*. New York: Russell Sage Foundation.

Portes, A. 1997. Immigration Theory for a New Century: Some Problems and Opportunities. *International Migration Review* 31(4):799-825.

Portes, A. and R.G. Rumbaut. 2001. *Legacies: The Story of the Immigrant Second Generation*. Berkeley : University of California Press ; New York : Russell Sage Foundation

Price, C.A. 1963a. *Southern Europeans in Australia*. Melbourne: Oxford University Press.

Price, C.A. 1963b. *The Method and Statistics of 'Southern Europeans in Australia'*. Canberra: Research School of Social Science – The Australian National University

Ram, B. and M.V. George. 1990. Immigrant Fertility Patterns in Canada, 1961-1986. *International Migration* 28 (4): 413-426

Ravuri, Evelyn D. 2004. Determinants of Migration to and from Bolivar State, Venezuela for 1961 and 1990: The Effect of Ciudad Guayana on Migration. *The Journal of Developing Areas*. 37(2): 155-167

Reynolds Farley and Richard Alba. 2002. The New Second Generation in the United States. *International Migration Review*. 36 (3): 669–701

Reimers, D.M. 1985. *Still the Golden Door: The Third World Comes to America*. New York: Columbia University Press

Reimers, D.M. 1992. *Still the Golden Door: The Third World Comes to America.(2nd ed.)* New York: Columbia University Press

Roberts, B.R., R. Frank, and F. Lozano-Ascencio. 1999. "Transnational Migrant Communities and Mexican Migration to the US." *Ethnic and Racial Studies* 22:238-66.

Rosenzweig, M. R. and T. P. Schultz. 1985. The Demand for and Supply of Births: Fertility and its Life Cycle Consequences. *American Economic Review*, 75 (5): 992-1005

Rowland, D.T. 2003. *Demographic Methods and Concepts.* Oxford: Oxford University Press.

Ruggles, S., M. Sobek, T. Alexander, C.A. Fitch, R. Goeken, P.K. Hall, M. King, and C. Ronnander. 2004. *Integrated Public Use Microdata Series: Version 3.0* [Machine-readable database]. Minneapolis, MN: Minnesota Population Center [producer and distributor].

Rundquist, F.M. and L.A. Brown. 1989. Migrant Fertility Differentials in Ecuador. *Geografiska Annaler Series B-Human Geography* 71 (2): 109-123

Schoorl, J. J. 1990. Fertility Adaptation of Turkish and Moroccan Women in the Netherlands. *International Migration* 28:477-504

SCIRP. 1981 *U.S. Immigration Policy and the National Interest.* The Final Report and Recommendation of the Select Commission on Immigration and Refugee Policy to the Congress and the President of the United States. Washington, DC: General Printing Office.

Serow, W.J., R.H. Weller, D.F. Sly and C.B. Nam (eds.) 1990. *Handbook on International Migration.* Westport, CT: Greenwood Press

Shah, N.M. and I. Menon. 1999. Chain Migration Through the Social Network: Experience of Labour Migrants in Kuwait. *International Migration* 37(2):361-382.

Simcox, D.E. (ed.) 1988. *U.S. Immigration in the 1980s.* Boulder, Colorado: Westview Press

Singhanetra-Renard, A. 1992. The Mobilization of Labor Migrants in Thailand: Present Links and Facilitating Networks. In M.M. Kritz, L.L. Lim and H. Zlotnik (eds.) *International Migration Systems: A Global Approach.* New York: Oxford University Press.

Singley, S.G. and N.S. Landale. 1998. Incorporating Origin and Process in Migration-Fertility Frameworks: The case of Puerto Rican Women. *Social Forces* 76(4): 1437-1470

Sjaastad, L.A. 1962. The Costs and Return of Human Migration. *American Economic Review* 75(2):173-178

Smith, J.P. and B. Edmonston, (eds.), 1997. *The New Americans: Economic, Demographic and Fiscal Impacts of Immigration.* Washington, DC: National Academy Press.

Stark, O. 1991. *The Migration of Labor.* Cambridge, MA: Basil Blackwell.

Stark, O. and J.E. Taylor. 1989. Relative Deprivation and International Migration. *Demography* 26(1): 1-14.

Stark, O. and J.E. Taylor. 1991. Relative Deprivation and Migration: Theory, Evidence, and Policy Implications. In S. Díaz-Briquets and S. Weintraub (eds.) *Determinants of Emigration from Mexico, Central America, and the Caribbean.* Boulder, CO: Westview Press.

Stephen, E.H. and F.D. Bean. 1992. Assimilation, Disruption and the Fertility of Mexican-Origin Women in the United States. *Internal Migration Review* 26:67-88

Suro, R. 1999. *Strangers Among Us: Latino Lives in a Changing America.* New York: Vintage Books.

Swicegood, G., F.D. Bean, E. H. Stephen and W. Opitz. 1988. Language Usage and Fertility in the Mexican-Origin Population of the United States. *Demography* 25:17-33

Taylor, J.E. 1986. Differential Migration, Networks, Information and Risk. In O. Stark (ed.) *Migration, Human Capital and Development.* Greenwich, Conn: JAI Press.

Taylor, J.E. 1987. Undocumented Mexico-U.S. Migration and the Returns to Households in Rural Mexico. *American Journal of Agricultural Economics* 69:616-638

Teitelbaum, M.S. 1989. Skeptical Noises about the Immigration Multiplier. *International Migration Review* 23(4): 893-899.

Tilly, C. and C.H. Brown. 1967. On Uprooting, Kinship, and the Auspices of Migration. *International Journal of Comparative Sociology* 8(2): 139-164

Todaro, M. 1969. A Model of Labor Migration and Urban Unemployment in Less Developed Countries. *American Economic Review* 59(1):138-148.

Todaro, M. 1976. *International Migration in Developing Countries.* Geneva: International Labor Organization.

Todaro, M. 1980. Internal Migration in Developing Countries: A Survey. In R.A. Easterlin (ed.) *Population and Economic Change in Developing Countries.* Chicago: University of Chicago Press.

Todaro, M. and L. Maruszko. 1987. Illegal Migration and U.S. Immigration Reform: A Conceptual Framework. *Population and Development Review* 13(1):101-114.

Torpey, J. 1998. Coming and Going: On the State Monopolization of the Legitimate "Means of Movement". *Sociological Theory* 16(3):239-259

Toulemon, Laurent. 2004. Fertility Among Immigrant Women: New Data, A New Approach. *Population and Societies.* No. 400 (April 2004)

U.S. Census Bureau. 1986. Statistical Abstract of the United States: 1986. Washington, DC.

U.S. Census Bureau. 1995. Statistical Abstract of the United States: 1995. Washington, DC.

U.S. Census Bureau. 2000. Statistical Abstract of the United States: 2000. Washington, DC.

U.S. Census Bureau. 2006. Statistical Abstract of the United States: 2000 Washington, DC.

U.S. Department of Homeland Security, Yearbook of Immigration Statistics: 2006: Immigrants, Table 2, retrieved on 4/5/2007 from http://www.dhs.gov/ximgtn/statistics/publications/LPR06.shtm

U.S. Department of Justice, USCIS. 1972 - 2000. *Immigrants Admitted to the United States, 1972 - 2000*: Annual Demographic File [Computer file]. Washington, DC: U.S. Dept. of Justice, Citizenship and Immigration Service [producer], 1972-2000. Ann Arbor, MI: Inter-university Consortium for Political and Social Research [distributor].

U.S. State Department, Visa Bulletin, retrieved on 4/18/2007 from http://travel.state.gov/visa/frvi/bulletin/bulletin_3219.html

U.S. State Department, Visa Types for Immigrants, retrieved on 4/8/2007 from http://www.travel.state.gov/visa/immigrants/types/types_1326.html

Uhlenberg, P. 1973. Fertility Patterns within the Mexican American Population. *Social Biology* 20: 30-39

Umezaki, M. and R. Ohtsuka. 1998. Impact of Rural-urban Migration on Fertility: A Population Ecology Analysis in the Kombio, Papua New Guinea. *Journal of Biosocial Science* 30(3): 411-422

Ware, H. 1975. Immigrant Fertility: Behavior and Attitudes. *International Migration Review* 9(3): 361-378.

Ware, H. 1988. Post-War Italian Immigration. In J. Jupp (ed.) *The Australian people : an encyclopedia of the nation, its people, and their origins.* Cambridge: Cambridge University Press.

Watsula, Michael. 2005. Naturalization in the United States: Who, Why, and How. *Multicultural Center Prague.* April, 2005

Wegge, S.A. 1998. Chain Migration and Information Networks: Evidence From Nineteenth-Century Hesse-Cassel. *The Journal of Economic History* 58(4): 957-986

White, M.J., Y.K. Djamba and D.N. Anh. 2001. Implications of Economic Reform and Spatial Mobility for Fertility in Vietnam. *Population Research and Policy Review* 20(3): 207-228

Williams, J.D. and A.J. Sofranko. 1979. Motivations for the Immigration Component of Population Turnaround in Nonmetropolitan Areas. *Demography* 16(2): 239–256.

Wilson, D.C. 1998. Markets, Networks, and Risk: An Analysis of Labor Remuneration in the Lake Victoria Fishing Industry. *Sociological Forum* 13(3): 425-456

Winters, P., A. De Janvry and E. Sadoulet. 2001. Family and Community Networks in Mexico-U.S. Migration. *The Journal of Human Resources* 36(1): 159-184

Yeh, Ling-Ling. 2004. Mexican Immigration and its Potential Impact on the Political Future of the United States. *The Journal of Social, Political and Economic Studies.* 29 (4): 409-431

Yoo, J.-K. 2000. Utilization of Social Networks for Immigrant Entrepreneurship: A Case Study of Korean Immigrants in the Atlanta Area. *International Review of Sociology* 10(3):347-363.

Yu, Bin. 2005. Immigration·Multiplier: A New Method of Measuring the Immigration Process. Providence, RI: Brown University.

Yu, Bin. 2006. Immigration Multiplier: A New Method of Measuring the Immigration Process. PAA Paper.

Yusuf, F. and I. Rockett. 1981. Immigrant Fertility Patterns and Differentials in Australia 1971-1976. *Population Studies* 35: 413-424

Yusuf F. and S. Siedlecky. 1996. Family Formation Patterns Among Migrant Women in Sydney. *Journal of Biosocial Science* 28 (1): 89-99

Zhao, Yaohui. 2003. The Role of Migrant Networks in Labor Migration: The Case of China. *Contemporary Economic Policy.* 21(4): 500-511

Zolberg, A.R. 1989. The Next Waves: Migration Theory for a Changing World. *International Migration Review* 23(3): 403-430.

Zolberg, A.R. 1999. Matters of State. In C. Hirschman, P. Kasinitz and J. DeWind (eds.) *The Handbook of International Migration: the American Experience.* New York: Russell Sage Foundation.

Zolberg, A.R. and P.M. Benda. 2001. *Global Migrants, Global Refugees: Problems and Solutions.* New York: Berghahn Books.

Index